The Palestine–
Israeli Conflict

A Beginner's Guide

Dan Cohn-Sherbok and
Dawoud El-Alami

ONEWORLD

A Oneworld Book

First published by Oneworld Publications, 2001
Reprinted 2002 (four times)
Revised edition 2003
Reprinted 2006 (twice)
Revised and updated 2008
Reprinted 2009
Reprinted 2011
Revised and updated 2015
Reprinted 2015

ISBN 978-1-78074-380-6
ISBN 978-1-78074-701-9 (eBook)

Typeset by Jayvee, Trivandrum, India
Cover design by Two Associates
Printed and bound in Great Britain by Clays Ltd, St Ives plc

Oneworld Publications
10 Bloomsbury Street
London WC1B 3SR
England

Contents

A Jewish perspective:
Dan Cohn-Sherbok

A Palestinian perspective:
Dawoud El-Alami

Preface to the fourth edition

Since the last edition of this book was published, much has taken place in the Middle East. Most significantly with regard to the Palestine–Israeli conflict, President Mahmoud Abbas addressed the United Nations on 23 September 2011, pleading for recognition of Palestine as a nation state. At the conclusion of his speech, he stated:

> The time has come for our men, women and children to live normal lives, for them to be able to sleep without waiting for the worst that the next day will bring; for mothers to be assured that their children will return home without fear of suffering, killing, arrest or humiliation; for students to be able to go to their schools and universities without checkpoints obstructing them. The time has come for sick people to be able to reach hospitals normally, and for our farmers to be able to take care of their good land without fear of the occupation seizing the land and its water, which the Wall prevents access to, or fear of the settlers, for whom settlements are being built on our land and who are uprooting and burning the olive trees that have existed for hundreds of years. The time has come for the thousands of prisoners to be released from the prisons to return to their families and their children to become part of building their homeland, for the freedom of which they have settled.

(Haaretz.com, 29 December 2011)

In his speech to the United Nations, delivered following this address, Israeli Prime Minister Benjamin Netanyahu extended the hand of peace to the Palestinian people. Yet he stressed that peace must be anchored in security. The truth, he stated, is that a solution to the Middle East crisis cannot be achieved through UN resolutions, but only through direct negotiations between the parties. Israel, he insisted, wants peace with a Palestinian state, but the Palestinians want a state without peace. As the prime minister of Israel, he was unprepared to risk the future of the Jewish state on wishful thinking. Serious peace talks, he insisted, can be properly addressed, but they will not be confronted without negotiations. Regrettably, negotiations collapsed after these events, and Israel's attempt to curtail rockets being fired by Hamas by launching Operation Protective Edge has intensified the conflict between Israel and the Palestinians. As this book goes to print, we can only hope that there can at long last – after a century of hatred and bloodshed – be a lasting peace.

Preface to the third edition

Over seven years ago, this book was first published as the Palestine–Israeli conflict intensified. In the second edition, published in 2003, we discussed further events that had profoundly affected Middle East politics: in particular, the terror attacks on the World Trade Center and the Pentagon had focused international attention on the significance of the struggle between Israelis and Palestinians. In the subsequent four years, major events have taken place in the Holy Land: Prime Minister Ariel Sharon suffered a severe stroke and was replaced by Ehud Olmert; Yasser Arafat died and Mahmoud Abbas was elected President of the Palestinian Authority; Israel launched an offensive against Hezbollah; and most recently Hamas won the majority of seats in the Palestinian Legislative Council. Today there is a major struggle between Hamas and Fatah for the hearts and minds of the Palestinian people. This revised version of our book highlights these most recent developments while presenting a history of the struggle between Jews and Palestinians for the land of their ancestors.

Dan Cohn-Sherbok, Dawoud El-Alami, 2008

Preface to the first edition

During recent years the conflict in the Middle East has exploded on to our television screens. Day after day images of violence and suffering have dominated the news. Scenes of heavily armed Israeli soldiers facing young Palestinian children hurling stones with slingshots – like Goliath facing David – have evoked dismay and confusion. The vehemence of the Palestinian reaction is a result of years of pent-up anger and frustration. The Israeli response has been swift and determined: Palestinian towns have been besieged, territories sealed off and negotiations suspended between the Israeli government and Palestinian representatives.

What are the causes of this bloody conflict? Is there any hope for peace in the Middle East? These are the questions that this book seeks to explore. Designed for the general reader with little knowledge of the modern history of the Middle East, this volume is unique in its approach, offering both a Jewish and a Palestinian perspective. Nearly all studies of the Arab–Israeli conflict are written by a single author, but here two differing accounts are presented from a Palestinian and a Jewish scholar with widely divergent views.

Dr Dawoud El-Alami is from a distinguished Palestinian family. Born in Jerusalem, Dr El-Alami was educated in Egypt and graduated from the University of Cairo with a degree in law. Initially he worked as a lawyer, only later becoming an academic. Over the years, he has held appointments at the

University of Kent in Canterbury, the University of Oxford, Al Al-Bayt University in Jordan and the University of Wales, Lampeter. An ardent advocate of the Palestinian cause, he is critical of both Israeli and Palestinian policy.

Professor Dan Cohn-Sherbok is an American rabbi who was ordained at the Hebrew Union College Jewish Institute of Religion, and later obtained a doctorate from the University of Cambridge. He has served Reform congregations in the United States, Australia, Britain and South Africa, and is currently Professor of Judaism at the University of Wales, Lampeter. He has written a study of Israel, *Israel: The History of an Idea*, in which he advocates the creation of a homeland for the Palestinians. Nonetheless, he is a strong advocate of a Jewish state in the Middle East.

In their presentations, both authors outline the history of Middle East politics, beginning with the origins of Zionism in the late nineteenth century. They adopt different perspectives about the same historical events. For Cohn-Sherbok, the creation of the State of Israel was an urgent necessity, given the terrible history of the Jews in Europe. In his view the Holocaust provides ample justification for the establishment of a Jewish nation. El-Alami, however, regards Israel's claims to Palestine as lacking any legal or moral foundation. Angrily, he protests the Jewish appropriation of Palestinian land. In his opinion, Israel must compensate the Palestinian people for nearly a century of hardship. In the concluding chapter of this volume, Cohn-Sherbok and El-Alami debate the central issues of the Middle East crisis. The aim of this study is thus to encourage readers to gain an informed understanding of both the Jewish and Palestinian viewpoints and to come to their own conclusions regarding the troubled and turbulent history of this part of the world.

Dan Cohn-Sherbok, Dawoud El-Alami

Chronology

1862	Publication of *Rome and Jerusalem* by Moses Hess.
1881	Assassination of Tsar Alexander II followed by persecution of Russian Jews.
1882	Publication of *Autoemancipation* by Leon Pinsker.
1882–1903	First Aliyah.
1891	Arab protests against Zionist settlers in Palestine.
1894–5	Alfred Dreyfus falsely charged with espionage.
1896	Publication of *The Jewish State* by Theodor Herzl.
1897	First International Congress of Zionists.
1903	Persecution of Jews in Kishinev.
1904	Beginning of Second Aliyah.
1905	Seventh Zionist Congress rejects alternative to Palestine as aim of Zionism.
1908–9	Arab opposition to Zionist settlements intensifies.
1914–18	First World War.
1915–16	Sykes-Picot agreement.
1917	Balfour Declaration.
	Arab Revolt: Lawrence takes Aqaba, Allenby enters Jerusalem.
1919	Chaim Weizmann leads Zionist delegation at Paris Peace Conference.
1919–23	Third Aliyah.
1920–1	Arab anti-Jewish riots in Palestine.
1924–32	Fourth Aliyah.
1929	Arab riots in Jerusalem, Hebron and Safed.
1930	Passfield White Paper seeks British disengagement from the Jewish National Home aspects

	of the Balfour Declaration and the Palestine Mandate.
1931	Irgun Tzevai Leumi established.
1933–5	Fifth Aliyah.
1937	Peel Commission recommends partition of Palestine.
1938	Evian Conference.
1939	Conference at St James's Palace.
	White Paper repudiates partition and favours an independent Palestinian state.
1939–42	Co-operation between British forces and Jews in Palestine.
1942	Loss of Struma. Biltmore Congress.
1943	Anglo–American Conference at Bermuda on refugees.
1944	Assassination of Lord Moyne in Cairo.
1945	President Truman supports the demand for a large number of immigrants to Palestine.
1946	Truman supports demand for admission of 100,000 refugees to Palestine. This is refused by the British. Jewish sabotage operations throughout Palestine. Irgun blows up King David Hotel in Jerusalem. Truman endorses partition of Palestine and creation of a Jewish state.
1947	British Foreign Secretary, Ernest Bevin, declares intention to refer the Palestine Mandate back to the United Nations. General Assembly votes for partition of Palestine into a Palestinian and a Jewish state.
	The British government expresses its intention to terminate its responsibility under the Mandate.
1948	Irgun, led by Menachem Begin, massacre villagers at Deir Yassin. Palestinian civilians flee *en masse* fearing a similar fate.

	Ben-Gurion declares the State of Israel.
	Termination of the British Mandate.
	Arab armies enter areas assigned to the Palestinian state under the partition plan to support Palestinian resistance.
	UN appoints as mediator Count Folke Bernadotte.
	Bernadotte assassinated.
	Fighting between Israel and Egypt.
	Moshe Dayan drives all Palestinian civilians from Lydda and Ramleh by force.
	UN Resolution 194 states that Palestinian refugees wishing to return to their homes should be permitted to do so and that compensation for loss or damage to property should be paid.
1949	Israel concludes armistice agreements with Egypt, Lebanon and Syria.
	UN votes in favour of internationalizing Jerusalem.
	Ben-Gurion declares Jerusalem the capital of Israel.
1950	Beginning of immigration to Israel of Jews from Arab countries.
	King Abdullah of Jordan formally annexes the West Bank.
	The Law of Return gives the right to settle in Israel to every Jew worldwide.
1951	King Abdullah assassinated in Jerusalem at Friday prayers.
1952	Coup in Egypt by 'Free Officers'; rise to power of Nasser.
1953	Ben-Gurion retires. Moshe Sharrett becomes Prime Minister of Israel.
1954	Increased fedayeen attacks on Israel.
	Israeli army attacks Nahalin in the West Bank.

1955	Israel launches major raid against Egyptians.
	Military pact between Egypt and Syria.
	Ben-Gurion becomes Prime Minister.
1956	Israel attacks in Sinai.
	Israeli border guards massacre forty-nine villagers at Kufr Kassem.
	UN Security Council Resolution calling for Israeli withdrawal from Sinai vetoed by Britain and France.
	British and French attack in the Canal Zone.
1957	Israel announces intention conditionally to with-draw from Sinai.
	Palestinian Liberation Party (Fatah) founded.
1958	Relations between Israel and United States strengthened.
1963	Levi Eshkol becomes Prime Minister.
1964	Palestine Liberation Organization (PLO) founded.
1966	Fedayeen activity against Israel increased.
1967	Nasser sends troops into Sinai.
	Nasser closes Strait of Tiran to Israeli shipping.
	Six-Day War.
	Summit at Khartoum.
	United Nations Security Council Resolution 242 issued.
1968	Golda Meir becomes Prime Minister.
	Egypt commences war of attrition against Israel.
	Yasser Arafat elected chairman of the executive committee of the PLO.
1970	Black September: Jordanian army acts against PLO guerrillas in Jordan.
1971	PLO guerrillas leave Jordan for Syria and south Lebanon.

1972	Black September organization seizes Israeli athletes at Munich Olympics. Nine Israelis die in airport shoot-out.
1973	Egypt and Syria launch full-scale war against Israeli forces occupying the Sinai Peninsula and Golan Heights.
1974	Summit meeting of Arab leaders in Rabat declares the PLO the only legitimate representative of the Palestinian people.
1975	Civil war breaks out in Lebanon. Palestinian guerrillas fight alongside Lebanese leftists and Muslims against Maronite Christians.
1976	Following Syrian intervention in the Lebanese civil war, Arab leaders agree to a cease-fire.
1977	Sadat goes to Jerusalem for peace offer.
1978	Israel invades south Lebanon and attacks Palestinian guerrilla bases. Camp David Accords signed by Egypt, Israel and USA.
1979	Egypt and Israel sign peace treaty.
1981	Katyusha war between the PLO and Israel in Lebanon. Sadat assassinated by Egyptian militants during a military parade celebrating victory in the 1973 war.
1982	Israel invades Lebanon again in an all-out offensive against the PLO. Israeli forces reach outskirts of Beirut. Following the siege, the PLO leaves Lebanon, establishes headquarters in Tunis and scatters its fighters throughout the Arab countries. Massacre of Palestinian refugees in Sabra and Shatila camps in Lebanon. Israeli Defence Minister Sharon forced from office. Lebanon–Israel truce.

1998	Wye River agreement between Netanyahu and Arafat.
1999	Netanyahu loses Israeli election to Ehud Barak. King Hussein of Jordan dies and is succeeded by his eldest son, Abdullah.
2000	Israel withdraws from Lebanon. Death of President Hafez al-Asad of Syria. Palestinian uprising. Final collapse of Wye Accords as Palestinians reject Israeli plan that would keep large areas of the West Bank under Israeli control. Visit by MK Ariel Sharon to al-Haram al-Sharif/Temple Mount triggers Al-Aqsa Intifada.
2001	Ariel Sharon elected Prime Minister of Israel. 'Dolphinarium' discotheque in Tel Aviv hit by suicide bomb. 'Sbarro' pizzeria suicide bombing in Jerusalem by Islamic Jihad. Israel assassinates Abu Ali Mustafa. Terror attacks on the World Trade Center. PFLP assassinates Israeli tourism minister Rehav'am Ze'evi.
2002	Saudi Prince Abdullah announces a Peace plan. Israel mounts operation 'Defensive Wall' in retaliation for suicide bombings. Invasion of Jenin refugee camp and West Bank towns. Chairman Arafat imprisoned in the 'Mukata' compound in Ramallah. End of sieges in Mukata and Church of Nativity. Chairman Arafat signs the 2002: PNA Basic Law. Israel commences building of the 'Separation Fence'. President Bush calls for Israeli withdrawal and a

	Palestinian state, but insists that PNA be reformed and current leaders replaced.
	Israel assassinates Saleh Shehadeh.
	Israel's government unstable due to resignations in the Labour party.
2003	Cairo conference of Palestinian groups.
	Ariel Sharon re-elected Prime Minister.
	United States and Britain invade Iraq overthrowing the regime of Saddam Hussein.
2003	Mahmoud Abbas appointed Prime Minister.
	Arafat under siege in Ramallah headquarters.
2004	Operation Rainbow.
	Operation Days of Penitence.
	Ramallah siege continues.
	Arafat delegates powers to Mahmoud Abbas.
	Death of Arafat.
2005	Mahmoud Abbas elected President.
	Ariel Sharon resigns as leader of Likud party and sets up Kadima. Israeli disengagement from the Gaza Strip.
2006	Ariel Sharon suffers haemorrhagic stroke.
	Ehud Olmert elected Prime Minister of Israel.
	Hamas wins a majority of seats in the Palestinian legislature.
	Israel–Lebanon War.
	Hamas and Fatah agree to a cease-fire.
2007	Fighting continues between Hamas and Fatah.
	The armed wing of Hamas announces that the truce with Israel has ended.
2008	Bush tours Middle East.
	Popular breakout from Gaza into Egypt to buy essential supplies.
2009	Barack Obama elected President of the United States of America.

US Secretary of State Hillary Clinton goes to Israel.

White House announces negotiations to take place between Israel and the Palestinians.

Israel imposes construction freeze on settlements in the West Bank.

2010   Israel carries out Gaza flotilla raid.

Negotiations take place between Israel and the Palestinians.

2011   Fatah and Hamas sign a unity agreement.

Mahmoud Abbas appeals to the UN General Assembly to recognize Palestine as a nation state.

2014   On 8 July Israel launches Operation Protective Edge in the Gaza Strip; its aim is to stop rocket attacks from Gaza.

Mahmoud Abbas appears before the UN General Assembly demanding an end to Israeli occupation and recognition of the Palestinian State.

Maps

A Jewish perspective

Dan Cohn-Sherbok

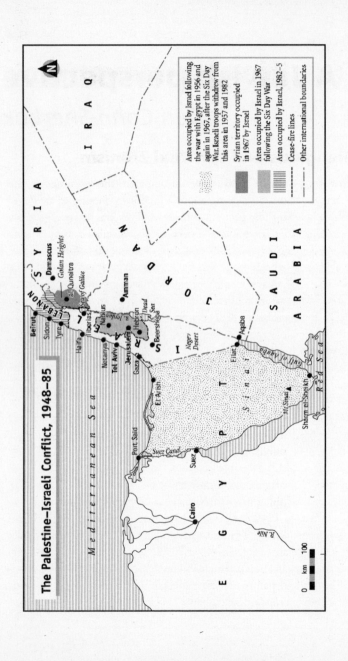

The Palestine–Israeli Conflict, 1948–85

Mediterranean Sea

LEBANON
Beirut
Sidon
Tyre

SYRIA
Damascus
Golan Heights
al-Quneitra
Sea of Galilee
Tiberias

Haifa
Netanya
Tel Aviv
Nablus
Jordan
Amman

JORDAN

Jerusalem
Gaza
Hebron
Dead Sea
Beersheba
El-Arish

ISRAEL

Negev Desert

IRAQ

SAUDI ARABIA

Aqaba
Eilat

EGYPT
Port Said
Suez Canal
Suez
Cairo
R. Nile

Sinai
Mt Sinai
Sharm el-Sheikh
Gulf of Aqaba
Red Sea

Area occupied by Israel following
the war with Egypt in 1956 and
again in 1967, after the Six Day
War. Israeli troops withdrew from
this area in 1957 and 1982

Syrian territory occupied
in 1967 by Israel

Area occupied by Israel in 1967
following the Six Day War

Area occupied by Israel, 1982–5

Cease-fire lines

Other international boundaries

0   km   100

The Zionist movement

Religious and spiritual Zionism

For thousands of years Jews anticipated the coming of the Messiah who would bring about a final in-gathering of the Jewish people to their ancient homeland. This was to be a divinely predetermined miraculous event which would inaugurate the messianic age. However, in the early nineteenth century within religious Orthodox circles there emerged a new trend, the advocacy of an active approach to Jewish messianism. A number of Jewish writers maintained that, rather than adopt a passive attitude towards the problem of redemption, the Jewish nation must engage in the creation of a homeland in anticipation of the advent of the Messiah.

Pre-eminent among such religious Zionists was Yehuda hai Alkalai, born in 1798 in Sarajevo to Rabbi Sholomo Alkalai, the spiritual leader of the local Jewish community. During his youth Yehuda lived in Palestine, where he was influenced by kabbalistic thought. In 1825 he served as a rabbi in Semlin in Serbia; in 1834 he published a booklet entitled *Shema Yisrael* in which he advocated the establishment of Jewish colonies in Palestine, a view at variance with the traditional Jewish belief that the Messiah would come through an act of divine deliverance.

When in 1840 the Jews of Damascus were charged with the blood libel (killing a child and using its blood in an act of ritual), Alkalai became convinced that the Jewish people could be secure only in their own land. Henceforth he published a series of books and pamphlets explaining his plan of self-redemption. In *Minhat Yehuda*, for example, he argued on the basis of the

Hebrew scriptures that the Messiah will not miraculously materialize; rather, he will be preceded by various preparatory events. In this light the Holy Land needs to be populated by Jewry in preparation for messianic deliverance.[1] For Alkalai, redemption is not simply a divine affair – it is also a human concern requiring labour and persistence.

This demystification of traditional messianic eschatology extends to Alkalai's advocacy of Hebrew as a language of communication. Traditionally, Hebrew was viewed as a sacred language; it was not to be profaned by daily use. Alkalai, however, recognized the practical importance of having a single language for ordinary life in Palestine. It would be a mistake, he believed, to think that God will send an angel to teach his people all seventy languages. Instead the Jewish people must ensure that Hebrew is studied so that it can be used for ordinary life.[2]

How can this process of redemption be accomplished? Alkalai stressed the importance of convening an assembly of those dedicated to the realization of this goal. Thus he asserted that the redemption must begin with efforts by Jews themselves. They must organize, choose leaders and leave the countries in which they reside. Since no community can exist without a governing body, the first step in this process of resettlement must be the appointment of elders of each district to oversee the affairs of the community.[3]

Another early pioneer of religious Zionism was Zwi Hirsch Kalischer, the rabbi of Toun in the province of Posen, in Poland. An early defender of Orthodoxy against the advances made by Reform Judaism, he championed the commandments in prescribing faith in the Messiah and devotion to the Holy Land. In 1836 he expressed his commitment to Jewish settlement in Palestine in a letter to the head of the Berlin branch of the Rothschild family. The beginning of redemption, he maintained, will come through natural causes by human effort to gather the scattered of Israel into the Holy Land.[4]

Such a conviction did not actively engage Kalischer until 1860 when a society was organized in Frankfurt on the Oder to encourage Jewish settlement in Palestine. After joining this group, he published a Zionist work, *Derishat Zion* (Seeking Zion), which appeared in 1862. The redemption of Israel, he argued, will not take place miraculously. Instead, the redemption of Israel will take place slowly through awakening support from philanthropists and gaining the consent of other nations to the gathering of the Jewish people into the Holy Land.[5]

For Kalischer practical steps must be taken to fulfil this dream of resettlement. What is required is that an organization be created to encourage emigration, and to purchase and cultivate farms and vineyards. Such a programme would be a ray of deliverance to those who were languishing in Palestine suffering poverty and famine; this situation would be utterly changed if those able to contribute to this effort were inspired by the vision of a Jewish homeland. An advantage of this scheme would be to bring to fruition those religious commandments that attach to working the soil of the Holy Land. But beyond all this, Kalischer was convinced that Jewish farming would be a spur to messianic redemption.

Following in the footsteps of such religious Zionists as Alkalai and Kalischer, Abraham Isaac Kook formulated a vision of messianic redemption integrating the creation of a Jewish state. Born in Greiva, Latvia, in 1865, Kook received a traditional Jewish education and in 1895 became rabbi of Bausk. In 1904 he emigrated to Palestine, eventually becoming the first Ashkenazi chief rabbi after the British Mandate. Unlike secularists who advocated practical efforts to secure a Jewish state, Kook embarked on the task of reinterpreting the Jewish religious tradition to transform religious messianic anticipation into the basis for collaboration with the aspirations of modern Zionism.

According to Kook, the centrality of Israel is a fundamental dimension of Jewish life and a crucial element of Jewish religious consciousness. Yet the fervent belief in messianic deliverance has not been accompanied by an active policy of resettlement. This disjunction between religious aspirations for the return from exile and the desire of most Jews to live in the diaspora highlights the confusion in Jewish thinking about the role of Israel in Jewish life. There is thus a contradiction between the messianic belief in a return to Zion and the accommodating attitude to exile of most Jews throughout history.

For Kook, this contradiction at the heart of Jewish existence must be confronted and resolved. Kook maintained that a Jewish person in the diaspora is able to observe all commandments of the Law and live as a devout Jew. Yet, because he lives outside the Jewish homeland, an essential dimension of Jewishness is missing from his life. Life in the diaspora involves one in unholiness whereas by settling in Palestine it is possible to live a spiritually unsullied life. Return to Zion is thus imperative for an authentic existence.[6] For Kook, attachment to the land must serve as the foundation of Jewish life in the modern world. Although the secular pioneers who came to Palestine were motivated by ideological convictions alien to traditional Judaism, their actions are paradoxically part of God's plan of redemption. In the cosmic scheme of the divine will, seemingly atheistic and secular actions are absorbed into the unfolding of God's plan for his chosen people. Therefore these pioneers unintentionally contributed to the advent of the Messiah.[7]

Like Alkalai and Kalischer and Kook, Asher Zvi Ginsberg (later known as Ahad Ha-Am) was concerned with the spiritual redemption of the Jewish people, although his thought is devoid of traditional Jewish ideas of messianic redemption. Born in Skvira in the Russian Ukraine on 18 August 1856, he received a traditional Jewish education. In 1868 his family moved to an estate that his wealthy father leased; there he studied the works of medieval Jewish philosophers and writers of the Enlightenment. Later he studied French and German literature and philosophy.

After attempting unsuccessfully to continue his study in various European capitals, he moved to Odessa in 1886, where he began to publish articles concerning contemporary Jewish life.

His first essay, *Wrong Way*, set the stage for his role within the *Hovevei Zion* (Lovers of Zion) movement. In this work he advocated a return to Zion, but remained critical of a number of aspects of the movement's platform. In a later essay, *The Jewish State and the Jewish Problem*, he discussed the notion of a Jewish settlement. According to Ahad Ha-Am, even if a Jewish state existed in Palestine, not all Jews would be able to settle there. What would be the result if only a small section of the world Jewish population emigrated? Ahad Ha-Am argued that the economic problems facing Eastern European Jewry would not be solved for those who remained behind. The Jewish state could only contribute to cultural and spiritual regeneration.

The central dilemma faced by Zionism is how the spiritual perplexities of Jews in the diaspora could be resolved by the creation of a Jewish homeland. For Ahad Ha-Am, Zionism is able to solve the problems of Western Jewry more readily than to ameliorate the condition of Jews in Eastern Europe. Jews in the West are separated from Jewish culture and simultaneously alienated from the society in which they reside. The existence of a Jewish state would enable them to solve the problems of national identity, compensating them for their lack of integration into the culture of the country in which they live.[8] This ideal can cure the Jews in the West of their social unease, their sense of inferiority in lands where they are aliens. Ahad Ha-Am was thus insistent that the Jewish state be infused with Jewish values, and not simply be a homeland for the Jewish people. It must embody the religious and cultural ideals of the Jewish past.

Although Ahad Ha-Am's vision of the return to the Jews' ancestral homeland was not filled with messianic longing, his idealization of the spiritual, religious and cultural dimensions of Judaism and their embodiment of a Jewish state was rooted in

Jewish messianism. For Ahad Ha-Am, it would not be a divinely appointed Messiah who would bring about the realization of God's kingdom on earth. Rather this would be the task of the Jewish people themselves. Through the creation of a Jewish state, the spiritual values of the faith are to materialize in the Holy Land.

Secular Zionism

In contrast with such figures as Alkalai, Kalischer, Kook and Ahad Ha-Am, modern secular Zionists have been preoccupied with the problem of anti-Semitism rather than religious and spiritual values. Modern secular Zionism begins with the writings of Moses Hess. Born in Bonn, Germany, Hess settled in Paris, where he was active in socialist circles. From 1842 to 1843 he served as the Paris correspondent of the *Rheinische Zeitung,* edited by Karl Marx. In 1862 he published *Rome and Jerusalem*, a systematic defence of Jewish nationalism. In this work, he argued that anti-Jewish sentiment is unavoidable. Progressive Jews think they can escape from Judeophobia by recoiling from any Jewish national expression, yet the hatred of Jews is inescapable.

For Hess, Jews will always remain strangers among the nations: nothing can alter this state of affairs. The only solution to the problem of Jew hatred is for the Jewish people to come to terms with their national identity. According to Hess, the restoration of Jewish nationalism will not deprive the world of the benefits promoted by Jewish reformers who wish to dissociate themselves from the particularistic dimensions of the Jewish heritage. On the contrary, the values of universalism will be championed by various aspects of Judaism's national character. What is required today, Hess asserted, is for Jewry to regenerate the Jewish nation and to keep alive the hope for the political rebirth of the Jewish people.[9]

For Hess, a Jewish renaissance is possible once national life reasserts itself in the Holy Land. In the past the creative energies of the people deserted Israel when Jews became ashamed of their nationality. But the holy spirit, he argued, will again animate Jewry once the nation awakens to a new life. The only question remaining is how it might be possible to stimulate the patriotic sentiments of modern Jewry as well as to liberate the Jewish masses by means of this revived national loyalty. This is a formidable challenge, yet Hess maintained that it must be tackled. Although he recognized that there could not be a total emigration of world Jewry to Palestine, Hess believed that the existence of a Jewish state would act as a spiritual centre for the Jewish people and all of humanity.

The Russian pogroms had a profound impact on another early Zionist, Leon Pinsker, driving him from an espousal of the ideas of the Enlightenment to the determination to create a Jewish homeland. Born in TomoaszF3w in Russian Poland in 1821, Pinsker attended a Russian high school, studied law in Odessa and later received a medical degree from the University of Moscow. Upon returning to Odessa, he was appointed to the staff of the local city hospital. After 1860, he contributed to Jewish weekly papers and was active in the Society for the Spread of Culture among the Jews of Russia. However, when Jews were massacred in the pogroms of 1881, he left the Society, convinced that a more radical remedy was required to solve the plight of Russian Jewry.

In 1882 he published *Autoemancipation,* in which he argued that the Jewish problem is as unresolved in the modern world as it was in former times. In essence, this dilemma concerns the unassimilable character of Jewish identity in countries where Jews are in the minority. In such cases there is no basis for mutual respect between Jews and non-Jews. Among the nations of the world, Pinsker argued, the Jews are like a nation long since dead. The fear of the Jewish ghost has been a typical reaction throughout the centuries, and has paved the way for current Judeophobia. This prejudice has through the years become rooted and naturalized among all peoples of the world.

Such Jew hatred has generated various charges against the Jewish people: throughout history Jews have been accused of crucifying Jesus, drinking the blood of Christians, poisoning wells, exacting usury and exploiting peasants. Such accusations are invariably groundless – they were trumped up to quiet the conscience of Jew baiters. Thus Judaism and anti–Semitism have been inseparable companions through the centuries, and any struggle against this aberration of the human mind is fruitless. Unlike other peoples, the Jews are inevitably aliens. They are not simply guests in a foreign country; they are more like beggars and refugees.

The isolation of the Jew, Pinsker continued, cannot be removed by any form of official emancipation, since the Jew is eternally an alien. Given this situation, the Jewish people have no choice but to reconstitute themselves as a separate people. The Jewish struggle to attain this goal has an inherent justification that belongs to the quest of every oppressed people. Although this endeavour may be opposed in various quarters, the battle must continue – the Jewish people have no other way out of their desperate position. There is a moral duty to ensure that persecuted Jews wherever they live will have a secure home.[10]

For Pinsker the present moment is a decisive time for the revival of national aspirations. History appears to be on the side of world Jewry in its longing for a national homeland. Even in the absence of a leader like Moses, the recognition of what Jewish people need most should arouse a number of energetic individuals to take on positions of responsibility. Already, he noted, there are societies that are pressing for the creation of a Jewish nation. They must now invoke a national congress and establish a national directorate to bring to fruition these plans. Not all Jews would be able to settle in this Jewish homeland.

Yet, it would serve as a refuge for those who seek to flee from oppression and persecution.

More than with any other figure, modern secular Zionism has become identified with Theodor Herzl. Born on 2 May 1860 in Budapest, Hungary, he was the only son of a rich merchant. After studying at a technical school and high school in Budapest, he went to Vienna, where he enrolled in the law faculty of the university. In 1884 he received a doctorate and worked for a year as a civil servant. Subsequently he wrote plays, and in 1892 was appointed to the staff of the *Neue Freie Presse*. As its Paris correspondent, he witnessed the Dreyfus affair and became convinced that the Jewish problem could be solved only by the creation of Jewish homeland.

In May 1895 Herzl requested an interview with Baron Maurice de Hirsch to interest him in the establishment of a Jewish state. When the Baron expressed little sympathy for the project, Herzl hoped the Rothschilds would be more receptive and wrote a sixty-five-page proposal outlining his views. This work was an outline of his *The Jewish State,* which appeared in February 1896; this was followed by a utopian study, *Alteneuland*, published in 1902. Herzl's analysis of modern Jewish existence was not original – many of his ideas were preceded in the writings of Moses Hess and Leon Pinsker. However, what was novel about Herzl's espousal of Zionism was his success in stimulating interest in and debate about a Jewish state in the highest diplomatic and political circles. This was due both to the force of his personality and to the passionate expression of his proposals.

Convinced of the importance of his views, Herzl insisted that the building of a Jewish homeland would transform Jewish life. In the preface to *The Jewish State* Herzl states that his advocacy of a Jewish homeland is not simply a utopian scheme; on the contrary, his plan is a realistic proposal arising out of the appalling conditions facing Jews living under oppression and persecution. The plan, he argued, would be impractical if only a single individual were to undertake it. But if many Jews were to agree on its importance, its implementation would be entirely reasonable. Like Pinsker, Herzl believed that the Jewish question can be solved only if the Jews constitute themselves as one people.[11]

Old prejudices against Jewry are ingrained in Western society – assimilation will not act as a cure for the ills that beset the Jewish people. There is only one remedy for the malady of anti-Semitism: the creation of a Jewish commonwealth. In *The Jewish State* Herzl outlined the nature of such a social and political entity. The plan, he argued, should be carried out by two agencies: the Society of Jews and the Jewish Company. The scientific programme and political policies that the Society of Jews will establish should be carried out by the Jewish Company. This body will be the liquidating agent for the business interests of departing Jews, and will organize trade and commerce in the new country. Given such a framework, immigration of Jews will be gradual. Their tasks will be to construct roads, bridges, railways and telephone installations; in addition, they will regulate rivers and provide themselves with homesteads.

Those Jews who agree with the concept of a Jewish state should rally round the Society of Jews and encourage its endeavours. In this way they will give it authority in the eyes of governments, and in time ensure that the state is recognized through international law. If other nations are willing to grant Jews sovereignty over a neutral land, then the Society will be able to enter into negotiations for its possession. In his novel *Alteneuland* Herzl discussed the social and economic structure of such a state in Palestine. These two works, one a passionate call for the building of a Jewish country and the other a novelistic proposal for Jewish existence in such a future society in Palestine, strengthened the case for political Zionism. Championing the concept of a Jewish refuge from persecution, Herzl laid the foundations for the creation of a Jewish homeland in the Middle East.

The origins of the Zionist movement

Anxious to pursue his Zionist vision, Theodor Herzl began a campaign to arouse interest in the creation of a Jewish homeland. In 1896 he established contact with *Hovevei Zion* in Russia and Poland. This was followed in the same year by a meeting with the Grand Duke of Baden. In the summer of 1896 Herzl travelled to Constantinople to meet with the Sultan. On route he encountered Sephardic and Ashkenazic Jews at the station in Sofia who hailed him as the 'Heart of Israel'. Joyously they declared *'Leshanah Haba Birushalayim'* (Next year in Jerusalem). Despite such enthusiasm, this mission accomplished little – Herzl failed to see the Sultan and instead met with the Grand Vizier.

Returning to Europe, he spoke to a gathering of poor immigrant Jews in Whitechapel, London. Sitting in their midst, he perceived that the masses saw him as their redeemer, a modern Messiah who would lead them back to the Promised Land. Nonetheless, the leaders of Eastern European Jewry became increasingly agitated about Herzl's appeal. Fearing the consequences of mass hysteria, like that which accompanied Shabbetai Zevi in the seventeenth century, they were wary of his political activities. In addition, members of *Hovevei Zion* became suspicious of what they perceived as Herzl's messianic pretensions.

By the autumn of 1896, Herzl was discouraged by these reactions. Yet, he quickly revived and renewed his labours. After conferring in Berlin with members of *Hovevei Zion* from Berlin, Herzl came to the view that a congress of Zionists should be convened in Switzerland. Once invitations to this gathering had been sent, delegates enthusiastically responded. Even the leaders of *Hovevei Zion* agreed to attend despite their reservations about Herzl's appeal among the Jewish masses. On 29 August 1897, the First Zionist Congress opened in the concert hall of Basle Municipal Casino. Over two hundred men and women attended, representing twenty-four states and territories.

Though only about half of the participants came from Eastern Europe, a large proportion of those from Western countries were of Eastern European origin. Half of those from Germany, for example, were originally from Russia. Herzl took special care not to dominate the Congress, and the most moving speech was given by Max Nordau, who spoke eloquently about the dismal conditions of European Jewry at the end of the nineteenth century. Anti-Semitism, he explained, dominated their lives. Not only do the Jews' fellow citizens repel them, but the Jews have no sense of belonging to the countries where they reside. Believing that the world hates them, they are unable to find a place where they can feel secure. In his speech to the Congress, Herzl emphasized that the creation of a Jewish homeland is an abiding feature of the Jewish tradition.[12]

Paradoxically, however, there was no mention made at the Congress of a Jewish state because mention of such a vision might endanger Jewish settlers in Palestine and prejudice future development of the movement. Delegates were well aware that the Sultan had no intention of handing back Palestine to the Jews. Further, even if this had been his intention, he would have feared the Russian response. As Rothschild had explained to Max Nordau several months previously, the Sultan feared Russia, and Russia would never permit Palestine to fall under Jewish control. This was so because the Russian Orthodox Church would never permit the Jews to become masters of Jerusalem.

In its programme the Congress adopted by acclamation the quest to establish a Jewish homeland in Palestine. Yet, after Basle there were two approaches to Zionism: political Zionism as espoused by Herzl, and practical Zionism, the official policy of *Hovevei Zion*. Dedicated to settling the land, *Hovevei Zion* continued with their small-scale settlements in Palestine, committed to the view that the development of a Jewish presence should be a gradual process. Herzl, however, believed that there must be a massive in-gathering into the Holy Land. Determined to save those Jews who were compelled to live in adverse conditions, Herzl sought to negotiate at the highest levels a grant of land sufficient for Jewish statehood.

In 1898 a Second Zionist Congress was held at Basle with nearly double the number of participants. Since the First Congress, the number of Zionist societies had grown to 913, most of them in Russia and Austria-Hungary. The total membership of these organizations was approximately one hundred thousand. In his address to this body, Herzl stressed that the emancipation of Jewry did not result in the elimination of anti-Semitism. Rather, Jews have continued to be oppressed and persecuted in the countries in which they reside. As a result, the historical intent of emancipation is to create a homeland for modern Jews. This was not possible in earlier times, but it can now become a reality.

Critical of Russian Jews who sought to smuggle settlers into Palestine, Herzl argued that a formal agreement must be reached with the Turkish authorities. In this address, Herzl alluded to the visit of Kaiser Wilhelm II to Constantinople, Jerusalem and Damascus in October and November 1898 – this, he believed, would provide an opportunity to enlist support for the movement, since Imperial Germany was emerging as the patron and protector of the Ottoman Empire. On 18 October 1898 the Kaiser met Herzl in Constantinople at the Yildiz Kosk, where the Kaiser was staying as the Sultan's guest. During their discussion, Herzl encouraged the Kaiser to ask the Sultan if a chartered company for Jews in Palestine under German protection could be created.

Initially it appears that the Kaiser viewed this plan favourably, but when he met with a Zionist delegation headed by Herzl in Jerusalem nothing was said about this plan. At the conclusion of his tour in Damascus, the Kaiser declared himself a friend of the Islamic people, and it became an official policy of Germany that no intervention in favour of Herzl's state should be undertaken because of the damage it would inflict on Germany's interests in Turkey. Following the Kaiser's visit, the Sultan announced his decision to award the Deutsche Bank the concession for a railway to Baghdad and the Persian Gulf.

At the Third Zionist Congress Herzl stressed that progress had been made toward creating a Jewish state. He had met the Kaiser, and all efforts must now be directed toward obtaining a charter from the Turkish government under the sovereignty of the Sultan. Such an agreement would enable Zionists to undertake widespread settlement in Palestine. In pursuit of this aim, Herzl met with the Sultan on 17 May 1901 at Yildiz Kiosk, where he had met the Kaiser two years before. Despite Herzl's enthusiasm for this meeting, the interview produced no positive results. Returning to Constantinople, he was conscious that he was up against an insuperable obstacle to his plans.

Not surprisingly the Sultan rejected Herzl's overtures. Herzl and other Zionists believed they could hide their ultimate objective – the establishment of a Jewish state – by focusing on the formation of a chartered company. Ottoman diplomats, however, were clear about the intentions of the Zionists. Reporting on the Sixth Zionist Congress, which took place in 1903, the Ottoman ambassador to Berlin, Ahmed Tevfik, encouraged his government to draw up special laws to prohibit the purchase of land in Palestine in order to prevent the colonization of the country. This, he declared, was the essential aim of the Zionists.

Undeterred by such resistance, Herzl concentrated on influencing British opinion. The Fourth Zionist Congress was to be held in London, and Herzl turned his attention to influencing British policy. Giving evidence before the Royal Commission on immigration, he stated that European Jews were subject to increasing anti-Semitism. How were they to escape such persecution? he asked. Emigration would be possible if a Jewish homeland were made available.[13] Joseph Chamberlain, a member of Balfour's Conservative government, was seriously interested in such a project. At a meeting with Herzl in October 1902, Chamberlain expressed his approval of a Jewish settlement at El Arish in the Sinai peninsula on the border of Palestine. The Foreign Office, however, was opposed to such a solution, as was the *de facto* governor of the area, Lord Cromer.

By this stage Herzl was suffering from heart disease, and pogroms in Russia became increasingly disastrous for the Jewish community. On 19–20 April 1903, the Jews of Kishinev were assaulted by an unruly mob which killed thirty-two men, six women and three children. In addition, 495 were injured and subsequently eight others died. Herzl's response to this onslaught was to go to St Petersburg to meet with the Tsar's Minister of the Interior, V.K. Plehve. Determined to divert Russian Jews from revolutionary activity and to rid the country of a Jewish presence, Plehve stated that Russia favoured the creation of a Jewish state in Palestine and would intervene in Constantinople to support the establishment of a Jewish settlement. Despite such assurances, little resulted from this meeting.

Returning from St Petersburg on 16 August 1903, Herzl stopped in Vilna, where he was met by crowds of enthusiastic Jews who had thronged to welcome him as their saviour. After encountering these Eastern European Jews, Herzl became even more convinced of the need for a Jewish homeland. Yet, he recognized the difficulties of creating a Jewish state in Palestine. The same month the British Foreign Secretary, Lord Lansdowne, told the Zionists that if a suitable site could be found in East Africa he would be prepared to entertain favourably proposals for the creation of a Jewish colony or settlement.

At the Sixth Zionist Congress in Basle in August 1903, Herzl encouraged sending a committee to East Africa to inves-tigate. Although this proposal was passed by 295 votes to 178 with 99 abstentions, Russian Zionists were bitterly opposed to such a development. In their view, this was a travesty of

Zionist aspirations. The delegates from Kishinev in particular were determined to thwart this scheme; in November 1903 they met at Kharkov and an ultimatum was sent to Herzl: he was to withdraw the East Africa project, or a new Independent Zionist organization would be formed.

Determined to carry on with negotiations, Herzl met with the King of Italy and Pope Pius X in Rome in January 1904 and explained the importance of creating a Jewish settlement in Palestine. The Pope, however, was insistent that the Jewish people embrace the Christian faith if he were to support the notion of a return to the Holy Land. On 3 July, Herzl died and was buried in Vienna. From throughout Europe thousands of supporters came to his funeral. The next year the Seventh Zionist Congress rejected the East Africa project and declared the movement's commitment to creating a Jewish National Home in *Eretz Israel*. This was to be the guiding policy of the Zionists throughout the century.

Jewish settlement in Palestine

While Herzl and others agitated for the creation of a Jewish state in Palestine, Jewish immigrants founded a variety of settlements and institutions in the Holy Land. By the middle of the nineteenth century approximately ten thousand Jews lived in Palestine. Most of these immigrants resided in Jerusalem; several hundred others settled in Safed, Acre and Jaffa. Most of these Jews had emigrated from Poland and Lithuania and survived on charity. In 1870 a French educator, Charles Netter, founded an agricultural school at Mikveh Israel (Hope of Israel) with the approval of the Turkish authorities. Eight years later a number of Jews from Jerusalem established Petah Tikvah (Gateway of Hope) on the coastal plain; in the same year religious Jews from Safed founded Rosh Pinah (Head Stone).

Following pogroms in Russia, members of *Hovevei Zion* emigrated to Palestine, where they established farms and villages. During the First Aliyah, from 1882 to 1903, about twenty-five thousand Jews reached Palestine. The first village created by settlers from outside Palestine was Rishon le-Zion (First to Zion), later supported by Baron Edmond de Rothschild – the first language kindergarten and elementary school in Palestine were opened there several years after its establishment. In 1882 the town of Zichron Yaakov (Memory of Jacob) was created by Romanian immigrants, again with the support of Baron Edmond de Rothschild; in the same year Hayyim Amzalak, a Jew from Gibraltar, bought the land on which Petah Tikvah had been built; this was given to Bilu, secular and socialist pioneers from Russia who took their name from the Hebrew initials of the biblical verse '*Beth Jacob Lechu Venelcha*' ('O House of Jacob, come and let us go').

In 1883 a Russian Jewish emigrant, Reuben Lehrer, built a house in an Arab village, Wadi Hanin, on the coastal plain; he was later joined by several other Jewish settlers. In 1884 another Russian Jew, Yehiel Michael Pines, bought land needed for Bilu pioneers to create another village, Gederah. In Jerusalem the population grew considerably through these waves of immigration. By the 1850s Jews were in the majority – by 1889 their numbers had risen to twenty-five thousand. In 1890 another Jewish village, Rehovot (Wide Expanses), was founded on the coastal plain. The same year, Russian Jews who had emigrated from Vilna, Riga and Kovno founded Hadera (The Green). At the same time a group of *Hovevei Zion* created a small farming settlement in Upper Galilee on the west bank of the River Jordan – Mishmar Ha-Yarden (Guard of the Jordan).

In 1903 Menachem Ussishkin travelled from Russia to Palestine to convene a convention at Zichron Yaakov, where he encouraged delegates to remain faithful to the Zionist vision. Before returning to Russia, he founded the Hebrew Teachers'

Federation in Palestine. From 1904 until the First World War a further wave of immigration – the Second Aliyah – took place. In 1906 the first Hebrew high school was founded in Jaffa. Two years later, Arthur Ruppin became head of the Palestine Office of the Zionist Executive and encouraged the creation of Jewish farming settlements; in addition, he arranged for the purchase of land and set up an agricultural training farm at Kinneret. The money for this acquisition came from the Jewish National Fund, as did funds that were used to buy farming land at Hulda in the Judean Hills. In 1910 Aaron Aaronsohn set up the Jewish Agricultural Experiment Station at Athlit.

During this period Tel Aviv (Hill of Spring) was founded just north of Jaffa on land purchased from Turks. The Jewish National Fund provided funds needed to build the first sixty houses, and foundations were laid for the creation of a Hebrew language high school, the Herzliya Gymnasium. In 1911 the first Jewish hospital was opened in the Arab port of Haifa by Elias Auerbach, a German-speaking doctor who had emigrated to Palestine. The following year the Hadassah Women's Zionist Organization of America sent two members to establish a clinic in Jerusalem. In the same year a girls' agricultural farm was created at Kinneret.

In 1914 supporters of the creation of the Hebrew University sought to persuade Sir John Gray Hill to sell them his house on Mount Scopus. Much of the money for this project was raised by the *Hovevei Zion* at the instigation of Menachem Ussishkin. On 9 March 1914 Arthur Ruppin recorded in his dairy that he had been successful in acquiring an option to purchase Sir John Gray Hill's property. Four years later this option was acted upon. Other early institutions founded in Palestine included the Bezalel art school, which was funded by Otto Warburg and a group of German Zionists. An American Jew, Nathan Straus, provided funds to establish a Jewish hospital in Jerusalem.

Simultaneously, Jewish settlements continued to be created in Palestine. In 1914 a group of *Hovevei Zion* from Russia
founded Nahalat Yehuda (the Inheritance of Yehuda) north of
Rishon le-Zion. By this stage there were approximately ninety
thousand Jews living in the Holy Land, of whom seventy-five
thousand were immigrants. In the years following the creation
of the Jewish National Fund at the beginning of the century,
forty-three settlements had been created with a population of
120,000. The majority of those who had emigrated to Palestine
were from Russia and Romania – they either worked on the
land as farmers or agricultural labourers or were employed as
shopkeepers, artisans and labourers. By contrast, the number of
Arabs in Palestine was about half a million.

Anxious about the influx of Jewish settlers, the Arab population began to engage in political activity. Two Jerusalem Arabs
were elected to the Ottoman Parliament in Constantinople as
anti-Zionists. In the summer of 1914 the Turkish government
imposed strict measures to curtail Jewish immigration. Later,
when Turkey entered the First World War on the side of the
Central Powers, France and Russia became Turkey's enemies.
As a result, the Jews of Palestine suffered great hardships as food
supplies dwindled and the Turkish government came to regard
the Jewish population with hostility, since large numbers of Jewish immigrants were Russian in origin.

The Turkish military commander, Jemal Pasha, sought to
quell both Jewish and Arab national sentiments. In Beirut and
Jerusalem several Arab leaders were hanged, and eighteen thousand Jews were expelled or fled from Palestine to Alexandria.
In addition, Jews known to have been active in Zionist circles,
including Arthur Ruppin, were expelled from the country. In
response to these developments, the Jaffa Group, consisting of
a number of Jewish fighters, was established to defend Jewish
settlements in Palestine. With the outbreak of war, a number
of Zionists were anxious to establish a Jewish legion to fight

alongside the Allies against the Turks. It was the aim of this group to participate in the liberation of Palestine from Turkish control and to convince the Allies of the need for a Jewish homeland. Pre-eminent among these Zionists, Vladimir Jabotinsky, a Russian correspondent of a Moscow newspaper who was based in Egypt, encouraged Zionists there to join in political and military alliance with the British, French and Russians against the Germans and Turks.

Another major Jewish figure in this campaign was Joseph Trumpeldor, a veteran of the Russo–Japanese war of 1904–5. Strongly in favour of a Jewish military force, he joined with Jabotinsky in an effort to persuade the British government to create a Jewish defence force, the Zion Mule Corps, to serve on the Gallipoli Peninsula, where an Anglo–French force had landed. Although the Allied offensive at Gallipoli was unsuccessful, the efforts of the Zion Mule Corps were appreciated by the British, an outcome that encouraged the Allies to include Jewish troops in the conquest of Palestine. Yet, as the war intensified, Turkish troops were successful in keeping the British out of the country.

Throughout the war, the defence of outlying settlements in the north became a priority. In 1916 Kibbutz Kfar Giladi was established by members of Ha-Shomer to guard the northern settlements against Arab attack. In Tel Aviv a committee headed by Meir Dizengoff, head of the local Israel council, was created to help those suffering in the war. Like other Jews, he was expelled by the Turks and sent to Damascus, where he remained until liberated in 1918 by the British. During this period, a spy ring working behind Turkish lines, known as Nili (from the initial letters of the Hebrew verse 'Nezah Yisrael Lo Yeshakker' ('The strength of Israel will not lie')), had been set up in Palestine to support the British. One of this faction, Aaron Aaronsohn, was instrumental in the quest to persuade the British government to allow Jews to create a national home in Palestine.

After more than a year of negotiations between the Zionists and the British government, the Balfour Declaration was issued. Such a solution to the Jewish problem was in line with the British aspiration of defeating Turkey and becoming the major power in the Middle East. In a letter from the British Foreign Secretary, Arthur Balfour, to Lord Rothschild, dated 2 November 1917, the British government resolved to create a National Home for the Jewish people in Palestine. Such a resolution was a cause for rejoicing throughout the Jewish world. In Odessa two hundred thousand Jews followed Ussishkin and his colleagues in a motor-car in a massive procession. However, in the United States, David Ben-Gurion, the future Prime Minister of Israel, was more reserved. Britain, he declared, had not given back Palestine to the Jewish people. The British had made a magnanimous gesture in recognizing the right of the Jewish population to their own country. But it was only the Jewish people, he emphasized, who could transform such a decree into a historical reality.

2
Beyond the First World War

Aftermath of the Balfour Declaration

Within a month of the Balfour Declaration, the British had driven the Turkish forces from Jerusalem. Only the northern half of Palestine remained in Turkish hands. Following this victory, it became possible for Zionists to work with the British in establishing a Jewish National Home as promised by the Balfour Declaration. As a result of the war the entire population of Palestine, including Jews, Muslims and Christians, had suffered considerably. The total population had fallen from about eight hundred thousand in 1914 to about 640,000 consisting of about 512,000 Muslims, 66,000 Jews and 61,000 Christians.[1]

In order to ensure that a Jewish National Home would be established in Palestine, a Jewish delegation headed by Chaim Weizmann addressed the Paris Peace Conference on 27 February 1919. After listening to impassioned speeches by the delegates, including Menachem Ussishkin, the Paris Peace Conference agreed to grant the Palestine Mandate to Great Britain, and accepted the need to establish a Jewish homeland in Palestine as outlined by the Balfour Declaration. In November of the same year, Ussishkin became Chairman of the Commission in Palestine; it was his responsibility to create an organizational structure for the Jewish Home. A Jewish National Assembly was created which elected a Jewish National Council.

In the meantime Jewish settlements in Upper Galilee were caught in the conflict between local Arabs and French

authorities who controlled the area following the war. Sub=
sequently the territory was transferred to Britain, yet Arabs
continued to attack the Jewish population. In response, Joseph
Trumpeldor, who had returned to Palestine, led the defence
of these northern settlements. On 1 January 1920 he began to
fortify Tel Hai; two months later this settlement was attacked
by armed Bedouin. Wounded in this conflict, Trumpeldor died
along with five other Jewish settlers.

In the years following the First World War, a further wave
of immigration – the Third Aliyah – took place; approximately
thirty-five thousand pioneers entered the country, including
Jews who were inspired by socialist values. These newcomers
worked on road building, set up *kibbutzim* and *moshavim* (villages of smallholders). The first *moshav* was founded in September 1921 at Nahalal in the Jezreel Valley; a second *moshav* was
created three months later at Kfar Yehezkel, east of Nahalal. In
the next ten years eight more *moshavim* had been established
nearby. Later Herzliya was established as a *moshav* on the coast.
During this period the kibbutz movement was also active. Ein
Harod (Herod Spring) was established at the foot of Mount Gil-
boa in the Jezreel Valley. Nearby Tel Yosaf was founded two
years later. Owing to the increase in Jewish population during
this period, other settlements were also created, such as Kiryat
Anavim (City of Grapes) located outside Jerusalem.

In order to unify the various Labour Zionist groups that had
developed since the First World War, the General Federation
of Jewish Labour, or Histadrut, was founded in December 1920
under the leadership of David Ben-Gurion. These steps towards
the creation of a Jewish homeland were met by increasing hostility on the part of the Arab population, which erupted into
the 1920 riots. After attempting to protect the Jewish population from attack, Vladimir Jabotinsky was arrested by the British and put in prison. At the Histadrut founding conference in
December 1920, it was agreed that a defence organization was

now needed. In March 1921 the Haganah was established as a secret body, acting without the consent of the British authorities. Initially it trained members and purchased arms in the quest to defend both Jewish property and life.

During this period of instability an English Jew, Sir Herbert Samuel, arrived on 30 June 1920 in Palestine as High Commissioner and Commander in Chief. Although Samuel was an ardent Zionist, he believed that Jews would be able to live harmoniously with the Arab population. In August 1920 Samuel authorized a Land Transfer Ordinance that made it possible for Zionists to acquire land; in September an Immigration Ordinance opened Palestine to legal Jewish immigration from those who obtained visas from the Zionist Organization. Initially Samuel sought to reconcile Arabs to these measures by pardoning the ringleaders of the Arab riots of 1920, including Hajj Amin al-Husseini, and creating an Advisory Council with an Arab majority in the unofficial membership. Such actions, however, did not pacify the Arab community.

In January 1921 Palestine was transferred from the Foreign Office to the Colonial Office under Winston Churchill. In March 1921 Churchill convened a conference of senior British officials in the Middle East in Cairo in order to reach a settlement with the leaders of Arab nationalism.[2] A focus of Arab resentment was the increasing number of Jews who had entered Palestine – by April 1921 nearly ten thousand Jews had come into the country under Samuel's Immigration Ordinance. Added to Arab fears about Zionist aspirations was the dispute about the election of the Grand Mufti of Jerusalem. Previously the post of Mufti was of little significance, since the Sultan served as both the supreme religious and temporal leader of the Muslim population. However, once the country was dominated by the British, the Grand Mufti became the supreme representative of Muslim Arabs.

Once the post of Grand Mufti became vacant, it was to be filled according to Ottoman procedures. An election took place in mid-April 1921, and Hajj Amin al-Husseini came fourth despite his notoriety as the principal instigator of the anti-Jewish riots of Easter 1920. Hajj Amin and his followers, however, declared that the elections had been rigged by the Jews in order to have a pro-Zionist Mufti. Although Samuel's major advisor on Arab affairs, Ernest Richmond, encouraged him to invalidate the elections, Samuel made no decision. While this matter remained unresolved, further anti-Jewish riots took place on 1 May in Jaffa. Jewish shops and a shelter for immigrants were attacked – twenty-seven Jews and three Arabs were killed and one hundred and four Jews and thirty-four Arabs wounded. In the next few days, rioting spread to other coastal centres. By 7 May forty-seven Jews had been killed and one hundred and forty-six wounded, and forty-eight Arabs killed and seventy-three wounded.

In order to calm Arab feeling, Samuel introduced a temporary suspension of immigration and agreed to Richmond's recommendation about the election of the Grand Mufti. One of the three Arabs who had been elected was encouraged to stand down, and on 8 May Hajj Amin was appointed Grand Mufti of Jerusalem. The Jewish community was incensed. In the same year the military sought to subvert the Balfour Declaration. At the end of June, General Sir Walter Congreve, commander of the British forces in the Middle East, went to London and argued against the Zionist cause.

In October, General Congreve issued a circular to officers under his command which supported the Arabs. Shortly after this letter was sent, Arabs in Jerusalem attacked Jews who were celebrating the fourth anniversary of the Balfour Declaration. Five Jews and three Arabs were killed. At Christmas 1921, after receiving a copy of Congreve's circular, Churchill resolved that the Air Ministry should assume responsibility for the defence of Palestine, and a squadron of the Air Force was stationed in the area and a British Gendarmerie set up. No longer was there to be a military presence on the ground which would be sympathetic to the Arab population in opposition to British policy.

During the years 1920–1 there were grave doubts about the possibility of establishing a Jewish National Home as proposed by the Balfour Declaration. Although Samuel sought to create representative institutions in Palestine, the Jewish population was fearful of representative institutions, since Jews constituted only eleven per cent of Palestine's population. In addition, the Arab birth rate was higher than that among Jews. In such conditions, it seemed certain that the Arabs would constitute the majority in any institution that would be established – and such a situation would inevitably undermine the Zionist programme. Samuel and Churchill, however, envisaged the creation of a Middle East Federation, of which the Jewish National Home would be a part. Although there was some support for this notion in Jewish circles, the *Yishuv* (the Jewish population in Palestine) was bitterly opposed.

Despite such resistance, Samuel initially established a nominated Advisory Council in October 1920 with a majority of Arab notables among its unofficial membership. After the May 1921 riots, he proposed that the Advisory Council be elected as a step towards self-government. At the same time Samuel declared that the Balfour Declaration did not imply that a Jewish government would be formed to rule over the Muslim and Christian majority. Rather, he insisted that the British government would never impose a policy that would be contrary to the religious, political and economic interests of those living in Palestine.[3] In August 1921 an Arab delegation went to London to meet with British officials; because the Arabs were not able to secure an assembly with legislative and executive powers, to control immigration and to receive a repudiation of the Balfour Declaration, they rejected the offer of an elected assembly.

Steps towards statehood

Despite the Arab rejection of a representative assembly, Samuel and Churchill were not deterred from their plans for Palestine. Once the League of Nations Council meeting in London on 24 July 1922 passed the Mandate for Palestine, the British government proposed a Palestinian Constitution which established a Legislative Council. Although such a body would have had an Arab majority, the Palestinian Constitution was accepted by the Jewish population. The Arabs adamantly rejected such a plan at a Palestinian Arab Congress in Nablus.

Undeterred by the Arab reaction, the British proceeded with elections. The Palestinian Arab Executive, elected by the Nablus Congress, decided on a boycott which effectively undermined the Legislative Council. Samuel then sought to reconstitute an Advisory Council and establish an Arab agency – both of these bodies were similarly rejected by the Arab representatives, who had adopted a policy of non-co-operation as long as the Balfour Declaration remained in force. The British government, however, was unable to overcome this impasse, since the Balfour Declaration was enshrined in the Palestinian Mandate.

With the fall of the Lloyd George government, the Arabs hoped to influence the new British leadership which had not been responsible for the Balfour Declaration. However, neither the British government of Bonar Law nor any future government had any intention of repudiating the Palestinian Mandate. As far as the Zionists were concerned, Arab non-co-operation suited their purposes. They had accepted the Palestine Constitution, and thereby proved to be co-operative partners in the quest to find a solution to the problems of the Middle East. The Arabs, on the other hand, were intractable in their opposition to the creation of a Jewish homeland as envisaged by the Balfour Declaration and the Mandate.

Samuel's lack of success in creating representative institutions meant that Palestine had to be ruled by the High Commissioner and his officials without any consultation with the Jewish and Arab communities. In the absence of such bodies, both Jews and Arabs were compelled to create their own institutions. On the Jewish side the most important organization was the Zionist Executive, which had been given official recognition under the Mandate. A further body, the National Council, represented the *Yishuv*, which itself had two specialized institutions: the Histadrut, which embraced the trade unionists and the co-operative movement, and the Haganah, the Jewish armed forces. On the Arab side, the Grand Mufti of Jerusalem became the president of a newly established Supreme Muslim Council in January 1922. It was this body which became responsible for financial and legal affairs, which had previously been under the purview of the Ottoman rulers. Thus by 1923 a tripartite system of government was established in Palestine which continued throughout the period of the Mandate – both the Arab and the Jewish communities were to look after their own affairs.

In the last year of Samuel's administration, there was a massive increase in Jewish immigration to Palestine. From 1920 to 1923 approximately eight thousand Jews a year had settled in the Holy Land. In 1924 the rate increased to about thirteen thousand. In 1925 it was over thirty-three thousand.[4] This increase was due to the political and economic crisis in Poland, the relaxation of Soviet immigration controls, and restrictions on immigration to America beginning in 1924. Such an influx of Jewish settlers – referred to as the Fourth Aliyah – resulted in a significant increase of Jews residing in Jerusalem, Haifa and Tel Aviv. Surprisingly, this did not give rise to public demonstrations as had occurred only a few years previously; similarly, when Arthur Balfour visited Palestine for the opening of the Hebrew University, there was little reaction from the Arab population.

With the retirement of Samuel in June 1925 and the appointment of Baron Plumer of Messines as High Commissioner, the British were anxious to ensure that the Mandate was upheld. According to Plumer, the commitment to a Jewish National Home was not inconsistent with the establishment of peace and order in Palestine. Unlike Samuel, Plumer did not seek to establish representative assemblies, nor to reconcile Jewish and Arab aspirations. Instead, he was anxious to ensure that peace was established in the land. Among Jews in the diaspora, Plumer's period in office marked a positive step towards settlement; it appeared that the Arab population had accepted the implications of the Balfour Declaration.

Within Palestine, however, the Jewish population continued to be aware of Arab hostility towards Jewish settlement. In the *Yishuv* two opposing approaches to the Arab problem emerged during this period. On the one hand, some Jews believed that some type of reconciliation might be possible. Pre-eminent among those who propounded a moderate policy was the Polish-born agronomist H.M. Kalvaryski, who served as an unofficial Minister for Arab Affairs; he had succeeded in creating a moderate organization, the Muslim National Association. It became clear, however, that this body lacked any substantial popular following among the Arabs. Other Zionists founded Berit Shalom (Covenant of Peace), which aimed to achieve peace with the Arabs through various concessions leading to the establishment of a bi-national state – but this approach received little support among either Arabs or Jews.

The second approach was of a pragmatic character: within the *Yishuv* a number of influential Zionists maintained that Arab hostility was inevitable and would eventually lead to armed conflict. The main proponent of such a view was Vladimir Jabotinsky owing to his role in the defence of Jews living in Jerusalem during the riots of April 1920. According to Jabotinsky and others, it was impossible to bridge the gap between Jewish and Arab intentions – instead the two communities should be isolated from one another. In the turbulent period of 1920–2, such a policy was widely accepted within the *Yishuv*, but under Plumer's firm control conflict between these two communities was suppressed.

Following the massive immigration from Poland and Russia in 1925, relatively few Jews arrived in Palestine. Between 1926 and 1931, the Jewish population increased only from 149,640 to 174,606. At the same time, the Arab population increased from 675,450 to 759,700.[5] Given such figures, it looked unlikely that there could ever be a Jewish majority in the land. Added to this difficulty, the *Yishuv* faced severe economic difficulties in the late 1920s. At the end of 1928, Plumer retired from the High Commissionership – and within a month the Arab population attacked the Jewish community, thereby renewing the conflict that had erupted at the beginning of the decade.

On the eve of Yom Kippur in September 1928, a police officer, Douglas Duff, and the District Commissioner of Jerusalem, Edward Keith Roach, took a walk around the Old City of Jerusalem. Looking down from the Dome of the Rock, they saw that Jews had placed a screen to separate men and women at prayers near the Wailing Wall. On the following day the police disrupted the prayer service and removed the screen. Furious with this decision, the Jewish population became incensed with the British. Such was the mood of the country when Sir John Chancellor arrived in Palestine. Intent on following the policy that H.C. Luke, the administrating officer, had initiated, Chancellor announced on 3 January 1929 that he would consider creating a legislative council.[6] This suggestion met with support from Arab leaders, who believed that by participating in representative institutions they would be able to control immigration to Palestine.

At this time, there was a change in Whitehall in London: the Conservative government fell and was replaced by a Labour government under Ramsay MacDonald. Britain was now governed by those who had no past links with the Balfour Declaration; in addition, the new Colonial Secretary, Lord Passfield, was unsympathetic to the notion of a Jewish National Home in Palestine. Throughout the year Luke carried on negotiations with the two main leaders of the Arab Executive, Musa Kazem al-Husseini and Raghib al-Nashashibi. In June 1929 an agreement was reached that the proposed legislative council would consist of ten Muslims, three Jews and two Christians.[7]

The Grand Mufti, however, had other plans. In his view the Holy Places in Palestine were under threat from the Jewish population. Following the Yom Kippur incident, he initiated a campaign against the Jews in the mosques and the press. In August a further incident inflamed both Arab and Jewish hatred. A Jewish boy kicked a ball into an Arab garden; in the ensuing fight he was stabbed and killed. After the boy's funeral, a Zionist demonstration took place at the Wall. This was followed by a sermon from the Mufti in the Mosque of Al-Aqsa. Then, on 22 and 23 August, large crowds of Arab peasants made their way to Jerusalem armed with clubs and knives. The Chief of Police in Jerusalem did not have enough men to disarm this mob, and the Jewish community was severely attacked in Jerusalem and later in other Jewish centres. In this conflict, 133 Jews were killed and 339 wounded, and 110 Arabs were killed and 232 wounded by reinforced police. Subsequently six Arabs were killed in a Jewish counter-attack near Tel Aviv.[8] It now appeared that confrontation between Jews and Arabs was inevitable in the Holy Land.

Jews and Arabs

The hostility between Jews and Arabs led to a reorganization of the Haganah. Supporters of military force emphasized that the Haganah had saved the Jewish communities of Jerusalem,

Tel Aviv and Haifa from mass destruction; others were critical of its efforts. As a result, a major restructuring of the Haganah took place. This, however, did not avert a split in its ranks. The political leadership of those who succeeded was furnished by the Betar, an activist movement founded in 1923 in Riga, Latvia under the influence of Vladimir Jabotinsky.

In 1931 a group of Haganah members left the organization in protest against its policies and joined forces with Betar in order to establish a more militant armed underground organization, the Irgun. The first Betar congress took place in 1931 in Danzig, where Jabotinsky was elected head of the movement. Rejecting the Histadrut and Haganah policy of self-restraint, Betar adopted retaliation as its strategy in dealing with the Arabs. From 1929 the politics of the *Yishuv* was divided between the Histadrut–Haganah movement led by David Ben-Gurion and the right-wing Revisionist movement led by Jabotinsky.

Among the Arabs the events of 1929 led to increased support for the Mufti. In Palestine and throughout the Arab world, the Grand Mufti was perceived as the leading figure in the struggle against the Zionist threat. In British circles, it became increasingly clear that a Jewish National Home was impossible because of the Arab reaction. Anxious to protect Jewish interests, Weizmann met in London with Lord Passfield, who insisted that mass immigration to Palestine would be impossible. Such a policy was subsequently enshrined in two Royal Commissions and a White Paper. The first Royal Commission, which addressed the events of August 1929, determined that the attacks on the Jewish population were not premeditated. Although it criticized the Grand Mufti for not doing more to deter the mobs, it did not conclude that he was responsible for the atrocities that took place. In the view of the Commission, more should be done to strengthen the control of Jewish immigration to the country.

The second Royal Commission applied the criterion of absorptive capacity in a more restrictive sense. Palestine, it was believed, was not able to absorb more than fifty thousand more Jewish immigrants. Lord Passfield now sought to reinterpret the Mandate. In a report to the Permanent Mandates Commission of the League of Nations, the British government argued that the lack of any self-government in Palestine did not result from a lack of goodwill on the part of the Mandatory power. Subsequently the conclusions of these reports were incorporated into a White Paper published on 21 October 1930. The White Paper also proposed the creation of a legislative council.

Concerned about the implications of governmental policy, Weizmann resigned as president of the Zionist Organization; this decision highlighted his view that the Balfour Declaration had been betrayed by the British. When the White Paper was debated in the House of Commons in November 1930, it was widely criticized. On 13 February 1931 the Prime Minister read to the House a letter he had written to Weizmann in which he emphasized that the Mandate had an obligation to facilitate Jewish immigration to Palestine without jeopardizing the rights of all sections of the population.[9] Among the Arabs, this communication became known as the 'Black Letter'.

Despite this success, many Zionists were not satisfied. They had hoped for a new White Paper, rather than a letter. Having resigned as the president of the Zionist Organization over the White Paper, Weizmann was eclipsed by Jabotinsky at the Seventh Zionist Congress in Basle from June to July 1931. During the session he was rebuked by the Congress for his statement in an interview that he had no sympathy with the demand for a Jewish majority in Palestine. This internal conflict within the Zionist Organization, however, was overshadowed by the rise of Nazism and the succession of Adolf Hitler as the Chancellor of the German Reich in January 1933.

From 1933 the Zionists and the Nazis co-operated in the emigration of Jews from Nazi Germany to Palestine. On 25 August 1933, Eliezer Siegfried Hoofien, general manager of the Anglo-Palestine Bank, agreed with the German Ministry of Economics that Jewish assets should be used to purchase material needed in Palestine. In the same year the Anglo-Palestine Bank created the Trust and Transfer Office Ha'avara Ltd in Tel Aviv. In Berlin a parallel body was created with the assistance of two Jewish bankers, Max Warburg and Siegmund Wassermann. This company was responsible for negotiating with the German government the settlement of the bills of German exports and contracts with German Jews who sought to settle in Palestine. Between 1933 and 1939 approximately fifty thousand Jews used the services of this organization.[10]

In Palestine, Jabotinsky and his colleagues denounced such arrangements because they violated the boycott against German goods. At the Eighteenth Zionist Congress held in Prague from August to September 1933, this issue was debated. Jabotinsky called for a worldwide boycott of Germany, but the majority were not in favour of such action. The transfer arrangements that allowed German Jews to settle in Palestine were defended, and the boycott resolution was not put to a vote. Undeterred by this setback, the Revisionists continued to attack this policy and sought to impose their own boycott.

During this period the immigration policy of the Mandatory power was relatively liberal, yet the number of those without capital who were allowed to immigrate was severely restricted. Such a policy was justified on the basis of the economic absorptive capacity of the country. Nonetheless, between 1933 and 1939 a significant amount of Jewish capital was imported into the country. As a result the *Yishuv* was far wealthier than at any other time in its history, and the notion of a Jewish state became more plausible.

As a result of the influx of new immigrants, the Arab population became increasingly agitated. Not only were the Jews viewed as enemies of the Arab cause, but the British also came under attack. In October 1933 anti-British disturbances broke out in Jaffa, Nablus, Haifa and Jerusalem. In the conflict twenty-six Arabs were killed. During the next few years the Arab press supported Italy in its struggle against Britain. During this period the Jews, too, rebelled against British rule. The Nineteenth Zionist Congress in Lucerne in 1935 rejected the notion of a legislative council in Palestine.

In Palestine itself, the conflict between Jews and Arabs intensified. In a terrorist operation, Sheikh Izz al-Din al-Qassam and his band were surrounded and killed. As a martyr to the Arab cause, al-Qassam's death put pressure on Hajj Amin to launch a Muslim revolt. On 15 April a group of armed Arabs took two Jews off a bus in the Nablus mountains and killed them. Two days later members of the nationalist Haganah, the parent body of the Irgun, murdered two Arabs in retaliation. Following these events, Arab demonstrations took place in Jaffa, Nablus and elsewhere throughout the country.

The shift from an anti-Jewish to an anti-British stance was not a simple option for Hajj Amin. If he complied with this policy, he risked losing his power as head of the Supreme Muslim Council, which was appointed by the British. However, if he failed to comply, he might forfeit his prestige as the leader of Muslim nationalism. As a consequence, he acceded to the demands of the young militants by becoming head of the Higher Arab Committee. Because this was a lawful body, such a position was reconcilable with his leadership of the Supreme Muslim Council. Hajj Amin, however, was aware that his position was precarious, and he was anxious to convince the British government that he was not directly involved in the Arab revolt.

Throughout June the Supreme Muslim Council encouraged Muslims to join in this rebellion. The Jews, they argued, aimed at reconstructing a Jewish Temple in the place of the Mosque of al-Aqsa. Having refused Muslim demands, Britain was perceived as supporting the Jewish people in this quest.

One major reason for this change in Muslim policy towards the British concerned the dispute between Italy and Ethiopia. In May, Mussolini had declared that the King of Italy was Emperor of Ethiopia; the same month Emperor Haile Selassie, who was in Jerusalem, appealed to the League for support. Such a spectacle of the head of a people whose cause Britain had failed to support had a powerful impact on the Muslim community in Palestine. Arguably, the Jewish people, who had relied on the British for the establishment of a Jewish National Home, would be treated in a similar fashion.

Throughout the summer the revolt spread throughout the country. In June attacks took place along the roads and against the Haifa–Lyddah railway line. The first major conflict between British troops and Arab forces occurred near Tulkarm. During the next two months, clashes continued and were accompanied by a general strike. Although British forces defended themselves, there was no concerted attempt to suppress the revolt. Any political solution to this conflict required concessions to Arab demands. During this period three Arab princes, Abdul Aziz Ibn Saud, King of Saudi Arabia, Ghazi, King of Iraq, and Abdullah of Transjordan became involved in the Mandatory government. All three detested Zionism and saw that personal political gains could be made from their participation in the affairs of Palestine.

Palestine before the Second World War

In the quest to stem the Arab revolt, the British hoped the Arab princes would encourage the rebels to desist. Yet because the Arab fighters perceived their struggle against the British as a holy war, they were undeterred by such foreign intervention. In the meantime, the British had created the Peel Commission, which was empowered to look into the roots of the Palestinian question. By 1937 the British had assembled a large military force in Palestine and decided to impose martial law on the country. Both the Higher Arab Committee and the Foreign Office did not wish it to appear that the rebels had accepted defeat. Hence, the Arab princes were encouraged to issue a joint appeal for public order which the Higher Arab Committee could accept.

When this appeal was made, the Higher Arab Committee published a manifesto urging the rebels to abandon their strike as well as public disorder. This opened the way to the arrival of the Peel Commission. In November 1936 the Royal Commission, headed by Lord Peel, arrived in Palestine. The Commission held sixty-six meetings, which were largely dominated by Jewish evidence, since the Arabs boycotted most of the proceedings. Appearing before the Commission on 25 November 1936, Weizmann spoke about the Jewish plight in Europe. In addition, he sought to reassure the Commission that Jews who had settled in Palestine sought to create a National Home for the Jewish people without causing undue suffering to the Arab population.[11] Later, on 7 January, David Ben-Gurion sought to persuade the Commission of the inherent right of the Jewish people to their ancestral homeland. A week later, Hajj Amin emphasized that the Jewish claim to Palestine was in direct conflict with Islam.

In July 1937 the Peel Commission published its report in which it declared that the Palestinian problem was insoluble. It arose within the narrow bounds of a small country in which approximately one million Arabs were in conflict against forty thousand Jews. Since in its view neither group could justly rule over all of Palestine, the Commission concluded that the country should be partitioned. In this light the Commission recommended that the Mandate for Palestine should be terminated and replaced by a Treaty System, and a new Mandate for the Holy Places be established. Further, it suggested that a Treaty of

Alliance should be negotiated between the government of Transjordan and the Arabs of Palestine, representing an expanded Transjordan, and that the Zionist organization should be responsible for a Jewish state. The Commission assigned to the Jewish state a coastal strip from the south of Jaffa to the north of Gaza along with Galilee from the sea to the Syrian border. Jerusalem, with a corridor to the sea, was to be placed under the new Mandate. The remainder of the country was to be the new Arab state.

Although this scheme was endorsed by the British government, it was strongly opposed by the Palestinian Arabs. On the Jewish side, Weizmann and Ben-Gurion favoured the principle of partition because it would have created a Jewish homeland. Under their influence, the Twentieth Zionist Congress held in Zurich in August 1937 approved the plan, and the Zionist Executive was authorized to negotiate with the Mandatory power for the purpose of ascertaining the British terms for the proposed establishment of a Jewish National Home.

There were, however, differing views within the Zionist movement about this plan. Jabotinsky and the Revisionists bitterly opposed partition. Weizmann viewed the boundaries as inadequate, but was willing to accept such a scheme. Ben-Gurion, on the other hand, viewed the establishment of a Jewish state in Palestine as simply a beginning. He stressed that the number of Jews entering the country would increase, and that a military force would be created to protect the Jews living in the land. He was sure that Jews would not be prevented from settling in other parts of the country either through agreement or other means.

In the summer of 1937 the Arab revolt, which had been suspended during the deliberations of the Peel Commission, was renewed following meetings of nationalists in Syria. During this period Lewis Andrews, acting District Commissioner of Galilee, was murdered. Despite the Higher Arab Committee's condemnation of this act, Hajj Amin was removed as head of this body and warrants were issued for the arrest of its members. Fleeing to Lebanon, Hajj Amin was given asylum by the French. On 13 October, Sir Arthur Wauchope was removed as High Commissioner, to be replaced by Sir Harold MacMichael in February 1938.

These events led to a full-scale Arab revolt which lasted until the end of 1938 and was severely repressed by the British government. At this time steps were taken towards abandoning the partition plan. In December 1937 the Prime Minister, Neville Chamberlain, supported the Foreign Office, which opposed partition as well as the creation of a Jewish state. Despite such a shift in policy, the British sought the support of the *Yishuv* in repressing the Arab uprising. Haganah volunteers formed Special Night Squads under Orde Charles Wingate.

In Palestine a section of the Jewish youth joined the National Military Organization, Irgun Tzevai Leumi, which was opposed to the Haganah policy of self-restraint. In June 1938 the British hanged a young Revisionist for attacking an Arab bus; in response, the Irgun exploded land mines in Haifa, killing seventy-four people and wounding another 129.[12] This act was condemned by both Zionist and Haganah leaders. On 17 September 1938 partition was reaffirmed by the League of Nations, and the British appeared to be committed to the Jewish state because of their repression of the Arab revolt. Although little Arab response to such action was made outside Palestine, hostility to Jews living in Arab lands was widespread.

In November the British government officially confirmed its intention to abandon the policy of partition and invited the governments of Iraq and Egypt to help prepare for a London conference on the future of Palestine. This gathering was held in St James Palace and was attended by representatives of five Arab countries – Egypt, Saudi Arabia, Iraq, Yemen and Transjordan – as well as a Palestinian delegation, the Zionist Executive and the British. The three bodies of delegates did not meet together; instead, the British met separately with the Arabs, and similarly with the Jews. The Palestinian Arabs refused to be in the same room with the Jewish delegates.

At one of the joint meetings between Zionists and leaders of the Arab states, Aly Maher of Egypt appealed to the Zionists to limit immigration. Although Weizmann was interested in this appeal, Ben-Gurion and the rest of the delegation adamantly supported the policy of Jewish immigration to Palestine. On 17 March 1939, two days after Hitler's occupation of Prague, the conference ended without any agreement between the various parties. In May 1939 a further White Paper was published which ruled out partition and the creation of a Jewish state. However, the White Paper decreed that a Palestine state be created within ten years, and that after five years Jewish immigration would not be allowed unless approved by the Palestinian Arabs. Despite this anti-Jewish bias, the White Paper allowed for seventy-five thousand more Jews to be allowed to settle in Palestine within the five-year period, and that the independence of a Palestinian state depended on adequate safeguards for the Jewish community.

In effect the White Paper endorsed a double veto: the Arabs were empowered to block the growth of the Jewish National Home, whereas the Jews could prevent the Arabs from having an independent state. Anxious to avert this change in policy, the Jews contested the legality of the White Paper. In its report to the Council of the League, the Permanent Mandates Commission stated that the White Paper was not in accord with the interpretation that the Commission had placed upon the Palestine Mandate. Under Article 27 of the Mandate, the Council's consent was required for any change in its terms. With the outbreak of war, however, the Council never met to debate this issue. Such a change of policy was profoundly disturbing to the *Yishuv*. The Zionists perceived that Britain had abandoned the Balfour Declaration. For many Zionists, it had become clear that force was now required to oppose the White Paper. Previously the Arab community had rebelled against British rule; now the White Paper reversed the situation. A Jewish revolt had begun.

3

The Jewish state

Revolt against the British

Despite the change in British policy, the Higher Arab Committee that met in Beirut rejected the White Paper. Hence, the British ruled in Palestine without the consent of either Jews or Arabs. From the Jewish side, immigration became the overriding concern in the light of the Nazi threat. In response the British terminated their relationship with the Haganah and increased their efforts to police entry into Palestine. Bitterly critical of such actions, the Jewish Agency repudiated the Mandatory policy limiting immigration, and a number of Revisionists insisted on the need for retaliation. On 26 August the Irgun killed two British police inspectors.

During this period the Twenty-First Zionist Congress met in Geneva on 16–26 August 1939 and declared its opposition to the policy of the White Paper. At the Congress, Ben-Gurion stated that the White Paper created a vacuum in Palestine, which would have to be filled by the Jewish community itself. The Jews, he maintained, should act as though they were an independent state.[1] During the Congress, Hitler announced the Nazi–Soviet pact. Aware of the implications for European Jewry, the delegates vowed to press Jewish interests in Palestine and to ensure that Germany be defeated in the war.

Before the end of 1941, 10,881 Jewish soldiers enlisted in the British forces; by the end of 1942 approximately eighteen thousand were serving in the military.[2] Owing to this increase in numbers, the Jews pressed for the creation of large Jewish units. Fearful of Arab resentment, the British refused. In Palestine the

Yishuv supported the British in the war effort. Not only did the Irgun suspend its pre-war terrorist activities, but a pro-British spirit became the dominant attitude of Jews living in the Holy Land. Inevitably, however, such a rapprochement between the Irgun and the British gave rise to serious misgivings. A section of the Irgun headed by Avraham Stern, know as Lehi or the Stern Gang, made an offer to Hitler to assist in the conquest of Palestine in exchange for the transfer of the Jews of Europe. Alarmed by this proposal, Stern's envoy, Naphtali Lubentchik, was arrested by the authorities in Acre on his return from Beirut, and a year later Stern was tracked down by the British police, aided by both the Haganah and the Irgun, and shot.

In the early years of the war, Ben-Gurion was the dominant figure in the *Yishuv,* with Irgun and Lehi on the margin. After the events of May 1940, Ben-Gurion focused on defeating the Germans rather than overturning the White Paper. Victory over Hitler, he believed, had become the key issue. Now that Churchill had replaced Chamberlain, the *Yishuv* believed that the White Paper would be discarded. Yet, once Italy entered the war, the British believed that the policy of restricting immigration should continue so as not to antagonize the Arabs. At the same time, the Nazi conquests increased the need for Jews to have a safe haven in the Middle East.

The event that turned many Jews against the British even during this phase of the war with Hitler concerned the sinking of the *Struma*. This ship carrying 769 Jewish refugees from the Romanian Black Sea port of Constanza landed in Istanbul, where the refugees applied for entry visas to Palestine. When the Colonial Office rejected these applications, the Turks turned the ship back into the Black Sea, where it sank. In the aftermath of this tragedy, Menachem Begin took over leadership of the Revisionist party and sought to initiate a war of liberation against the British despite the participation of Jewish soldiers in the struggle against Hitler.

Paradoxically, the sinking of the *Struma* occurred when British–Jewish military co-operation was at its height. Having suffered the loss of Greece and Crete, the British trained Jewish commando units to fight in the campaigns of Iraq and Syria in the summer of 1941. As Rommel's forces advanced on Egypt, the British set up a military school at Kibbutz Mishmar Haemek (Guard of the Valley) where Jewish volunteers were trained throughout the summer of 1942. By the autumn, the danger of a German invasion of Palestine receded. But in the meantime the British had inadvertently created an independent Jewish force that was to become an essential element in the defence of the *Yishuv*.

During this period, the British feared that the Arabs under the influence of Hajj Amin, who was living in exile, might again stage a revolt. In October 1939 the Grand Mufti left Beirut for Baghdad, where he was greeted as a hero. Working on behalf of a pro-Axis war effort which culminated in a coup headed by Rashid Ali, he issued a *fatwa* (an official ruling) on 9 May 1941 which was broadcast over Iraqi and Axis radios. Proclaiming *jihad* (holy war) against the British, he declared that they had profaned the al-Aqsa Mosque and had been waging a war against Islam.[3] When the British defeated Rashid Ali's forces, nearly two hundred Jews living in Baghdad were killed by the Mufti's followers.

Escaping from Baghdad along with Rashid Ali, he fled to Teheran; however, when Soviet and British forces occupied Iran in September 1941, the Mufti made his way to Berlin. On 21 November 1941 Hitler received the Mufti, who told the Führer about his struggle with the Jewish people. Hitler stated that he was not at present prepared to help the Arabs in this conflict. Such co-operation could not take place until the defeat of Russia. When German forces reached the southern Caucasus, he stated, then the hour of the liberation of the Arabs would have arrived.[4] For the rest of the war the Mufti continued to reside in Germany, but once Germany was defeated he escaped again to Beirut, via Berne and Paris, and proclaimed a *jihad* against the new State of Israel.

As the conflict with Germany progressed, it became increasingly clear that American support of the war effort was vital if the Allies were to prevail. In the summer of 1940 Churchill encouraged Weizmann to travel to America to stimulate Jewish opinion in favour of the anti-Nazi cause. At this stage, however, American Jews were unable to influence foreign policy. But from December 1941, after America's entry into the war, general opinion towards the Jewish cause became increasingly favourable. Anti-Semitism was the ideology of the enemies of the United States. By 1942 Jewish opinion had become much more favourable to the Zionist cause, resulting in a major Zionist effort. In May 1942 a conference of representatives of all American Zionists took place at the Biltmore Hotel in New York and was addressed by Weizmann and Ben-Gurion. At this conference, the Biltmore Resolution was endorsed, which declared that the Jews in Palestine should form a Jewish Commonwealth and should regulate immigration into the country. On the basis of this declaration, Ben-Gurion demanded the admission of two million Jews into Palestine.

In November 1942 a group of Palestinian citizens were permitted to leave Poland and return to Palestine; they brought news about the Nazi persecution of the Jews. In December this report was confirmed by the Allied governments. In a speech at the Berlin Sports Palace on 30 September 1942, Hitler recalled a prophecy he made three years earlier that if Jewry were to start a world war in order to eliminate Aryans from Europe, it would be the Jews who would be eliminated instead. Previously, he stated, the Jews laughed at his policies but they will laugh no more.[5] By the end of the year the *Yishuv* was aware of Hitler's intentions concerning Jews living in Europe.

During this period a number of Jews were helped to escape from Europe by the United Rescue Committee. This body represented all factions in the *Yishuv* and worked together with the Jewish underground operating in Europe. In 1943–4 Haganah volunteers were parachuted into the Balkans to collect military evidence and to aid in this escape work. Through their actions about ten thousand people were able to emigrate to Palestine. Within the *Yishuv,* however, the Allies' apparent indifference to the plight of European Jewry as well as Britain's support of limited immigration caused considerable frustration. At this time an Anglo–American conference took place in Bermuda to consider the question of aid to refugees from Nazi occupation. The Americans, however, insisted that US immigration laws should not be discussed, and the British were opposed to any deliberation about Jewish immigration to Palestine.

Such actions evoked a hostile response from the Jewish population in Palestine. Lehi intensified its activities, winning recruits from young Jews as well as illegal immigrants. Joining these new recruits, the Irgun increased its numbers as well. Ironically, at this stage the Churchill government was contemplating repudiating the 1939 White Paper, and on 20 December 1943 a Cabinet committee recommended the partition of Palestine on the basis of the 1937 Peel Report. Despite this development, terrorism continued throughout 1944, and in August an attempt was made on the life of the High Commissioner, Sir Harold MacMichael. The Zionist establishment condemned such action, and Weizmann continued his negotiations with the British. These talks were interrupted on 6 November by the murder of Lord Moyne, British Minister Resident in Cairo, by Lehi. This led to the full co-operation of the Zionists with the British to curtail terrorism. When the war ended, the British remained committed to the policy of the White Paper despite the encouraging steps towards partition in the last years of the war.

Post-war developments

The election of a Labour government after the war appeared to offer hope to the Zionist cause. Repeatedly the Labour Party had been opposed to the White Paper, and in 1944 and 1945 it expressed its commitment to the creation of a Jewish National Home as well as unlimited immigration to Palestine. Nonetheless, when President Truman indicated his wish that the British government lift the White Paper's restrictions on Jewish immigration, the new Prime Minister, Clement Attlee, sent back an ambiguous response. Truman continued to apply pressure on the British, and in August 1945 he sent Attlee a report on the conditions of one hundred thousand Jewish survivors of the concentration camps who were now housed in camps in Germany and Austria.

In reply Attlee stated that the Jews had little more to complain about than many other peoples who were compelled to endure such conditions. The Jews, he stated, should not receive favourable treatment.[6] By September it had become apparent that the Labour Party would not alter the restrictions of the White Paper, and only fifteen hundred Jews would be allowed into Palestine. Bitterly opposed to such a stance, Ben-Gurion warned the Jews would fight against the British if such attitudes prevailed. On 1 October, Ben-Gurion sent a telegram instructing the Haganah to instigate armed uprisings against British forces. Subsequently the Haganah issued daily broadcasts over its illegal Voice of Israel radio station. Simultaneously, the Haganah re-established links with the Irgun and Lehi. On 31 October 1945 the Palestine railway system was blown up, an act of defiance defended by all segments of the *Yishuv*.

This guerrilla war evoked a positive response from Jews in Palestine and in the United States. The British remained intransigent. When an Anglo–American Committee was established to examine the refugee problem, the Foreign Secretary, Ernest

Bevin, insisted that the Jews should not receive special treatment. Such a statement inflamed Jewish anger in Palestine and abroad. In Tel Aviv riots took place for two days; in response the British fired on the crowd, killing six Jews. In March the Anglo–American Committee recommended the admission of one hundred thousand Jews to Palestine, and Truman encouraged the British to comply with this recommendation. The Attlee government refused until the Jews disarmed.

In May 1946 the Anglo–American Committee of Inquiry recommended that Palestine become a bi-national state and the immediate admission of one hundred thousand Jews. This proposal was welcomed by Truman. In a statement to the House of Commons, Attlee declared that Britain would not implement this recommendation unless the United States was prepared to share the added military and financial responsibilities. The next month Ernest Bevin explained to the Labour Party Conference that the reason why the Americans were anxious that Jews immigrate to Palestine was because the United States did not want to absorb so many new immigrants.[7] During the same month the Attlee government authorized the High Commissioner, Sir Alan Cunningham, to carry out searches in the main Jewish centres. As a consequence, thousands of Jews were arrested, including members of the Jewish Agency. Although the Agency had previously condemned acts of terrorism, it had refused to co-operate with the authorities against the Irgun and Lehi.

By the end of June, Britain had resolved to suspend such disciplinary action even though it had not disarmed the Haganah. Such a change in policy was a result of pressure applied by American Jews on public opinion regarding the post-war loan to Britain which was before Congress. One of the most prominent American Zionists, Dr Abba Hillel Silver, had urged Jews to ask their congressman whether the United States should make a loan to Britain given its policies in Palestine.[8] Under such pressure, the British reversed their policy towards the Jewish Agency and the Haganah. At the end of July the Irgun blew up the government offices in the King David Hotel, killing about eighty British, Jewish and Arab civil servants and wounding about seventy others. A four-day curfew was imposed and the British carried out intense searches. In the United States, anti-British feeling intensified.

In the Muslim world, pressure was initially applied on Britain through agitation against American investment in Arab lands. Yet, when it became clear that such actions would adversely affect Arab interests, the plan to impose Arab sanctions in support of the Palestinian cause disintegrated. Nonetheless, the Arab states were anxious to help the Palestinian cause. In May the Mufti arrived in Cairo. Although he was not allowed to travel to Palestine, he was able to influence Arab affairs in Palestine through the Higher Executive Committee. This body was supported by the Arab states, and with British encouragement had formed the Arab League. At a conference with the British in London in September, the Arab nations demanded that an independent Arab state be created in Palestine no later than 31 December 1948.

Meanwhile the Twenty-Second Zionist Congress met in Basle in December 1946. The Congress endorsed the Biltmore Programme with explicit reference to a Jewish state. At the Congress, Weizmann attacked the terrorists in Palestine as well as their American supporters. Although his speech made a strong impact on the delegates, the majority rejected his suggestion that the Zionists participate in the London conference to be held in January. Perceived as pro-British, Weizmann was no longer suitable as president of the Congress, and the office remained unfilled. Ben-Gurion hence became Executive Chairman with regard to *Yishuv* affairs, and Rabbi Abba Hillel Silver was elected Executive Chairman with regard to America.

From 1947 the political climate in Britain underwent a transformation. For some time the opposition had urged that the Mandate be rescinded. With the failure of the London talks, Churchill urged that the United Nations take over control of Palestine. On 18 February 1947 the government announced that the British government had no power under the Mandate to determine whether Palestine belonged to the Arabs or the Jews. As a consequence, the only course open was to submit the problem to the United Nations. To facilitate this transition, Britain requested that a Special Session of the General Assembly consider this issue.

This meeting, which took place from 28 April to 15 May 1947, resolved to set up an investigating eleven-member body – the United Nations Special Committee on Palestine (UNSCOP) – which was to report by the autumn. During these deliberations the Soviet Deputy Foreign Minister, Andrei Gromyko, attacked the Mandatory system in Palestine and endorsed Zionist aspirations to create a homeland in the Middle East. Although Gromyko preferred a bi-national solution, he indicated that if this were not feasible Palestine should be partitioned into a Jewish and an Arab state.[9]

During the summer, members of the Special Committee went to Palestine. On the day they arrived a British military court sentenced three members of the Irgun to death. Although the Committee appealed against this decree, its plea was ignored. The Irgun then captured two British sergeants on 12 July and threatened to kill them if the British carried out these sentences. At the end of the month the Irgun members were executed; in retaliation the Irgun hanged the two sergeants. This event evoked widespread antipathy in Britain towards Zionism, and British troops in Tel Aviv rioted. Five Jews were killed, but no one was ever charged for these murders. During this period of unrest Jewish refugees continued to flood into Palestine. Between July 1945 and the end of 1946 approximately thirty ships arrived from Europe.[10] Most of the larger ships were intercepted by the Royal Navy and their passengers were interned.

On 31 August UNSCOP completed its report, recommending the end of the British Mandate. A majority report recommended that Palestine be partitioned into an Arab and a Jewish state with an international zone for the Holy Places. The British expressed disdain for the report, and the Arabs were bitterly opposed. On 17 October 1947 the British government made it clear that it would not accept responsibility for the enforcement of such a settlement. On 29 November the General Assembly formally considered the report: thirty-three delegates voted in favour; thirteen were opposed, including the eleven Muslim states. There were also ten abstentions. A two-thirds majority had thus been achieved.

In December the British indicated that they would continue to rule Palestine until 15 May 1948. The Mandate would then come to an end. In the remaining months British forces would be used only in self-defence; this meant that they would not intervene in any conflict between Arab and Jew. In November the Jewish population was subjected to a number of attacks; these were followed by retaliation against the Arabs in which both the Haganah and the Irgun played a role. In these new circumstances the policy of self-restraint was abandoned. In April 1948 the Irgun attacked Deir Yassin, an Arab village near Jerusalem, killing 107 citizens. This onslaught led to the flight of the Arab population from areas with large Jewish populations. By mid-May about three hundred thousand Arabs had fled, seeking refuge in neighbouring countries. In retaliation for this massacre, the Arabs ambushed a medical convoy, killing seventy-seven doctors, nurses, teachers and students.

Jewish statehood

During this period Weizmann was active in Washington attempting to persuade President Truman of the need for a

Jewish state. Despite the threat of Arab attack, on 14 May 1948 in Tel Aviv, Ben-Gurion and other leaders put their signatures to Israel's Declaration of Independence. The document opened by describing the Land of Israel as the birthplace of the Jewish people, and looked back to the Jewish past. It went on to explain that the Jewish people had prayed and hoped for their return to the land of their ancestors, and strove in every generation to re-establish themselves in their ancient homeland. In recent times they had returned as pioneers and defenders and had recreated a thriving community.

Recounting the stages of historical development, the Declaration emphasized the destruction of European Jewry under the Nazi regime and the urgency of creating a Jewish nation. Through the partition resolution of 1947, the United Nations had recognized the right of the Jewish people to establish their own state, which would henceforth be known as the State of Israel. This Jewish state, the Declaration concluded, would be open for immigration and would be based on freedom, justice and peace as envisaged by the prophets of Israel. It was hoped that the Arabs of Israel would be active participants in the creation of the state on the basis of full and equal citizenship and representation in all its institutions. To Israel's Arab neighbours, the state extended an offer of peace and good neighbourliness, and to Jews living in the diaspora it appealed for support.[11]

On the day of independence, notices were posted throughout Tel Aviv by the Haganah indicating that the new state was in imminent danger. Immediately Egyptian planes bombed Tel Aviv. The next day began the intervention of five Arab states. Syrian troops attacked in the Jordan Valley, capturing the town of Zemah. On 20 May they attacked Degania, which managed to drive the Syrians back; by 23 May the Syrians had withdrawn. In the north the Lebanese army invaded northern Galilee but was stopped by an Israeli counter-attack. Other Arab forces, however, penetrated into central Galilee, where they were greeted by Palestinian Arabs. At the same time the Syrians continued their assault, capturing the border settlement of Mishmar Hayarden.

To the south of the Syrian, Lebanese and so called 'Liberation armies', the Iraq army attacked Gesher but was repulsed; nonetheless, the Iraqis captured the settlement of Geulim but were later driven out by Israeli forces, who captured Arab villages and the town of Jenin. In the Negev desert, Israel was attacked by the Egyptian army, which was halted at the settlement of Yad Mordechai, south of Ashdod. On 24 May the settlement was evacuated. By 29 May the first Israeli fighter planes, four Messerschmitts, attacked the Egyptian column.

During this period Jerusalem consisted of a New City composed largely of Jews and the Old City with a largely Arab population. On 15 May Transjordanian forces crossed the Jordan and attacked the New City. On 24 May the assault was repelled; the Transjordanians then continued their assault on the Jewish Quarter of the Old City. On 28 May the Israeli garrison surrendered. The siege of the New City continued with the Transjordanians holding Latrun in the Valley of Ayalon on the main road from the coast to Jerusalem. This position was attacked but the Israelis were driven back.

Of central importance in this conflict was the fact that President Truman had recognized the State of Israel on 15 May; three days later the Soviet Union gave its recognition. On 17 May the United States introduced a Security Council draft resolution, stating that the situation in Palestine was a breach of the peace under Article 39 of the United Nations Charter. Britain added an amendment to this resolution, deleting the reference to Article 39. This intervention caused the pro-Israel lobby in the United States to pressurize the government to suppress the American loan to Britain under the Marshall Plan. In response the Attlee government agreed to stop its arms shipments to Arab states. On 29 May the Security Council called for a cease-fire and also prohibited the importation of arms or military personnel into Palestine or any Arab nations. On 11 June the cease-fire came into effect.

This cease-fire was interrupted by an internal dispute within Israel. On 28 May the Israel Defence Forces were created and this prohibited the existence of any other military force. Yet it was impossible to implement this edict during the conflict with the Arabs, and Irgun continued to exist as a separate unit after the truce was declared. When a ship, the *Altalena*, was commissioned by the Irgun to bring in volunteers and arms, the Israeli government decided to prevent it from landing. On 21 June the Haganah – now the Israel Defence Force – set the ship on fire on the beach at Tel Aviv, causing the death of fifteen men. Though civil war seemed imminent, Menachem Begin, who had been aboard the *Altalena* when it was set alight, stated that although Irgun soldiers would not engage in conflict with the state, they would continue their political activities.

The truce declared on 11 June lasted for nearly a month; during this period the United Nations attempted to establish a lasting peace in the area. The mediator in this conflict, Count Folke Bernadotte, who had been appointed by the Security Council, evoked hostility among the Jewish population owing to his belief that he was not bound by the General Assembly's resolution of 29 November 1947. On 27 June the mediator submitted a plan providing for a union involving the whole of Mandate Palestine in a partnership between the kingdom of Jordan and the Jewish state. According to this proposal, Jordan would continue its possession of the West Bank territory including East Jerusalem; the Arabs would acquire the entire Negev; and Israel was to be allocated western Galilee. Jewish immigration would be unlimited for two years; subsequently it would be controlled by a United Nations agency. Finally, all Arabs were to be allowed to return to their former homes.

Not surprisingly, such a plan was unacceptable to both Jews and Arabs. From the Israeli side, the lack of sovereignty was a fundamental obstacle; for the Arabs, such a proposal was perceived as granting too many concessions to the Jews as well as to Abdullah, the ruler of Transjordan. On 8 July, the day before the truce was due to expire, fighting broke out in the Negev, which lasted for ten days. As a result of this conflict, the Israelis succeeded in widening the Jerusalem corridor; in addition they captured large areas of Lower Galilee, including Lydda and Ramle.

When the second truce was established, more than half a million Arab refugees had fled from Israeli territory. Although some were forced to leave, a large number, including the Palestinian Arab leadership, left of their own accord. Most of the refugees went to Jordan; others escaped to the Gaza Strip. From the earliest stage, the Israeli government was opposed to the return of these refugees to their homes. On 16 June Ben-Gurion declared to his Cabinet that those who had taken up arms against the Jewish nation would have to bear the consequences. By mid-July general hostilities had ceased, but occasional conflicts took place in August and September, particularly in Jerusalem. On 17 September 1948 Count Bernadotte was murdered by members of Lehi, provoking international condemnation of the Jewish state. In response, Ben-Gurion disbanded the Irgun and detained members of Lehi.

Just before Bernadotte's death, the General Assembly proposed a revised version of his plan. The unification of Israel and Jordan was eliminated, and it was suggested that Palestine be partitioned between Israel and Jordan; Jerusalem and the Negev were to be allocated to Jordan, and Israel was to retain western Galilee. Although this proposal was supported by the United States and Britain, Israel viewed it as granting too much to the Jordanians. Within the Arab world the Grand Mufti and the Egyptians roused opinion against the plan. The Russians, too, regarded this new plan as detrimental to their interests in the Middle East. As a result of such opposition coupled with the response of a number of Catholic states who sought to internationalize Jerusalem, this proposal was defeated in the General Assembly.

During this period while the Bernadotte plan was being considered, Ben-Gurion sought to lay claim to the Negev, which the United Nations had awarded to Israel in November. Although he might have wished to drive Abdullah back as well as drive the Egyptians out of the Negev, his military advisers insisted that the two aims could not be achieved simultaneously. As a result, Ben-Gurion focused on the Negev. A first attack was launched in October, driving the Egyptians out of much of the Negev; two months later the Israelis completed this task and also dislodged small Transjordanian forces stationed in the area. The Israelis then pushed on into the Sinai desert.

This invasion brought a strong response from Britain. On 31 December 1948 Britain offered to invoke the Anglo– Egyptian Treaty of 1936. The Egyptians, however, preferred to seek an armistice with Israel. When RAF planes went on reconnaissance missions over Israeli-held territory on the border between Israel and Egypt, the Israeli military shot five of these planes down. At this time, when it appeared that Britain and Israel might go to war, the Israelis withdrew from Egyptian territory in preparation for an armistice agreement with Egypt. Under pressure, the British retreated. On 26 January 1949 in a Commons debate on Palestine, Bevin emphasized that the British had not sought to undo the State of Israel. During the debate Churchill attacked Bevin for mishandling the Palestine question. Three days later Ben-Gurion called in Israel's unofficial representative in Britain, Joseph Linton, reminding him of the conversation in which Ernest Bevin told him of Britain's decision to grant *de facto* recognition to Israel.

The first years of independence

With the defeat of the Egyptian forces, other Arab states sought
to establish armistice agreements with Israel. Until this time
the United Nations intervention had sought to co-ordinate
the policies of the United States and Britain. Such actions had
prompted both of Bernadotte's plans. By the end of January
1949 the course of Middle East negotiations had undergone
a major transformation. Each of the armistice agreements was
reached on a bilateral basis, thereby avoiding the type of separate
negotiations favoured by the London Conference of 1939. On
24 February 1949 an armistice with Egypt was reached, followed
by armistices with Lebanon on 23 March, Jordan on 3 April, and
Syria on 20 July.

Through such settlements, Israel had come to be seen as
a major presence in the Middle East. With fierce indignation
the Arab world recoiled from these agreements and attacked
the regimes, alliances and leaders who had brought about such
defeat. In Egypt, Premier Nokrashy was assassinated in December 1948; King Farouk's reign ended with a military coup nearly
four years later. In Syria, a series of coups took place, and in
Jordan Abdullah was assassinated. Those who led such rebel-
lions were hostile to the old regimes. Pre-eminent among these
radicals was Gamal Abdel Nasser, who led the coup against King
Farouk, coming to power in 1954.

In January 1949 elections to the Knesset took place with
Ben-Gurion's party, Mapai, taking a dominant role. With the
support of a number of small parties, most of a religious character, Ben-Gurion formed a government. Although various
concessions were made to these parties, Ben-Gurion judged
that such accommodations were necessary to secure a strong
and effective government. The largest opposition party was
Mapam, which had connections with various Communist states.
The next largest party was Herut, led by Menachem Begin. At

Ben-Gurion's invitation, Weizmann became President of Israel, a largely ceremonial position.

At this point, Israel was surrounded by Arab states bitterly opposed to the creation of a Jewish homeland. In an attempt to drive the Zionists from their midst, a total economic boycott was established: trade between Israel and the Arab world was forbidden, and other countries were put on notice that any government that established trade relations with Israel would be excluded from trade with Arab nations. Border crossings were barred, and Arab air space was closed to aircraft flying to Israel. Determined to overcome this boycott, the Israeli government embarked on a four-year plan aimed at ensuring agricultural self-sufficiency. By the winter of 1950, Israelis were surviving on a subsistence economy with rationing of vital food and goods. In the face of such harsh conditions, some Jewish pioneers left the country, warning those who remained of future dangers.

By 1953, however, the programme of economic auster-ity began to halt ruinous inflation; in addition, foreign capital largely from the United States and Western Europe helped to bolster the flagging economy. Such conditions led to a resump-tion of immigration, and by the mid-1950s a considerable number of immigrants from the Maghreb, Tunisia and Morocco had entered the country. Israel, however, remained fearful that the United States would not continue to support the growing Jewish state, particularly when in October 1953 the Ameri-can Secretary of State, John Foster Dulles, decided to suspend American aid to Israel in response to Israeli raids on Arab border villages.

Anxious to protect the new state from such changes in pol-icy, Ben-Gurion sought to establish an alliance with France. In the autumn of 1956, Ben-Gurion together with the army chief of staff, Moshe Dayan, and an administrator from the Defence Ministry, Shimon Peres, flew to a military airfield south-west of Paris for a meeting with the French Prime Minister, Guy Mollet.

Later in the afternoon the British Foreign Secretary, Selwyn Lloyd, joined the conference. At this meeting the governments of France, Britain and Israel agreed to a plan of action to wrest control of the Suez Canal and the Sinai Peninsula from Egypt.

On 29 October, Israel launched an attack with a paratroop drop deep inside Sinai. Under the command of Moshe Dayan, Israel's attack resulted in the expulsion of Egyptian forces from all of Sinai. On the political front, however, the Israeli offensive gave rise to hostile reactions from Israel's allies. President Eisenhower sent Ben-Gurion a message asking that Israel withdraw its forces after liquidating the fedayeen bases and return to its original borders. When Ben-Gurion delayed responding to this request, Eisenhower proposed to the Security Council of the United Nations that an immediate cease-fire come into effect and that Israel withdraw its troops behind armistice lines.

This resolution was firmly rejected by Britain and France, since they had jointly expressed their own ultimatum addressed to both Israel and Egypt, threatening direct intervention. Angered by Britain's and France's failure to consult the United States before embarking on a joint operation in Suez, Eisenhower brought the matter before the General Assembly, where the Suez venture was vehemently criticized. On 4 November an Israeli representative informed the General Assembly that Israeli would agree to a cease-fire as long as a similar response was made by Egypt. However, on 6 November the British and French landed in the Canal Zone, determined to separate the combatants. Their aim was to withdraw having accomplished this mission.

In the meantime all those involved in this conflict were in danger of evoking Soviet intervention. On 5 November Premier Bulganin sent Israel a note stating that the Jewish state's actions placed into question the very existence of Israel. The following day, the US ambassador in Paris informed Prime Minister Guy Mollet that a Soviet attack on Britain and France

would lead to American retaliation. On 7 November the CIA
leaked a report that Moscow intended to destroy Israel the following day. Although this Soviet threat was taken seriously by
the Israeli leadership, Ben-Gurion was more concerned with
Israel's triumph over the Egyptian military. On 7 November
he delivered a victory speech in which he declared that the
armistice lines were no longer of any consequence. Further, he
stated that Israel would not agree to the stationing of a United
Nations force within her territory or in any of the occupied
territories.[12]

Undeterred by such vehemence, the General Assembly
voted for immediate withdrawal of the Israeli forces. In addition, Eisenhower informed Ben-Gurion of his deep concern
about the victory speech, implying that if Israel chose to ignore
the United States' concern, governmental aid would cease and
sanctions against Israel would be taken by the United Nations.
From the Jewish side, Nahum Goldman, the president of the
World Zionist Organization, indicated that the pro-Israel lobby
in the United States would not support Ben-Gurion's attitude.[13]
Unnerved by these reactions, the Israeli government meeting
on 8 November stated that Israel would withdraw her forces
from Sinai when satisfactory arrangements had been made with
the international force that was about to enter the Canal Zone.
The government also agreed that, if this failed, unconditional
withdrawal would have to be accepted.

Between November 1956 and March 1957 Abba Eban,
Israel's permanent representative at the United Nations and
Ambassador in Washington, engaged in negotiations about Israel's withdrawal. Following the Suez crisis, there was widespread
feeling that the West had been humiliated and that the Soviet
Union had increased its international influence. Further, it was
felt that the United States government had let down its allies. In
this context, the pro-Israel lobby was able to gain a greater hearing. Eban sought to ensure that the international force should be

used to ensure that the fedayeen raids should cease and that the Straits of Tiran should be opened to Israeli shipping. Eventually a consensus was established between Israel, the United Nations, the United States and Egypt that Israel would withdraw from Sinai on the assumption that the fedayeen raids would stop and the straits be reopened.

These arrangements afforded Israel ten years of peace with Egypt, thereby providing the opportunity for the Jewish state to absorb thousands of immigrants and improve its relations with the United States. Further, this agreement reinforced Israel's legitimacy, implying that the United States would not seek to inhibit Israel's right to armed resistance if Egypt sought to return to the pre-Suez situation by closing the straits. During this ten-year period Israel grew considerably in size; from 1956 to 1957 over 120,000 immigrants arrived mainly from Egypt and North Africa. In addition, there was an influx of immigrants from Eastern Europe. By 1965 Israel's GNP had increased two and a half times since 1952. These developments greatly strengthened Israel's position in the Middle East.[14]

During this period Jordan, which had essentially become a tributary of Egypt, became dependent on the United States after Hussein dismissed his pro-Nasser government in 1957. Syria, however, posed a major threat to Israel – under the influence of leftist-nationalist governments from 1962, it continued to agitate against the Jewish state. Joining this protest, Jordanians and Egyptians encouraged Palestinian exiles to establish their own organization. In 1964 an assembly of Palestinian Arabs meeting in East Jerusalem established the Palestine Liberation Organization. This body subsequently set up the Palestinian Liberation Army, whose aim was to liquidate Israel. This led to the resumption of fedayeen raids throughout the country.

4

The Six-Day War and its aftermath

Prelude to war

During the period of growth and expansion of the Jewish state, Germany undertook to pay reparations to Israel as compensation for property seized by the Nazis. The first stages to such an arrangement occurred in the early 1950s. When Ben-Gurion accepted this offer, Begin and the Herut party denounced such a financial agreement. Violent scenes took place in the Knesset, yet Ben-Gurion remained unmoved. By the end of 1965 nearly five billion dollars had been received, providing twenty per cent of Israel's state development budget.

Israeli society was further shaken by the extradition in the early 1960s of Adolf Eichmann, who had been responsible for implementing the Final Solution during the Second World War. Tracked down to an obscure place of hiding in Argentina where he had been living under a false identity, Eichmann was kidnapped by a shock force and flown to Tel Aviv. Over six months, Eichmann's trial reawakened memories of the Nazi regime; reported daily by the media, both Jews and non-Jews were compelled to confront the tragic crimes inflicted by the Germans on millions of innocent victims. On 15 December 1961, Eichmann was sentenced to death, and executed the next May.

Israel itself underwent internal conflict during this period of economic renewal. In 1950 the Law of Return, which guaranteed entry for Jews living in the diaspora, came under serious scrutiny by the religious parties. Determined to ensure the dominance of religious law in the Jewish state, these parties sought to impose their own definition of Jewishness upon the state. According to traditional Judaism, only those of maternal Jewish descent or individuals converted under Orthodox Jewish auspices are to be regarded as Jewish. Such a definition ruled out Jews converted by the non-Orthodox Jewish movements as well as any persons of doubtful descent.

Remaining aloof from such rulings, the secular Labour leadership expressed no interest in these technical distinctions. Nonetheless, because Labour was dependent on the support of marginal parties, in 1960 pragmatic politicians accepted the rabbinical definition of Jewishness along with its strictures against those of mixed origin. Ten years later the Supreme Court ruled that children of mixed marriages could be registered as Jews by nationality. Nonetheless, this measure was overturned by the Knesset under pressure from the militant right. In the years since, this issue has continued to fester in Israeli society, causing inevitable rifts between those of Orthodox and non-Orthodox conviction.

At the end of the 1960s the conflict between Jews and Arabs reached a climax with the Six-Day War. At this time the United States was deeply involved in the Vietnam War. For months China had been encouraging the Soviet Union to intensify its involvement in Middle East affairs in order to pressure the United States to reduce the bombing of North Vietnam and seek a peaceful settlement. On 12 May 1967 the Soviet Ambassador in Cairo provided the Egyptian government with fabricated intelligence about Israeli troop movements along the northern border. Two days later Egyptian troops and artillery paraded through the streets of Cairo, the country was placed on a war footing, and units were sent across the Suez Canal into Sinai. On 17 May, Nasser demanded the withdrawal of UN troops. This was followed by a decision to dispatch torpedo boats and submarines into the Gulf of Aqaba and to close the Straits of Tiran to Israeli shipping.

Although France had provided Israel with weaponry during this period, the French government did not express a formal objection to this development. When Abba Eban went to the Elysée Palace to seek French support, President Charles de Gaulle cautioned him against embarking on a war. The Four Powers, he stated, must be left to resolve the dispute, and France would influence the Soviet Union.[1] Such intervention, however, was rebuffed by the Soviet Union, and nine days after their meeting de Gaulle halted the emergency airlift to Israel.

The British and American governments were more support-ive. Prime Minister Harold Wilson stated that Britain would not allow the blockade of the Straits of Tiran to remain in force. Similarly, President Lyndon Johnson expressed the view that the straits should be opened by force if required. Yet, burdened by the war in Vietnam, the President refused to act without the consent of Congress and the United Nations. In the meantime Iraq, Kuwait and Algeria sent troops to Jordan and Egypt, and the Arab world grew increasingly impatient. Under pressure from Syria and Egypt, King Hussein of Jordan signed a mutual defence agreement with Nasser, and an Egyptian general was assigned as joint commander of the Jordanian forces.

In Israel agitation for military engagement increased. Yet Eban persuaded the Cabinet not to act, evoking support from Europe and the United States. However, by 4 June it was acknowledged that it was pointless to delay any further, par-ticularly since the Western powers had abandoned the 1957 agreement to keep the Straits of Tiran open. On the morning of 5 June, Israeli planes flew low across Egypt, avoiding radar detection, and discovered that most Egyptian planes were on the ground as Israeli intelligence had expected. In approximately five hundred sorties Israeli aircraft destroyed 309 out of Egypt's 340 planes.[2]

Although Moshe Dayan had instructed that Jordan and Syria should not be attacked, these countries conducted air strikes on Israeli targets. In response, Israel destroyed nearly the entire Jordanian and Syrian air forces. By the end of the second day, Israeli officials were convinced that the war had been won. Israeli planes attacked Egyptian bases, and Israeli ground forces penetrated the border in northern Sinai. Having eliminated the Egyptian air force, the Israeli army continued its onslaught under air protection. Israeli tanks outmanoeuvred the Egyptians, and Israeli planes attacked convoys of retreating tanks and trucks. On 7 June, Israeli paratroopers descended on Sharm el-Sheikh, which overlooks the Straits of Tiran; the Egyptian fortress there was abandoned. By dusk Israeli forces had reached Rumani, ten miles from the canal; the next day Israeli troops reached the waterway.

Initially Nasser remained unaware of this onslaught; however, when he learnt that the Egyptian air force had been devastated, he contacted Hussein to co-ordinate their actions. Alleging that American and British planes had participated in the attack on Egypt, Hussein shelled Tel Aviv and other Israeli towns and *kibbutzim* on 5 June; he subsequently sent a unit into Jerusalem's demilitarized zone to secure a position from which he could shell West Jerusalem. In response, Israel moved into the West Bank and seized the mountain ridge and road between Jerusalem and Ramallah.

In addition to this victory, Israel fought for control of other important routes through the West Bank, seizing the roads that ran south-west from Jerusalem to Latrun, north to Nablus and Jenin and south through Bethlehem and Hebron. Israeli planes were also reported as having hit Palestinian refugee camps near Jericho. It was reported that about one hundred thousand Palestinian civilians had been ordered out of this territory and had fled eastwards across the Jordan, although some later returned and settled elsewhere on the West Bank.[3] In this conflict Israeli forces cut off the main road from Jerusalem and hit Jordanian reinforcements with air strikes.

Since 1948 the Old City had been in Jordanian hands, but Hussein's attack on Israel provided an opportunity for Israel to seize Jerusalem. On 7 June, a battle for supremacy took place which lasted for nearly two days. Israeli troops broke through St Stephen's Gate, moved along the Via Dolorosa and eventually took all of Jerusalem. After three days, Syria remained undefeated despite its central role in waging a virulent anti-Israeli campaign. From the Golan Heights, Syria had been attacking Israeli villages. On 8 June plans were approved to initiate an attack against the Syrian forces; two days later the Israeli army was in control of the Golan Heights. This marked the end of the war.

Israel's military victory had a shattering effect on the Arab world; the Jewish state had emerged as the most powerful force in the Middle East. On the international stage, the Soviet Union requested the Secretary General of the United Nations to convene an Emergency Session of the General Assembly to secure the withdrawal of Israeli forces behind the armistice lines. Under the influence of the United States, all resolutions calling on Israel to undertake this withdrawal failed to win a two-thirds majority. However, when the issue was referred to the Security Council, a compromise resolution was passed unanimously which called for the withdrawal of the Israeli armed forces from territories occupied in the recent conflict and the termination of all claims of belligerency and an acknowledgement of the sovereignty and political independence of every state in the area. Such conditions constituted a major victory for the Jewish state.

The Arab world

In the wake of the Six-Day War three categories of Palestinian Arabs existed: Arab residents of Israel; Arab inhabitants of territories occupied by Israel in 1967; Palestinian refugees living in Arab states. The first group consisted of a small number of Palestinian Arabs who became citizens of Israel; although Israel has no written constitution, the Declaration of Independence guarantees social and political equality to all its citizens. Despite this guarantee of freedom, from the beginning Israelis were ambivalent about the Arab population residing in their midst. Although there was a desire to honour the guarantee of equality, other factors mitigated against its implementation.

Zionists insisted that Israel should be a Jewish state – there was no place, they argued, for non-Jews within the mainstream of national life even if Arabs were granted citizenship. For many, the Arab remnant in Israel was perceived as a potential threat to the stability of the country. Concentrated in border areas, they were viewed as in sympathy with Arabs living outside the Jewish state. Ben-Gurion, for example, was adamant that the Arab minority was a dangerous presence. Throughout his tenure as Prime Minister, he continually pointed to the inherent danger posed by the Arab population. It was, he believed, a hotbed of conspiracy.

From the beginning, Israel's policies towards the Arabs were in accord with this perception: they were seen as implacable enemies of the state. From 1948 ninety per cent of the Arabs lived under Military Government with three regional councils – the Northern Command, the Central Command and the Southern Command. Between 1949 and 1950 Military Government was granted full legal form, a governmental structure that lasted 18 years.[4] The most important aspect of Military Government was the restriction of movement: Article 125 of the Emergency Regulations of 1949 granted military governors the power to declare any area or place a forbidden area that no one was allowed to enter or leave without a written permit. Under such a provision, nearly one hundred Arab villages were designated closed areas out of which no one was permitted to move without a permit.[5] The Bedouin in the Negev were subject to similar restrictions.

Other powers granted to military governors included the right to banish, restrict the residence of or detain Arabs without trial, and to impose a curfew. The justification for such regulations was state security. Of particular concern to Israeli authorities was the threat of nationalistic gatherings; for this reason local sports were forbidden (although countrywide associations of sport were permitted). In addition, any expressions of Arab nationalism or anti-Zionism could be suppressed by the military authorities. Such emergency provisions were seen as vital for Jewish survival given the nature of Palestinian resentment.

Such restrictions might appear to undermine the principle of equality of citizenship. But the Israeli government was determined to protect the new Jewish state at all costs. It should be stressed also that these restrictions applied to areas rather than individuals. Nonetheless, the main objective was to ensure that any form of Arab insurrection would be thwarted and that the Arab population would be strictly controlled. Despite these limitations, the generation of Arabs who remained in Israel generally accepted such restrictions. Under Ottoman rule, and later under the Mandate, they had not been granted democratic rights. Rather than rebel against Israeli rule, they accommodated themselves to the status of a subject people. Their children, however, were keenly aware that they had been denied the right to equal treatment within the Jewish state.

Nonetheless, the first generation of Arabs in Israel were aware of their loss of land. During the fighting between Jews and Arabs, a sizeable area of Arab territory had been seized and this was later legalized by the Knesset under the Land Acquisition Law of 1953. In addition, Arab lands were taken by the military authorities on military grounds and given to Jewish settlers. Financial compensation was offered, but those who had lost their property refused to accept such payment in the hope that the land would be returned.

The majority of land and houses taken belonged to Palestinian Arabs who had fled during the fighting; this was confiscated under the Absentees' Property Law of 1950. This property was given to Israel's new immigrants, some of whom were themselves refugees from Arab lands. Approximately 418 Arab towns were taken over during this period. Dismayed by this state of affairs, dispossessed Arabs harboured deep resentment against those who had seized their land that had been inherited from ancient times and their ownership of which the British Mandate had respected.

This transformation of Arab life in Palestine was coupled with the loss of Arab control. Arabs had had no political power under Ottoman rule or during the British Mandate. Nevertheless, Arabs did have high social status as well as wealth which they were able to transform into collective political power. Under Hajj Amin, for example, the Supreme Muslim Council had exercised considerable authority in Palestine. The main source of such control resulted from the religious endowment (*waqf*) to which rich Arabs contributed for the benefit of the faithful. After Israel's defeat of Arab states during the 1949 campaign, Ben-Gurion instituted the law of abandoned property in 1950, resulting in the acquisition of agricultural land, urban real estate, houses and shops. In this way Arab wealth and influence were totally undermined. Within this framework, Israel also assumed responsibility over the mosques within its borders.

During the ten years following the creation of the Jewish state, there was little Arab unrest; however, in the summer of 1958 rioting took place in Nazareth. The following year Arab militants established their own Arab nationalist party, which was later suppressed by the Israeli authorities. Arab support then shifted to the Communist Party. Following the 1967 war Israel was in control of large territories populated by Arabs. East

Jerusalem and 28 Arab villages on the West Bank were annexed to the state, and the newly occupied territories included the West Bank, formerly held by Jordan, and the Gaza Strip, previously under Egyptian control. In a census taken in 1967 nearly a million Arabs lived in these territories – 595,000 in the West Bank and 389,700 in Gaza.[6]

During the first few years after the Israeli victory, the Israelis were faced with a serious security threat in the occupied territories. The Palestine Liberation Organization, which was supported by all Arab nations, initiated a war of liberation. Yasser Arafat, who had emerged as a significant figure in the Palestinian struggle for liberation, recruited young people to the resistance movement. In 1970 Palestinian freedom fighters took control of the Gaza Strip, but through a series of searches and the demolition of refugee camps PLO rule in Gaza was ended by 1972.

During this period, the PLO had emerged as the main body representing Palestinian interests. After the Six Day War, there were nearly the same number of Palestinians living under Israeli rule (1.6 million) as lived outside the Jewish state (1.5 million). Of those living outside Israel, 644,200 resided in Jordan (East Bank); 288,000 in Lebanon; 183,00 in Syria; 39,000 in Egypt; 194,000 in Kuwait; 59,000 in Saudi Arabia; 35,000 in Iraq; and 67,000 in other countries.[7] The first group that gained recognition among this diverse population was Fatah, founded in Kuwait in 1958–9 by Palestinian students, including Yasser Arafat. Other Palestinian organizations included the Democratic Front for the Liberation of Palestine (DFLP) headed by George Habash and the Popular Democratic Front for the Liberation of Palestine headed by Nayif Hawatmeh (PDFLP).

The Palestine Liberation Organization was established in Jerusalem in May 1964 under the auspices of the Arab League. Four years later the PLO became a federation of fedayeen organizations, of which Fatah was the largest. The next year

Arafat as leader of Fatah became chairman of the executive committee of the Palestine National Council, in effect the leader of the PLO. After the Six-Day War, the headquarters of the PLO were moved from Damascus to Amman. On 3 November 1969 the PLO was granted the right to act from Lebanon against Israel.

During 1971–3 various acts of terrorism took place supported by the PFLP (Popular Front for the Liberation of Palestine) and DFLP. Fatah similarly set up its own terrorist group: the Black September Organization. This body was responsible for the assassination of the Jordanian Prime Minister Wasfi al-Tal and the murder of Israeli athletes at the Munich Olympics. After the Yom Kippur War of 1973 the PLO was officially recognized as the sole representative body of the Palestinian people at the seventh Arab Summit Conference at Rabat on 26–9 October 1974. On 13 November, Yasser Arafat spoke at the United Nations on behalf of Palestinians worldwide.

Renewed conflict between Israel and the Arabs

Following the Six-Day War the government of National Unity, led by Levi Eshkol, was prepared to give up large areas of the occupied territories in exchange for peace. On 19 June 1967 the Israeli Cabinet agreed upon a four-point resolution stating that Israel was willing to withdraw to the international border with Egypt in exchange for a peace treaty. It was understood, however, that such an agreement was dependent on the recognition that Israel be allowed freedom of movement in the Straits of Tiran and the Suez Canal. This resolution also stated that Israel was prepared to withdraw to the international border with Syria as long as the Golan Heights were demilitarized. No mention was made of the West Bank and Gaza Strip – these were to be dealt with at a later stage.

Despite Israel's flexibility concerning these various territories, the Arab states were unwilling to engage in negotiation. At the first meeting of Arab nations after the war, at the Khartoum Conference from 19 August to 1 September 1967, it was resolved that there should be no peace or negotiation with and no recognition of the Jewish state. At this conference Nasser and the oil-rich states had reached an accommodation: in exchange for an annual subsidy of $225 million, Nasser agreed to halt his campaign against the monarchical and reactionary regimes in the Arab world. By such an arrangement, Nasser abandoned his quest to establish a Pan-Arab federation across the Arab world.

The Arab defeat led to widespread resentment against Israel. The loss of the Golan Heights and the West Bank and the continued presence of Israeli troops along the east bank of the Suez Canal evoked outrage among Arab leaders. Throughout 1968 Egypt carried out bombardments against Israeli positions along the canal; the following year it announced a policy of constant military activity along the canal. This war of attrition between Israel and Egypt was a serious problem for the Jewish state – Israel could not afford to sustain constant casualties along its border. In response to this Egyptian initiative, Israel embarked on a sustained policy of retaliation.

During this period the United States was following an inconsistent policy towards the conflict. The Secretary of State, William Rogers, pressed for a cease-fire in the Middle East, whereas the President's National Security Advisor, Henry Kissinger, encouraged Israel's activities. On 19 September 1969 Yitzhak Rabin, Israel's Ambassador to Washington, sent a cable to Jerusalem stating that the United States was prepared to supply Israel with arms if military actions against Egypt were increased.[8]

In the same month, Prime Minister Golda Meir established a system of direct communication through Rabin and Kissinger which bypassed both the Israeli Foreign Office and the State Department. On 25 October 1969 Rabin recommended deep penetration of Egyptian targets, advice that appeared to emanate from President Richard Nixon through Kissinger. However, such a plan was curtailed by an initiative taken by William Rogers on 29 October. On the basis of Security Council Resolution 242, he proposed an international frontier between Egypt and Israel. On 17 November, Israel rejected this suggestion, and two months later the Israeli Air Force struck at targets deep inside Egypt.

On 22 January 1970, Nasser flew to Moscow to obtain air-defence surface-to-air missiles along with Russian crews. Although initially reluctant to agree, the Soviet government finally concurred, thereby committing the Soviet Union to strengthening the Egyptian military. Reversing its previous policy, the United States began to apply pressure on Israel to cease its deep penetration of Egypt and to negotiate on the basis of the Rogers proposal. Although the United States had agreed to deliver arms to Israel, the State Department made it clear that the delivery of such weapons would be delayed. Eventually Israel accepted a cease-fire and the application of Resolution 242.

With the death of Nasser in 1971, Anwar el-Sadat came to power in Egypt. Unlike Nasser, Sadat ended his country's dependence on the Soviet Union and sought to reach an accommodation with Israel. In this quest, his main objective was to recover the Sinai Peninsula from Israeli control. To test Israeli defences, he launched several military offensives, and in addition strengthened the armed forces. Acknowledging that Israel was unwilling to relinquish this area, he decided that war would be inevitable. In early 1973 Israel became aware of increased Egyptian military activity, and the country was put on alert. By late September the Israeli political establishment was divided about whether further military movements signified that war was imminent.

On Yom Kippur, 6 October 1973, Israeli intelligence became aware that Egypt and Syria were preparing to attack the country. Although the Israeli air force was ready to launch air strikes, the Defence Minister, Moshe Dayan, and the Prime Minister, Golda Meir, came to the view that Israel should not strike first, since this would make it difficult for the United States to provide assistance. By 2.00 p.m. the Arab offensive had commenced; as a consequence, Israel suffered considerable loss of life and property. In the first month, 2500 Israelis were killed.

In the end, Syria and Egypt were defeated, but within Israel there was widespread criticism of the way in which the military had handled this conflict. Nonetheless, Israeli troops penetrated into Syria, and on the Suez front the Israeli army established a superior position. As a consequence, the cease-fire that commenced at the end of October was unstable, and the United States feared that conflict would be resumed. Anxious to protect American interests in the Middle East as well as to reduce Soviet influence in the area, the United States was determined that peace should be established in the region.

Initially negotiations between Israel and the Arab states were undertaken by the American Secretary of State, Henry Kissinger. At this stage the Israelis were recovering from the difficulties of the war. Although Sadat did not believe he could actually drive the Israelis out of Sinai, he had hoped that this could be achieved through diplomatic negotiations. The Syrians believed that the United States would curtail the Israeli incursion into their territory. Kissinger's first task was to ensure there would be no further conflict. Although many Israelis were anxious to secure peace, there was considerable reluctance to reward the Arabs for starting the war. Fearing Arab intentions, the Israelis were reluctant to withdraw from the territory they had conquered.

Despite such reservations, an agreement between Israel and Egypt was reached in January 1974. As a result of Kissinger's shuttle diplomacy between Jerusalem and Aswan, Egypt was willing to cede a narrow strip of land on the eastern bank of the Suez Canal as long as Israel retreated beyond the UN buffer zone in Sinai. Kissinger then flew repeatedly between Jerusalem and Damascus in pursuit of an agreement.

During this time Golda Meir resigned and was succeeded by Yitzhak Rabin, leading to a degree of instability in Israel. In Syria, President Hafez al-Assad sought the withdrawal of Israel from his country; Israel, however, was unwilling to comply. Despite such difficulties, both sides agreed that a buffer zone between Israeli and Syrian troops should be established. Further, it was accepted that a cease-fire line similar to that of 1967 would be created and that Israel would give up a small amount of land as well as the town of Kuneitra. In exchange, Israel would be allowed to use force in the event of guerrilla attacks launched from Syria. Both sides also agreed that their troops should be limited near the border. Although further diplomatic initiatives ceased, the peace process was revived by American President Jimmy Carter.

In the election of 17 May 1977 Menachem Begin and the Likud bloc were elected to power, breaking Labour's hold on the Jewish state. Adopting a right-wing policy, Begin argued that Israel had the right to control Judea and Samaria (the West Bank). In his view, though Resolution 242 obliged Israel to withdraw from occupied territories, the resolution did not specify that this should be done on all fronts. Hence any Israeli withdrawal from the Sinai would fulfil this requirement. Undeterred, Sadat, addressing the Egyptian Parliament on 9 November 1977, declared that he was prepared to go anywhere in search of peace.

Following this initiative, Begin invited Sadat to visit Israel. On 19 November, Sadat arrived in the Jewish state, and spoke to the Knesset the next day. Determined that Israeli forces leave all occupied territories as well as grant Palestinians the right of self-determination, Sadat urged the Israeli government to comply with these requests so that peace could be established in the Middle East. Although Israelis were anxious to establish a peace treaty with Egypt, there was considerable disagreement between Begin and Sadat.

Throughout 1978 the United States sought to negotiate a settlement; eventually a summit took place at Camp David from 5 to 17 September. Eventually Sadat accepted a general outline for West Bank and Gaza autonomy in return for the return of Sinai. Although the Camp David agreement set a goal of three months to determine a peace treaty, it took until March 1979 for differences between the countries to be resolved. On 26 March 1979, Begin, Sadat and Carter assembled at the White House to sign a peace treaty between Israel and Egypt.

The Palestinian problem

Following the Camp David agreement, many Israelis hoped that peace could be established with the Arab world. Yet, it soon became clear that the Arab nations had no desire to make concessions to the Jewish nation. When the Israeli Ambassador to Egypt sought to find a residence in Cairo, no one would lease him land for an embassy or house. In addition, as Ambassador he was shunned by the diplomatic community. Even though a considerable number of Israelis went on tours of Egypt, few Egyptians visited the Jewish state. Yet, though normal relations were not established between the two countries, Israelis no longer feared attack by the Egyptian army.

On the domestic front, Israel was beset with economic difficulties – every year the inflation rate rose by nearly one hundred per cent. As a consequence, class distinctions became greater, with Ashkenazi Jews becoming richer while Sephardi Jews from Mediterranean lands and elsewhere formed the poor sectors of society. In an attempt to control inflation, the government repeatedly curtailed food subsidies. As opinion polls reported increased dissatisfaction with the Begin government, import tariffs were cut on numerous goods, which precipitated widespread spending. In addition, foreign currency reserves were used to restore the value of the shekel, and subsidies on food, housing and education were restored.

In June 1981, several weeks before the general election, the Israeli air force attacked a nuclear reactor in Iraq. Although this action was condemned by the international community, Israelis were profoundly relieved that Iraq was rendered incapable of producing a nuclear bomb. In the ensuing election Likud was strongly supported, and Begin formed a new government with several ultra-Orthodox parties.

Among those included in the cabinet was Ariel Sharon, the new Minister of Defence. Previously, Sharon had served as Minister of Agriculture and Chairman of the Settlement Committee. Under his leadership, the number of Jewish settlers on the West Bank rose to about eighteen thousand.[9] Despite this increase, Sharon was committed to increasing substantially the Jewish presence in the occupied territories. Beginning in 1981 the government launched an extensive building programme. Attracted by low-interest mortgages and tax incentives, Jews from Tel Aviv and Jerusalem moved to these settlements where houses could be bought for the same price as an apartment in the cities.

By 1982 Israel had withdrawn from the Sinai despite repeated protests from Jews who had settled there. Despite Sadat's assassination by Egyptian fundamentalists in September 1981, the Egyptian borders were largely peaceful, as were the border areas with Syria and Jordan. In the north, however, Israel faced renewed difficulties. The Palestine Liberation Organization had established its headquarters in Beirut and southern Lebanon, from where it launched repeated attacks on

northern Israel; in addition, PLO terrorists managed to penetrate Israeli borders and carry out attacks on innocent victims.

In retaliation Israel struck at Palestinian refugee camps
and other targets. Determined to defend the nation against its
enemies in the north, Sharon devised a plan to drive the PLO
out of Lebanon as well as to strengthen the Lebanese Christians
who might be persuaded to expel both the PLO as well as Syrian
troops who had been stationed in the country. In a meeting with
Sharon in January 1982, the head of the Phalange (the Lebanese
Christian forces), Bashir Gemayel, agreed to join Israel in taking
action against the Palestinians.[10]

On 6 June 1982 eighty thousand Israeli soldiers invaded
Lebanon in an attempt to establish a twenty-five-mile security zone. However, by the third day the Israeli army had
penetrated twenty-five miles north with the aim of joining
Phalangist forces in Beirut so as to cut the Beirut–Damascus
highway. Troubled by this advance, Syria halted the Israeli
incursion. But in the Beirut area Israeli troops were able to link
up with the Phalangists. After a week's fighting, Israeli troops
camped outside Beirut.

As a result of this battle, PLO forces returned into the western side of Beirut. Although Sharon was anxious to drive out
these fighters, there was a reluctance to risk the lives of Israeli
soldiers. Though it was agreed that Phalangists should undertake this operation, they refused to do so. When Begin insisted
that the Palestinians withdraw, Arafat refused. The Israelis then
launched an offensive that they hoped would persuade the PLO
to leave. Owing to American intervention, the fighters withdrew by sea. Although this retreat appeared to be a defeat for
the PLO, they departed as triumphant guerrillas.

Sharon, however, was determined that all PLO forces be
expelled from Lebanon. In the face of Palestinian denials, he
insisted that about two thousand men were hiding in refugee
camps. Gemayel was determined to search the camps, but he was

assassinated within the month. With the concurrence of the Israeli army, Phalangist troops moved into the Sabra and Shatila Palestinian camps in southern Beirut. According to witnesses, these soldiers made no attempt to distinguish between Palestinians and Lebanese or between men, women and children. More than three hundred refugees were massacred.[11]

When news of this onslaught reached Israel, there was widespread criticism of the government. On 24 September a mass demonstration was held to protest against the war in Lebanon. Wearied by such criticism, Begin announced that he would resign as Prime Minister in August 1983. Following his election as Prime Minister, Yitzhak Shamir led Israel during a period of widespread discontent exacerbated by inflation, which rose at a rate of four hundred per cent every year. Eventually the Labour Party was able to bring down the Likud government, and an election was called for 23 July 1984. Under its leader, Shimon Peres, Labour formed a coalition with Likud. It was agreed that Peres would serve as Prime Minister for two years while Shamir served as Foreign Minister; these offices would then be exchanged.

Under Labour, Israel was subjected to severe wage and price control; eventually inflation was cut to about twenty per cent. During this period the government also declared that a security zone be established in south Lebanon. Together with Christian militia, Israeli soldiers patrolled an area along Israel's northern border about twenty miles deep. In the occupied territories, however, Palestinians rebelled against Israeli rule. In December 1986 in Ramallah, a Palestinian youth struck an Israeli soldier on the head with an axe. The soldier was taken to hospital and the youth was imprisoned.

Similar incidents took place the following year. The young Palestinians involved were from the post-1967 generation who had suffered under Israeli rule in the occupied West Bank and Gaza Strip. At the beginning of December 1987 after four Arab workers from the Gaza Strip were fatally run over by an Israeli truck, Israeli soldiers were attacked throughout the occupied territories. Attempts were made to block the entry of Israeli troops into Arab villages; strikes were declared; and pamphlets encouraging conflict with the authorities were circulated. At various points the Palestinian flag was raised, an illegal action under Israeli law.

Almost all the Palestinian population in the territories occupied by Israel took part in the resistance to occupation – men, women and children from all cities, towns and villages and the refugee camps housing nearly a quarter of a million refugees. Another quarter of a million refugees lived in the Gaza Strip. In the West Bank there were over 350,000 refugees, of whom one hundred thousand were housed in camps. Outside the country there were about a quarter of a million Palestinian refugees in Lebanon, of whom about 150,000 lived in camps; another quarter of a million in Syria, with about seventy-five thousand in camps; and over eight hundred thousand in Jordan, with over two hundred thousand in camps.[12]

To suppress this uprising, the Israelis deployed tear gas, rubber bullets, plastic bullets and in some cases live ammunition. Arabs were beaten, and some Israeli soldiers were arrested and punished. Attempting to control the Palestinian population became a major problem for the authorities. In the first two months over fifty Arabs were killed and hundreds wounded. In protest, one of the leading Arab members of the Knesset, Abdel Wahab Darawshe, left the Labour Party and founded the Arab Democratic Party, which pressed for the creation of a Palestinian state in the West Bank, the Gaza Strip and East Jerusalem.

Outside Israel, the *Intifada* was widely supported, and on 22 December 1987 the Security Council passed a resolution condemning Israeli action in the occupied territories. Spurred by such criticism, the Arab states established a fund to support the *Intifada*. Determined to find a solution to the Palestinian problem, the United States Assistant Under-Secretary of State, Richard Murphy, embarked on a visit to the Middle East on 5 February 1988 with a plan for the region. According to the Murphy proposals, two delegations – one from Israel and another composed of Jordanians and Palestinians – would discuss the possibilities of temporary autonomy for the Palestinians; this would be accompanied by Israeli redeployment and municipal elections for the Palestinian population. Later an international conference would be convened to discuss the outcome of these deliberations and within three years Palestinian autonomy would be established. On his departure, however, Hamas (the Movement of the Islamic Resistance) was founded, committed to Islamic rule for all of Palestine.

5

The road to peace

Intensification of the uprising

Operating as an independent body, Hamas instigated strikes, punished Palestinians who did not comply with its policies and created a network to help those in need. In August 1988 Hamas published its covenant, which rejected the legitimacy of the PLO as the sole representative of the Palestinian people. In addition, it rejected any compromise with the State of Israel. All of Palestine, it stated, belonged to Muslims, and Hamas proclaimed a holy war against Israel as well as corrupt elements within Palestinian society. Another group, Islamic Jihad, from the Egyptian-based Muslim Brotherhood in the Gaza Strip, similarly supported military action against the Jewish state. In Jordan, the Sudan and southern Lebanon other splinter groups supported the Palestinian cause.

In the election that took place on 1 November 1988, Likud retained the largest number of seats, with Labour second. However, in order to form a government, it was necessary to form a coalition. In an attempt to integrate the various factions within society, Likud formed a National Unity government. On 22 December 1988 Yitzhak Shamir became Prime Minister, Shimon Peres was appointed Minister of Finance and Yitzhak Rabin became Defence Minister. The leader of the ultra-Orthodox Shas party, Arye Deri, was appointed Minister of the Interior. The political leader of Shas, Rabbi Yitzhak Peretz, became Minister of Immigrant Absorption. The leader of the National Religious Party, Zvulun Hammer, became Minister of

Religious Affairs. Excluded from government, the left-wing parties combined into one party, Meretz.

Within Israel there was increasing sympathy for the plight of the Palestinians in the occupied territories. In 1988 a human rights organization, Betselem, was created which criticized breaches of human rights by the Israeli forces. Another human rights organization, Hotline: Centre for the Defence of the Individual, was established to aid Palestinians who had been denied the right to leave the country. In April 1989 the Israeli police reported that they had uncovered a network of illegal classes held by two West Bank universities at private schools in East Jerusalem, all schools in the University and the West Bank and the Gaza Strip having been closed by military order as a collective punishment because of resistance to the occupation. These meetings were closed down. In protest an expert on criminology, Professor Stanley Cohen of the Hebrew University, declared that such an action was an infringement of Jordanian law and a violation of the Geneva Convention and the Universal Declaration of Human Rights.[1]

During this period the emigration of Soviet Jews had dramatically receded because of instability within Israel; many Soviet Jews chose instead to live in the United States. On 1 October 1989 the United States adopted a new policy insisting that any Soviet Jew who sought to settle in the United States would no longer be able to use an Israel exit visa; instead, the person would be compelled to apply to the United States Embassy. As a consequence, the Israeli government drafted plans to integrate hundreds of thousands of new settlers. Another, smaller immigration took place in the 1990s, the arrival of 4137 Ethiopian Jews.

As the *Intifada* intensified, Yitzhak Rabin recommended that elections should take place in the West Bank and the Gaza Strip. On 14 May 1989 this scheme was presented by the National Unity government as one of several proposals: to strengthen peace between Egypt and Israel, to seek peace agreements with other Arab states, and to attempt to resolve the problem of Arab refugees in camps outside Israel. This peace initiative, however, was dependent on several conditions: Israel would negotiate only with Palestinians not connected with the PLO who resided in the occupied territories; there would be no change in the status of the occupied territories; Israel would not agree to an additional Palestinian state in the Gaza district and in the area between Israel and Jordan.

Such conditions were not acceptable to the PLO, and as a consequence the *Intifada* continued. On 20 May the leadership distributed a leaflet calling on Palestinians to kill a soldier or settler for every Palestinian killed in a conflict with Israeli troops. In addition, this document criticized the United States for supporting Israel's election proposal. The leaflet also encouraged attacks on Palestinian collaborators who were perceived as enemies of the Palestinian people.[2]

During the year thirty-five Palestinians were killed, and one Israeli soldier. To stem such hostility, the Israeli government attempted to quell Israeli actions in the occupied territories. In May a group of Israeli soldiers were criticized for desecrating the Qur'an; orders were also given to prevent Jewish settlers from damaging Arab property. Nonetheless, in July students at a *yeshiva* near Nablus attacked local Arabs, killing a thirteen-year-old Palestinian girl.

In the following months Palestinian schools were closed, since they were perceived as focal points of insurrection, leading to conflict between Palestinian youth and Israeli troops. In the wake of such violence a number of Palestinian moderates were murdered. Anxious about such increasing violence, a number of Israelis and Palestinians established the Israeli–Palestine Centre for Research and Information in an attempt to discover a way forward. On 6 December the United States Secretary of State, James Baker, acted as a facilitator in this crisis, issuing a five-point statement which proposed that Israel engage in talks with acceptable Palestinians.

As the *Intifada* continued, Jews were reluctant to walk in the Old City, particularly after Professor Menachem Stern was stabbed to death in West Jerusalem. At the beginning of July an Arab passenger on the 405 bus service outside Jerusalem forced the bus off the road, killing 16 people. During the next three days, 24 Jews were arrested by Jerusalem police for hurling stones at Arab cars and trying to attack Arabs in the streets. In response Arabs threw petrol bombs at Jewish buses. On 28 July an Israeli unit crossed into southern Lebanon and abducted an important Hizbullah cleric, Sheikh Abd al-Karim Obeid.

In the view of Yitzhak Rabin, the *Intifada* represented the will of small groups who sought to discover their national identity and insist on its recognition. Such an acknowledgement was officially given by the American Secretary of State at the beginning of March 1990. Seeking to find a solution to the Palestinian problem, he asked the government of Israel if they were ready to engage in negotiations with Palestinian representatives about the West Bank and the Gaza Strip. The Israeli Foreign Minister, Moshe Arens, was anxious for such discussion to take place, but Prime Minister Shamir objected. Angered by such intransigence, the Labour Party withdrew its support from the National Unity government.

Shamir's government was then defeated on a vote of no confidence; the President then called on Peres to form a government. During this period Arafat called on the Palestinians to renew violence against Jewish immigrants. Despite this, Peres sought to form a new coalition with the Sephardi religious party, Shas. When this attempt failed, he turned to other religious groups but in the end Likud was able to form a government with Shamir as Prime Minister.

Such internal turmoil was interrupted by international events that directly affected Israel. On 2 August 1990 the Iraqi leader

Saddam Hussein decided to invade Kuwait. Joining with the United States, Israel demanded Iraq's withdrawal from Kuwait. In response, Saddam agreed to an Iraqi withdrawal as long as Israel and Syria withdrew from southern Lebanon and Israel also departed from the occupied territories. At a summit in Helsinki on 8 September, President George Bush and Mikhail Gorbachev discussed this proposal; although Gorbachev wished to accept it, the Americans disagreed. Several weeks later Iraq threatened to deploy missiles against Israel; in response, the Israeli government distributed gas masks to the entire country, although they were not handed out to Palestinians living in the West Bank.

On 17 January 1991 a coalition of Allied forces attacked the Iraqi army in Kuwait. Israel was encouraged not to participate in this conflict. Although there was resistance among leading figures in the government, Israel complied despite Iraq's use of Scud missiles against the country. When Saddam was defeated, the population of Israel was greatly relieved. Nonetheless, the *Intifada* continued throughout the year. Throughout 1991 attacks on Jews and Palestinian collaborators intensified. By September 1225 Arabs had died, of whom 697 had been killed by Israeli forces; the others were killed by fellow Arabs. In addition, thirteen Israeli soldiers had been killed by Arabs.[3]

Israel was determined not to recognize the PLO. Hence, when Ezer Weizman met with Arafat in Vienna, he was sacked by Shamir. Yet, through James Baker's intervention, it was agreed that the Palestinians would be represented by persons from the occupied territories who would form a joint Jordanian–Palestinian delegation. On 18 October 1991 invitations were sent for a conference which was to be held in Spain. At the end of the month the Madrid Conference was opened with President Bush and President Gorbachev as the main speakers. At the conference Israel was represented by Prime Minister Yitzhak Shamir, and the Arab states were represented by their foreign ministers.

Arab–Israeli negotiations

In December 1991 another conference took place in Washington dealing with the procedures for future talks. Israel insisted it was not willing to discuss territorial concessions; rather it desired to focus on Palestinian autonomy. The Palestinians, however, were not content with such a limitation. After these talks, Jews and Arabs met in a number of cities to explore various practical issues. The first of these talks took place in Moscow and focused on water sharing and economic co-operation. In Ottawa the refugee problem was of central importance, whereas in Vienna water sharing was of critical importance. In Brussels the main topic was economic co-operation.

Such collaborative ventures were interrupted by the Israeli election, in which Labour became the largest party, forming an alliance with the left-wing party Meretz and the Arab Democratic Party. Shas, too, joined the coalition. As Prime Minister, Yitzhak Rabin was committed to continuing the peace process as well as the absorption of Russian immigrants into the country. In his opening speech as Prime Minister, Rabin emphasized that the peace process would be reactivated and that Palestinians would be partners with Israelis in this quest.[4]

Seeking to extend the agenda beyond the subjects discussed at Madrid and Washington, Rabin stated that the Israeli government would propose a continuation of the talks based on the framework of the Madrid Conference. Aware of Palestinian suffering in previous decades, Rabin proposed a form of Palestinian self-government in the West Bank and Gaza Strip. Anxious to win Palestinian support for this proposal, he refused to grant permission for the army to enter the Palestinian university campus at Nablus to search for six armed Palestinians who were allegedly attempting to influence student elections. In addition, he ordered a freeze on all new building of Jewish settlements in the West Bank and the Gaza Strip.

On 19 July, James Baker arrived in the Middle East to seek a solution to the conflict between Israel and its neighbours. Two days later Rabin went to Cairo in order to renew negotiations for a peace settlement. The next month he travelled to the United States to meet President Bush. On 24 August, Israel cancelled deportation orders for eleven Palestinians; the same day, talks between Israel and the Palestinians were resumed in Washington. Several days later Israel released eight hundred Palestinians who had been kept in detention. Simultaneously, Peres, acting as Foreign Minister, engaged in renewed negotiation. In September he met Prime Minister John Major in London, who agreed to end the arms embargo as well as the ban on British companies selling North Sea oil to Israel. In addition, Major agreed to intercede to end the boycott on British and European companies doing business with Israel.

Despite these steps, tension mounted in the West Bank and Jerusalem during November and December. These efforts to renew the peace process inflamed members of Hamas and Islamic Jihad who were bitterly opposed to compromise. With the encouragement of Iran, Hamas condemned the Israeli occupation while improving its educational, welfare and health care of the Palestinian population. During this period Israeli soldiers were occasionally trapped by gangs of Palestinian youths and fired on them with live ammunition. At the beginning of November in Khan Yunis, Israeli soldiers killed three Palestinians during a demonstration. Several days later in Beit Omar, Israeli troops killed a Palestinian youth who threw stones at the military. Two days later in Hebron another youth was shot dead. On 23 November in A-Ram a young Palestinian boy was killed during an attack. At the beginning of December in the Balata refugee camp, another youth was killed when a bomb he was handling exploded.

On 7 December 1992 three Israeli soldiers were killed in Gaza City; several days later Hamas kidnapped and killed an

Israeli sergeant. Determined to suppress such violence, the government took action against Hamas and Islamic Jihad. On 17 December 415 of their leaders who had been detained in prison or were at home were deported to Lebanon. When the Lebanese government refused to allow them to enter the country, these leaders created a tented encampment on the Lebanese side of the border. Eventually the United Nations Security Council demanded they be returned to Israel.

On 18 December, Israeli troops shot a Palestinian youth in the Askar refugee camp and another youth in the El-Arroub refugee camp near Hebron. The next day Israeli troops killed six Palestinians in Khan Yunis. Three days later another young boy was shot and killed. On 30 December, Israel admitted that some of the Hamas deportees should not have been expelled from the country. Acts of violence continued. On 15 January 1993 a Palestinian stabbed to death four people at the Tel Aviv Central Bus Station and at a café.

Despite such acts of violence, talks between Israel and the PLO began on 20 January. At a villa outside Oslo, representatives met for three days. At the meeting several of the PLO submitted proposals involving the Israeli withdrawal from the Gaza Strip, a mini Marshall Plan for the West Bank and Gaza, and economic co-operation between Israel and the Palestinian authorities. In Israel seventeen deportees were allowed to return home; however, an Israeli offer to take back 101 deportees was rejected. As the *Intifada* resumed, Israeli troops killed an armed Palestinian in Gaza City. On 5 February, Israeli troops killed a youth in the Nusseirat refugee camp in the Gaza Strip. In addition, three other Palestinians in the Bureij refugee camp were shot. On 6 February Israeli troops killed another youth when confronted by an Arab mob.

Such killings provoked debate within the country. According to the army, two-thirds of the deaths of Palestinians took place between August 1992 and January 1993 when the lives of Israeli soldiers were threatened. Because army regulations did not permit lethal shooting in such contexts, the troops were not complying with the regulations designed to regulate their conduct. Amidst such controversy, Peres and Rabin continued to engage in negotiations with the Palestinians. On 9 February the Oslo talks reached a new stage. Meeting with Rabin, Peres argued that Israel should seek to induce Arafat to leave Tunis and return to the West Bank and Gaza. He then set out the advantages of the proposals that had been presented by the Arab delegates.

On 11 February the Oslo talks continued, and a draft declaration of principles was drawn up as well as a paper establishing guidelines for a regional Marshall Plan. Nonetheless, on 1 March two young civilians were stabbed to death in Tel Aviv. On the next day Yehoshua Weissbroad was stoned and then shot in his car in the Gaza Strip. On 8 March a gardener was stabbed. On 12 March a young immigrant from Canada was shot. The next day a woman driver who took Palestinians from the Gaza Strip to their jobs was killed. Several days later two Israeli soldiers were shot dead.

Between 20 and 22 March secret meetings took place in Oslo in which it seemed that an accord between Israel and the PLO might emerge. This was followed by another meeting on 14 June in Oslo; two months later the Oslo Accords were approved by both the Israelis and the Palestinians. After the PLO had been required to renounce terrorism, a ceremony took place in Washington on 13 September 1993 with Yitzhak Rabin and Yasser Arafat as the main representatives. After the signing Rabin reluctantly shook hands with Yasser Arafat. In the following months Israel and the PLO engaged in active negotiations for an Israeli withdrawal from the West Bank and the Gaza Strip.

Despite these steps towards peace, Hamas and Islamic Jihad pressed for a more radical solution to the Middle East problem. In an attempt to stem further violence, Rabin felt that an approach should be made to Syria for an agreement concerning the Golan Heights. Peres, however, believed that Jordan should be consulted first about its desire that all the land should be returned, that Israel should cease taking water from the River Jordan, and that Palestinian refugees should be allowed to return to their former homes.

The Oslo Accords served as the framework for the peace process and a basis for Israeli–Arab co-operation. The form of self-government authorized at Oslo and the withdrawal plans provided a basis for eventual Palestinian statehood. In Arafat's view, such self-governing institutions were vital to the future of Palestine as a nation state. However, just as in 1947, the Palestinian Arabs were being encouraged by more radical groups to oppose a two-state solution. Israeli extremists were also set to sabotage the Oslo Accords. In January 1994 Yehoshafat Harkabi, former head of the Israeli military intelligence, told researchers from Ben-Gurion University that the internal debate about Israeli withdrawal from the West Bank could have serious consequences. Even though he was a supporter of the peace process, he feared that extremists would resort to violence.[5] On 25 February an Israeli gunman, Baruch Goldstein, opened fire on Palestinian Arabs inside the main mosque in Hebron, killing twenty-five people.

Negotiations and terrorism

In response to the massacre at Hebron, Arafat broke off negotiations with Israel, yet after several weeks of pressure the talks were resumed. Discontented Palestinians, however, actively sought to undermine the peace process. On 6 April a member of Hamas blew himself up with a bomb in Afula, killing eight Israelis. According to Hamas, this was to be the first in a series of terrorist attacks in retaliation for the murders at Hebron. A week later another member of Hamas detonated a bomb, killing himself and six other people in a bus in Hadera.

Determined to continue with negotiations, Rabin warned that such acts of terrorism would not deter the Israeli government from seeking an agreement with the PLO. On 3 May, Rabin and Arafat met in Cairo to finalize a peace agreement. Just after midnight Arafat added a number of territorial alterations to the maps that had previously been agreed upon. Once Rabin had agreed to these changes, a signing ceremony took place on 4 May. Under the Cairo agreement, a Palestinian authority headed by Arafat was given legislative, executive and judicial powers as well as responsibility for security, education, health and welfare. Israel would retain control of foreign affairs and defence.

Several days later Arafat flew to Johannesburg, where he declared that the Palestinians would not give up their *jihad* until Jerusalem was liberated. *Jihad*, he explained, did not mean holy war, but rather a sacred campaign. On 13 May, Israeli troops as well as administrators left Jericho; four days later they withdrew from the Gaza Strip. The Palestinian flag was raised over Jericho and Gaza City. During this period, a United Nations force took up positions between the Jewish and Arab sections of Hebron. Once Gaza and Jericho were transferred to the Palestinian Authority, Rabin and Peres engaged in discussion with Jordan; on 24 July, Rabin and King Hussein signed a peace declaration in Washington.

Despite these advances, four Hamas kidnappers seized an Israeli soldier in October, determined to murder him unless two hundred Hamas prisoners were released including Sheikh Ahmed Yassin. Determined not to negotiate with Hamas, Rabin refused to comply and suspended the Egyptian–Israeli negotiations. As Israeli commando units tried to rescue the soldier, he was killed along with one of the commandos. In consequence, discussions concerning Palestinian autonomy were suspended, but negotiations with Jordan continued. On 16 October, Rabin visited Jordan, where he and Hussein discussed border modifications that were to be part of the peace agreement. On 19 October another suicide bomber detonated a bomb on a bus in Ramat Gan, killing twenty-two people. Angered by this event, the leader of the opposition, Benjamin Netanyahu, condemned the peace process.

Following the incident at Ramat Gan, public support for the government's efforts began to decline. To deter further acts of violence, Rabin sealed off Gaza and the West Bank from Israel. Inside the Palestinian territories, Arafat arrested Hamas extremists. At the end of the month, President Clinton travelled to Cairo, where he held discussions with President Mubarak and Yasser Arafat. He then flew to Wadi Araba for the signing of the Israeli–Jordan Treaty of Peace, and then on to Amman and Damascus. Finally he flew to Israel, where he addressed the Knesset.

Several days after the signing of the Israel–Jordan treaty, a meeting of 2500 Israeli, Arab, American and European politicians and business people met in Casablanca for an economic summit which was addressed by Peres and Rabin.[6] These efforts to secure peace, however, were marred by further attacks. On 22 January 1995 twenty-nine Israeli soldiers and a civilian were killed at Beit Lid by a suicide bomber. Both Rabin and Arafat resolved that further efforts should be made to curtail such violence. Throughout Gaza a number of Islamic fundamentalist leaders were arrested.

Despite such setbacks Rabin pressed on with the peace process. Peres was to engage in negotiations with the Palestinians, and Rabin would focus on terrorism. On 29 March 1995 John Major arrived in Israel for a meeting with Rabin. Among the Palestinians, there was bitter conflict between those who supported efforts to achieve autonomy and those who rejected any form of negotiation with Israel. On 2 April two members of Hamas accidentally blew themselves up while preparing for an attack, killing six Palestinians. In response to these deaths, the chief of Gaza's civil police appealed to Hamas to desist from further acts of terror. Seven days later six Israelis were killed in suicide bombings in Kfar Daron.

Determined to continue the peace process, Peres went to Gaza on 4 July for a meeting with Arafat to finalize Oslo II, the extension of Palestinian rule to the West Bank accompanied by the withdrawal of Israeli troops. Under this scheme the West Bank would eventually be ruled by Palestinian authorities. Several weeks later six Israelis were killed in Tel Aviv. This act of terrorism, however, was not allowed to interrupt the peace process. Negotiations continued, and Israeli–Palestinian committees discussed the withdrawal of Israeli troops, Palestinian rule, the release of Palestinian prisoners, and the territory to be handed over to the Palestinian Authority.

Throughout the year the Israeli government had transferred a number of areas of government to the Palestinians in both the West Bank and the Gaza Strip: education, health, taxation, tourism and welfare. On 20 August 1995 several more spheres of responsibility were transferred: commerce, industry, agriculture, government, fuel, postal services, labour, insurance and statistics. Subsequently, with the help of an American negotiator, further aspects of Palestinian life were discussed. In Israel, however, there was growing alarm about these developments. According to Likud, Rabin had no authority to make such decisions, since his majority depended on Arab support within the country.

On 22 September Peres and Arafat went to an Egyptian resort and discussed the final aspects of Palestinian rule in the West Bank. The next week Rabin flew to Washington, where he signed the Oslo II agreement. The opposition parties denounced Rabin, calling him a traitor to his country. At the beginning of October the Knesset debated the Oslo treaty; at a rally in Jerusalem right-wing demonstrators protested against the government. In their view, Oslo II was a betrayal of the biblical Land of Israel. The leader of Likud, Netanyahu, attacked Rabin for reaching this accord with the support of Arab Knesset members. Despite such disturbances, Oslo II was narrowly passed in the Knesset.

Nonetheless, criticism of Oslo II continued. The President of Israel maintained that the treaty had been accepted too quickly. Undeterred, Rabin pressed on with plans for Palestinian autonomy. At the end of October he flew to Amman for the Amman Economic Conference; in his speech to the delegates, he supported economic co-operation between Israel and its Arab neighbours. In Israel, opposition mounted. At a rally in Jerusalem on 28 October, Rabin was denounced as a traitor to the Jewish state. The next week, Rabin and Peres appeared at a rally in Tel Aviv in support of the peace process. At the end of the rally Rabin left the platform and was shot dead by a religious Jew, Yigal Amir, a student at Bar-Ilan University.

The same evening at a meeting of the Israeli Cabinet, Peres was elected Prime Minister. Rabin's body had been placed in the Knesset forecourt; nearly a million people passed by his coffin during the afternoon and evening of 4 November and the early hours of the next day. Rabin's funeral was attended by a wide variety of representatives, including King Hussein, President Mubarak, the Prime Minister of Morocco, Prince Charles and representatives of over eighty countries. Although Arafat had wanted to attend, it was felt that his presence might cause difficulty at the ceremony. Throughout the Jewish world, memorial ceremonies were held to commemorate the Israeli leader. Eight days after Rabin's assassination a memorial meeting was held in Tel Aviv.

Despite such mourning, the peace process was disrupted when a West Bank university graduate student was killed in Gaza City on 5 January 1996. The next month a suicide bomber killed twenty-five people on a bus in Jerusalem. Later in the day another suicide bomber killed himself at a bus stop, killing one Israeli. Arafat's adviser, Ahmed Tibi, condemned these murders, insisting that the cycle of terrorism must come to an end. Despite his plea, thirteen Israelis were killed on 13 March by a suicide bomber in Jerusalem. The next day another suicide bomber attacked a crowd in Tel Aviv, killing eighteen people.

After the 13 March bus bomb, Peres told Arafat that the future of the peace process was at risk unless the Palestinian Authority was prepared to act against Hamas. Anxious to enlist international support against terrorism as well as to stop the funding of terrorist groups by Iran and Libya, Israel and Egypt held an international conference at Sharm el-Sheikh. Subsequently President Clinton flew to Israel to express sympathy for families that had lost relatives in the bombings.

Undermining Oslo

In the face of renewed attacks on Israel, the Oslo agreement came under increasing pressure. Although both Rabin and Peres were adamant that terrorism would not be allowed to undermine the peace process, the opposition parties unleashed a frenzied campaign against the Oslo Accords. In the midst of such uncertainty about government policy, Peres called an election, thereby inviting the Israel public to express its views about peace. On the night before the election Peres launched Operation Grapes of Wrath against Israel's enemies. For over two weeks Israeli forces bombed fundamentalist positions north of the security zone, killing twenty Lebanese civilians. Subsequently a civilian shelter was hit and 105 Lebanese died. Faced with international condemnation, Israel halted this attack.

In the election campaign, *yeshiva* students and young members of Likud roamed the streets denouncing Peres.

Within the Labour opposition, however, Meretz evoked considerable anxiety by stressing its secular character. Among the religious parties Likud's nationalism exerted a strong attraction for the right. In the campaign the leader of Likud, Benjamin Netanyahu, declared that he would ensure that the Oslo Accords were upheld, even though he was intent on slowing down the process. On 29 May 1996, elections were held.

Labour had the largest number of seats in the Knesset, totalling 34 seats. However, in the vote for Prime Minister, Benjamin Netanyahu narrowly won the election. Together with parties opposed to the Oslo peace process, as well as the religious bloc, a new Russian immigrant party and the centrist Third Way Party, Netanyahu was able to form a coalition government. Following the election, further conflict took place between Israel and the Palestinians as well as within Israel. Despite his defeat, Peres pressed forward with his peace plans. However, Netanyahu delayed completing the arrangements for Israel's withdrawal from the occupied territories.

Unable to achieve the type of co-operation attained by Rabin and Peres with Palestinian authorities, Netanyahu further exacerbated relations with the Palestinians by opening the exit of an ancient tunnel that ran under the Old City next to the Temple Mount – before Labour's defeat, Peres had been negotiating with Muslim authorities to transform an area of the Mount into another mosque in return for the opening of the tunnel. In response, Palestinians engaged in acts of violence that resulted in the death of fifteen Israeli soldiers and around eighty Palestinians. To salvage the situation, President Clinton invited Netanyahu, Arafat and King Hussein to Washington. On 7 October, in a speech to the Knesset, Peres warned of the dangers of allowing the peace process to collapse. Eventually an agreement was reached on 17 January that eighty per cent of the city of Hebron should come under the Palestinian Authority. As part of this agreement, it was accepted that Israel would with-draw more troops from the West Bank.

During this period there was considerable discussion about Israel's presence in southern Lebanon. On 4 February 1997 two helicopters crashed in northern Israel on their way to southern Lebanon – an event that caused further anguish about troops stationed there. On 13 March seven girls were shot by a Jordanian soldier. On the day after this attack, the Cabinet agreed to initiate a building project on West Bank land that had been annexed to Jerusalem. This decision provoked both Palestinian and Jewish left-wing protests as well as the condemnation of the United Nations.

On 21 March a West Bank Arab killed three people in Tel Aviv. At the beginning of May the Palestinian Authority issued an order imposing the death penalty on any Arab who sold land to a Jew. Two months later Israel observed Memorial Day. To the dismay of the population, the ultra-Orthodox refused to stand in silence to pay respects to those who had died for the Jewish state. In June a group of Jews praying at the Wailing Wall were attacked by ultra-Orthodox Jews. A week later members of the ultra-Orthodox attacked a Jewish pub in Jerusalem.

Despite the agitation of various peace groups, there was no change in governmental policy regarding Lebanon. In the summer of 1997 liberal Israelis protested against efforts to reduce the Palestinian population in Jerusalem: in their view the Israeli quest to claim all of Jerusalem had taken on an anti-democratic and anti-humanistic character. During this period further Jewish settlement took place in the West Bank. In the same month the government dramatically altered the maps from the Oslo Accords under which the vast majority of the West Bank would be transferred to the Palestinians. Instead the government based its view on the map previously introduced by Clinton Bailey which envisaged three self-governing Palestinian enclaves, with an Israeli corridor in Samaria. According to Netanyahu, Israel would annex a large part of the territory captured from Jordan in 1967. The Palestinian area would lack statehood and possess no common borders with Jordan. Rather it would be between territories annexed by Israel and intersected by a series of highways controlled by the army.

In accord with the Oslo agreement, Israel had vacated six Palestinian cities as well as Hebron. Most of the West Bank continued to remain under Israeli control. The transfer of further territory was halted. Friction between Israel and the Palestinians was further exacerbated by a suicide bombing on 30 July in Jerusalem, which killed sixteen victims. Reacting to such terrorism, the government stopped the movement of Palestinian workers into Israeli territory and suspended all financial transfers to the Palestinian Authority. In September a bombing in Jerusalem killed five people; the next day twelve Israeli naval commandos were killed during an attack in Lebanon. During the same month Israel asked the British Prime Minister, Tony Blair, to discuss with President Yeltsin the sale of weapons technology from the former Soviet arsenal to Iran. Simultaneously Israel agitated for the Americans to end aid to Russia while the sale of missile technology from Russia to Iran was continuing.

Despite such a shift in foreign policy, a number of Israelis still agitated for the continuation of the peace process, and during the autumn Peres founded the Peres Centre for Peace. Such agitation ran counter to the government's determination to create Jewish homes on land purchased in 1990 near the Dome of the Rock. When three Jewish families moved into these dwellings, the American Secretary of State, Madeleine Albright, pressed for them to be moved. Agreeing to this demand, the Netanyahu government insisted that religious students should be allowed to use these houses for prayer. This was followed by an expansion of the Etzon bloc settlements despite criticism from the American government. At the end of September a Jordanian terrorist wounded two Israeli embassy guards in Amman during an assassination attempt against a Hamas political representative. In response to this failed action, Israel agreed to release the spiritual leader of Hamas, Sheikh Ahmed Yassin, from prison.

In October 1998 Prime Minister Netanyahu and Yasser Arafat met in Washington to discuss the peace process. After prolonged argument, Israel and the Palestinians agreed to embark on a new stage of co-operation. According to the Wye agreement, Israel would effect a further West Bank redeployment, involving 27.2 per cent of the occupied territory. Thirteen per cent of this area would pass from Israeli occupation to Palestinian civil control. The remaining 14.2 per cent, which was previously under joint Israel–Palestinian Authority control, would come under Palestinian rule. In addition, the Israelis and Palestinians would together establish a committee to consider the third-phase redeployment that was mandated by the 1995 interim agreement.

Arafat agreed that the Palestinian authorities would take all measures necessary to prevent acts of terrorism, crime and hostilities. This would include a Palestinian security plan, shared with the United States, to ensure systematic and effective combat of terrorist organizations and infrastructure. To ensure peace in the region, bilateral Israeli–Palestinian security co-ordination would be restored, and a US–Palestinian committee would be created to monitor militant groups. The Palestinians further agreed to apprehend, investigate and prosecute specific individuals suspected of violence. It was accepted that they would collect all illegally held weapons in areas they controlled, and issue a decree barring any form of incitement to violence or terror. To ensure the implementation of this policy, a US–Palestinian–Israeli committee would monitor any cases of incitement.

Conflict between Israel and its Arab neighbours has thus not been overcome through the settlement initiated by Rabin and Peres, and the peace process has been undermined by intransigent attitudes on both sides, despite the steps taken by the new Prime Minister of Israel, Ehud Barak, elected in the summer of 1999. The events that took place in September and October 2000 have undermined attempts to create peace in the Middle East. On 28 September Israel's hardline leader Ariel Sharon angered Palestinians by visiting a Jerusalem shrine sacred to Jews and Muslims. Dozens of police and several Palestinians were injured in the riots that followed. The following day six Palestinians were killed and close to two hundred were wounded in clashes at the shrine, known as the Temple Mount to Jews and the Noble Sanctuary to Muslims.

Subsequently, clashes erupted in the West Bank and the Gaza Strip. On 30 September fourteen Palestinians were killed by Israeli firing, including twelve-year-old Mohammed al-Durrah, whose death was captured by a television cameraman and broadcast throughout the world. On 2 October nineteen people were killed in a day of heavy fighting. Israeli Arabs protested in solidarity with Palestinians, and Israelis were barred from travelling in the Palestinian territories. On 4 October Ehud Barak and Yasser Arafat flew to France to meet the US secretary of state Madeleine Albright and French President Jacques Chirac. Despite this political activity, fighting between the two sides continued. On 6 October, Israel sealed the West Bank and Gaza Strip, and the next day demonstrators stormed Joseph's Tomb in Nablus. Fighting in Jerusalem, Nazareth and Hebron continued through the Jewish holy day of Yom Kippur on 9 October, and in the following weeks the violence continued amid a flurry of diplomatic activity. As hostility between Israelis and Palestinians intensified, Barak called for an election to take place later in the year resulting in the election of Ariel Sharon as Prime Minister. These terrible events have made it increasingly difficult to see how Jews and Palestinians can ever reach any accommodation of their conflicting claims to the Holy Land.

6

Before and after September 11

Renewed peace negotiations

As we have seen, negotiations for a final settlement resulted in a deadlock in July 2000. Palestinians insisted that refugees should have the right to return to their former homeland – this would have led to a Palestinian majority in the country. Israel insisted on annexing key portions of the Palestinian areas, leaving most settlements intact, and offered only a limited form of Palestinian statehood. On 28 September 2000 violence erupted when Ariel Sharon made a visit to the Temple mount in Jerusalem. Nonetheless, in January 2001 peace talks were held at Taba, an Egyptian resort town.

At this meeting Israeli and Palestinian representatives agreed that in accordance with the UN Security Council Resolution 242, the 4 June 1967 lines would form the basis for borders between Israel and the State of Palestine. For the first time both sides presented their own maps regarding the West Bank. The Israelis stated that they did not need to maintain settlements in the Jordan Valley for security purposes, and both sides accepted the principle of land exchange and sovereignty for their respective areas. Concerning the future of Jerusalem, both sides accepted in principle the suggestion that the Palestinians should have sovereignty over Arab neighbourhoods and Israel should have sovereignty over Jewish sections. The Israelis accepted that Jerusalem should become the capital of both states: Jerusalem the capital of Israel, and Al-Quds, the capital of the State of

Palestine. Further, both parties accepted the principle of respective control over each side's holy sites. The refugee problem was to be resolved in accordance with UN Security Council Resolution 242 and General Assembly Resolution 194. It was accepted that Israelis should have three early warning stations on Palestinian territory subject to certain conditions. Finally, the Israeli side maintained that the State of Palestine would be non-militarized; the Palestinian side was prepared to accept limitation on its acquisition of arms. This meeting was followed by an Israeli election in which the Prime Minister, Ehud Barak, was voted out of office and replaced by a right-wing government headed by Ariel Sharon. Following this victory, Ariel Sharon rejected Palestinian demands to resume peace talks where they had left off with the outgoing administration of Ehud Barak. On 8 February 2001 Ariel Sharon's diplomatic adviser, Zalman Shoval, stated that the Prime Minister had ruled out resuming negotiations with the Palestinians since no final peace deal was concluded at Taba. 'There was no accord concluded at Taba', he said. 'What was discussed does not commit the government that Mr Sharon will form . . . This government will only be held by signed accords.' Responding to these remarks, the Palestinian negotiator Saeb Erakat, echoing the views of the Palestinian leadership, declared that if Sharon sought to resume the peace process it must be from where it was suspended by Barak. Erakat warned the new Israeli leader not to implement his political programme, saying this would only complicate the situation.[1]

Determined to continue the peace process, the United States sought to persuade Palestinians and Israelis that a negotiated settlement was vital to security in the Middle East. In April 2001 the Mitchell report was published which made a series of wide-ranging recommendations. The report concluded that it was vital that the Government of Israel and the Palestinian Authority act swiftly and decisively to halt violence. The immediate objective of the report was to rebuild confidence and resume negotiations. The report explained that during the committee's mission, their aim had been to fulfil the mandate agreed at Sharm al-Shaykh. The report stated:

> We value the support given our work by the participants at the summit, and we commend the parties for their co-operation. Our principal recommendation is that they recommit themselves to the Sharm al-Shaykh spirit and that they implement the decisions made there in 1999 and 2000. We believe that the summit participants will support bold action by the parties to achieve these objectives.
>
> The restoration of trust is essential, and the parties should take affirmative steps to this end. Given the high level of hostility and mistrust, the timing and sequence of these steps are obviously crucial . . . We urge them to begin the process of decision immediately.
>
> Accordingly, we recommend that steps be taken to:
>
> End the violence
>
> - The GOI [Government of Israel] and PA [Palestinian Authority] should reaffirm their commitment to existing agreements and undertakings and should immediately implement an unconditional cessation of violence.
> - The GOI and PA should immediately resume security co-operation.
>
> Rebuild confidence
>
> - The PA and GOI should work together to establish a meaningful 'cooling-off period' and implement confidence-building measures, some of which were detailed in the October 2000 Sharm al-Shaykh Statement and some of which were offered by the US on January 7, 2001 in Cairo.

- The PA and GOI should resume their efforts to identify, condemn and discourage incitement in all its forms.
- The PA should make clear through concrete action to Palestinians and Israelis alike that terrorism is reprehensible and unacceptable, and that the PA will make a 100 per cent effort to prevent terrorist operations and to punish perpetrators. This effort should include immediate steps to apprehend and incarcerate terrorists operating within the PA's jurisdiction.
- The GOI should freeze all settlement activity, including the 'natural growth' of existing settlements.
- The GOI should ensure that the IDF adopt and enforce policies and procedures encouraging non-lethal responses to unarmed demonstrators, with a view to minimizing casualties and friction between the two communities.
- The PA should prevent gunmen from using Palestinian populated areas to fire upon Israeli populated areas and IDF [Israel Defence Forces] positions. This tactic places civilians on both sides at unnecessary risk.
- The GOI should lift closures, transfer to the PA all tax revenues owed, and permit Palestinians who had been employed in Israel to return to their jobs, and should ensure that security forces and settlers refrain from the destruction of homes and roads, as well as trees and other agricultural property in Palestinian areas. We acknowledge the GOI's position that actions of this nature have been taken for security reasons. Nevertheless, the economic effects will persist for years.
- The PA should renew co-operation with Israeli security agencies to ensure, to the maximum extent possible, that Palestinian workers employed within Israel are fully vetted and free of connections to organizations and individuals connected to terrorism.
- The PA and GOI should consider a joint undertaking to preserve and protect holy places sacred to the traditions of Jews, Muslims and Christians.

- The GOI and PA should jointly endorse and support the work of Palestinian and Israeli non-governmental organizations involved in cross-community initiatives linking the two peoples.[2]

The attack on the World Trade Center

Violence continued into 2001 and 2002 despite attempts by the Mitchell commission and others to restore peace. On September 11, 2001 al-Qaeda terrorists hijacked airliners and flew them into the World Trade Center in New York and the Pentagon outside Washington. A fourth hijacked plane, apparently heading for the White House, crashed into a field in Pennsylvania after passengers attacked the terrorists to prevent them from carrying out their mission. The death toll in the attacks numbered more than 3000. Among the dead were 19 hijackers, 15 of whom were from Saudi Arabia. An alleged further hijacker, Zacarias Moussaoui, was arrested in Minnesota after raising suspicions among his flight instructors where he said he wished to learn how to fly but not how to land or take off.

Previously the Arab terrorist and leader of al-Qaeda, Osama Bin Laden, had stated his intention to wage war against America and Israel. Following this attack, he issued statements implying that this event was related to US support for Israel. His goals, he stated, were based on a desire to depose the Saudi monarchy, which he viewed as unfaithful to his interpretation of Islam. His aim was to recreate an Islamic empire and establish a Palestinian state. Traumatized by this onslaught, the United States government was determined to hunt down the terrorists in a long, unrelenting war. President Bush warned that governments would now have to choose to support the United States in this war on terror, or be regarded as enemies. He cautioned that there would be serious consequences for those who opposed the American government's efforts.

Immediately the president warned the Taliban rulers in Afghanistan, where al-Qaeda was based, that they should hand over Bin Laden or face a massive assault. When the Taliban refused to comply, the United States waged a war in Afghanistan, which brought an end to Taliban rule and destroyed the al-Qaeda organization. Despite the American advance, Bin Laden escaped with a number of his aides, and the United States has continued to try to discover his whereabouts. In addition to a direct attack on al-Qaeda, the Bush administration mobilized other countries in support of a global war on terrorism. Assets of individual terrorists, as well as terrorist organizations, were frozen, and intelligence agencies of Western countries joined together in the quest to thwart further terrorist attacks. Inevitably, the United States and other Western countries have become more security conscious in the light of September 11. United in their determination to overcome the terrorist threat, these countries have increased security at airports, governmental facilities and public gatherings.

As a result of such increased security, many Americans and others began to view terrorist actions in Israel itself in a new light given that such organizations as Hamas and Hizbulla appeared to be linked with al-Qaeda. Especially damaging for the Palestinians were the demonstrations held in favour of Bin Laden following the attack on the World Trade Center. By contrast a number of figures such as the leader of the Nation of Islam, Louis Farrakhan, sought to defend the Palestinian reaction. Seeking to explain the reaction of Palestinians to this tragedy, he stated, 'Some Palestinians danced in the streets, not because they have no feeling for American life, they danced because they wanted America to feel what they feel, what they have lived with.' Yet, in the West, the overwhelming reaction was one of bewilderment and disgust.

A few days before the war against Bin Laden began, President Bush announced that the idea of a Palestinian state had been part of the US vision for the Middle East as long as the right of Israel to exist is respected. According to the *New York Times* and the *Washington Post*, this was the first time that a Republican US President had acknowledged the need for Palestinian statehood. Neither the Palestinians nor the Israelis reacted with enthusiasm to Bush's statement. Most Palestinians questioned his motives. Moussa Abul-Marzouq, a Hamas leader, for example, regarded Bush's statement as a manoeuvre aimed at deceiving the Palestinian National Authority and driving it to end the Intifada. 'It is', he declared, 'an American attempt to persuade Arabs and Muslims to join the international alliance against Bin Laden.'[3] A statement issued by the Democratic Front for the Liberation of Palestine regarded Bush's proposal as a step in the right direction, but noted that it would not be useful unless it was reinforced by effective, practical measures. The Popular Front for the Liberation of Palestine also described the statement as a manoeuvre.

From the Israeli side Ariel Sharon issued a diatribe accusing the Bush administration of opportunism. Calling on Western countries, in particular the United States, not to repeat the mistake that triggered the Second World War, he pledged that Israel would never be a second Czechoslovakia, and would accordingly have to rely on itself. He concluded by stating that Israel would resume its assassination campaign against Palestinian activists who support the Intifada, and abandon the policy of restraint which it had been committed to under the terms of the cease-fire agreement.

In response, Bush dismissed Sharon's reaction as unacceptable. Categorically rejecting his claim that the US was appeasing the Arabs at Israel's expense, he denounced the Israeli Prime Minister's attempt to compare him to Chamberlain and Daladier, the European leaders who sought to appease Hitler at the Munich summit by ceding Czechoslovakia's Sudentenland to Germany. Twenty-four hours later, just before the military attack on Afghanistan, Sharon changed his approach, downplaying his differences with the American administration. Instead, he extolled the strong relations between the US and Israel and reiterated his support for Washington's campaign against terrorism. By offering the Palestinians hope for their own state, Bush was acknowledging the centrality of the Palestinian problem in fuelling Islamic terrorism. As President Mubarak observed, fifty per cent of this wave of violence stems from the situation in Israel.

Continuing conflict

Following the attack on the twin towers of the World Trade Center and the offensive against Bin Laden, Arab and Islamic countries stressed the need for their co-operation in the war against terrorism in order to obtain concessions from Israel. However, many Americans began to lose sympathy for the Palestinian cause, identifying Hamas and Hizbulla with the al-Qaeda group of terrorists. Palestinians were criticized for their apparent support of Bin Laden, and evidence emerged linking a boatload of illegal arms, intercepted by Israel, with Iranian support for the PNA. This boat was intercepted on 3 January 2002, the day that US envoy Antony Zinni sought to reach a peace settlement. Against this background, the US and the EU appeared to give Israel wider latitude for actions against the Palestinians. Israel continued to make incursions into Palestinian areas, and confined PNA Chairman Arafat to his compound in Ramallah. In the wake of such actions, Palestinians increased attacks on soldiers as well as suicide bombings.

On 12 March 2002 the UN Security Council passed Resolution 1397, a US-drafted resolution, referring for the first time to a Palestinian state existing side by side with Israel. The 14–0 vote, with Syria abstaining, marked the first time the fifteen-nation council had approved a resolution on the Middle East since October 2000. The Resolution consisted of a number of recommendations:

The Security Council

- recalling all its previous relevant resolutions, in particular 242 and 338,
- affirming a vision of a region where two States, Israel and Palestine, live side by side within secure and recognized borders,
- expressing its grave concern at the continuation of the tragic and violent events that have taken place since September 2001 especially the recent attacks and the increased number of casualties,
- stressing the need for all concerned to ensure the safety of civilians,
- stressing also the need to respect the universally accepted norms of international humanitarian law . . .

1. Demands immediate cessation of all acts of violence, including all acts of terror, provocation, incitement and destruction;
2. Calls upon the Israeli and Palestinian sides and their leaders to co-operate in the implementation of the Tenet work plan and Mitchell Report recommendations with the aim of resuming negotiations on a political settlement;
3. Expresses support for the efforts of the Secretary-General and others to assist the parties to halt the violence and to resume the peace process.

Although Yasser Arafat declared a cessation of violence on numerous occasions, this did not seem to affect the frequency of suicide bombings and ambushes. For their part, the Israelis continued with the policy of assassinating Palestinians. During the last week in March, as General Zinni was on his way to the Middle East, the Palestinians launched a successful suicide attack nearly every day. During this period a bombing at the Park Hotel in Netanya killed 27 people as they were celebrating Passover. In retaliation, Israel launched a massive raid intended to root out the terror network, including reoccupation of Ramallah, Nablus, Jenin, Tulkarm and other towns. In this onslaught a significant number of Palestinians were killed, including civilians. In contrast with the Palestinian claim that hundreds were killed in this action, Israel alleges that only about fifty were killed in Jenin, mostly members of the Fatah Al-Aqsa Martyrs suicide brigades. Even though these figures seem to be borne out by independent sources, they are not accepted in the Arab world.

This Israeli onslaught, referred to as Operation Defensive Shield, commenced on 28 March 2002. Its goal was to dismantle the terrorist infrastructure developed by the Palestinian Authority, or allowed to operate in territory under PA control. The operation consisted of moving Israeli forces into the West Bank and Gaza for the purpose of arresting terrorists, finding and confiscating weapons and destroying facilities for the manufacture of explosives. On 8 April Prime Minister Ariel Sharon gave this summary of the operational goals:

> IDF soldiers and officers have been given clear orders: to enter cities and villages which have become havens for terrorists; to catch and arrest terrorists and, primarily, their dispatchers and those who finance and support them; to confiscate weapons intended to be used against Israeli citizens; to expose and destroy terrorist facilities and explosives, laboratories, weapons production factories and secret installations. The orders are clear: target and paralyze anyone who takes up weapons and

tries to oppose our troops, resists them or endanger them – and to avoid harming the civilian population.[4]

Defending this operation, Sharon blamed Yasser Arafat for the actions taken against Israel:

> There is one dispatcher: Palestinian Authority Chairman Yasser Arafat. He is the man who, in a series of agreements, promised to abandon the path of terrorism, refrain from committing murder, use his forces to prevent it – and betrayed all his promises. Because of his promises Israel agreed to the establishment of the Palestinian Authority. That is why Israel agreed to transfer security responsibility to the areas given to its control. Thus, Israel agreed to the establishment of Palestinian security forces. We hoped that the Palestinians would understand, as they promised, that ruling does not mean license to kill, but rather the assumption of responsibility for the prevention of killing. But what was merely apprehension at the beginning, and intensified into suspicion, has turned into solid facts which nobody can deny. In the territories under his rule, Arafat has established a regime of terror, which nationally and officially trains terrorists and incites, finances, arms and sends them to perpetuate murderous operations across Israel.[5]

Despite the arrival of US Secretary of State Colin Powell, the violence continued. Powell's mission failed: he was unable to persuade the Palestinians to agree to a cease-fire. Demonstrations and public outrage in Arab countries, fuelled by charges of a massacre, prompted UN action. UN Resolution 1402 directed that Israel withdraw from the territories immediately. By the time Powell left, Israel had withdrawn from some towns, but Yasser Arafat was still imprisoned in Ramallah, and the Israelis were besieging the church of the Nativity in Bethlehem, where armed Palestinians had sought refuge from the Israel Defence

Force. The UN Security Council adopted Resolution 1403, expressing its dismay that Resolution 1402 had not been implemented. Palestinians charged that the Israelis had committed a massacre in the Jenin refugee camp.

On 19 April the Security Council adopted Resolution 1405, calling for an impartial investigative team to be sent to determine the truth of these claims. Although Israel at first agreed to this investigation, it later blocked it, claiming that the composition and procedures of the investigation would not be impartial. Opposition to the investigation was intensified by Israeli memories of the recent Durban conference as well as by the infamous 'Zionism is Racism' resolution of the UN which was recalled repeatedly in public debate. In May 2002 Prime Minister Sharon visited the US under pressure from Washington. During this meeting discussions took place concerning a regional summit to be held later in 2002. Yet the Israelis claimed they could prove the involvement of Yasser Arafat and the PNA in terrorist activities. When it was reported that a suicide bombing had been committed by Hamas, the Israeli Prime Minister returned to Israel.

Final stages of aggression

The sieges of Muqata'a and the Church of Nativity were also resolved in May 2002. Militants in the Church of Nativity were exiled to Cyprus and Europe and the wanted men in the Muqata'a compound in Ramallah were imprisoned in Jericho. The head of the PFLP allegedly coordinated a suicide attack from his cell in Jericho, and by the end of May, Yasser Arafat signed into law the Basic Law or constitution of the Palestinian transitional state. This law guaranteed basic rights, but stated that Palestinian legislation will be based on the principles of Islamic Shari'a law. Beginning with a declaration that Palestine is part of the large Arab World, and that the Palestinian people are part of the Arab nation, this constitution stresses that Arab unity is an ideal which the Palestinians seek to achieve. The Constitution continues by emphasizing that the Palestinian people are the source of all power which shall be exercised through the legislative, executive and judicial authorities. Following this declaration, the basic law makes a wide range of assertions about the creation of a Palestinian state. Among these regulations are the following stipulations:

Article 3. Jerusalem is the capital of Palestine.

Article 4. Islam is the official religion of Palestine.

Article 5. The principles of Islamic Shari'a shall be the main source of legislation.

Article 6. The governing system in Palestine shall be a democratic parliamentary system.

Article 7. Palestinian citizenship shall be regulated by law.

There follows a series of principles governing public rights and freedoms including the following:

Article 9. All Palestinians are equal under the law.

Article 11. It is unlawful to arrest, search, imprison, restrict the freedom, or prevent the movement of any person.

Article 13. No person shall be subject to any duress or torture.

Article 14. The accused is innocent until proven guilty in a court of law.

Article 15. Punishment shall only be imposed on individuals.

Article 17. Homes shall be inviolable.

Article 18. Freedom of belief and the performance of religious rituals are guaranteed.

Article 19. Every person shall have the right to freedom of thought.

Article 21. The economic system in Palestine shall be based on the principle of free market economy.

Article 23. Proper housing is a right for every citizen.

Article 24. Every citizen has the right to education.

Article 26. Palestinians shall have the right to participate in the political life individually and in groups.

Article 28. No Palestinian may be deported from the homeland.

Article 30. Litigation is a protected and guaranteed right to all people.

Article 31. An independent commission for human rights shall be established by law.

Articles 34–49 stipulate rules governing the legislative authority; they are followed by articles 50–87, concerning the executive authority; articles 88–100 regulate the judicial authority. Articles 101–105 focus on rules of the state of emergency. And, finally, general and transitional provisions are covered in Articles 106–112.[6]

In June, following a wave of Palestinian suicide attacks, Israeli forces reoccupied the West Bank. Even though the Israeli government claimed that this reoccupation would not continue indefinitely, it later altered its plans. At this stage President Bush made a speech concerning the Middle East in which he outlined plans for a Palestinian state following democratic reform. It is untenable, he stated, for Israeli citizens to live in terror. Further, it is unreasonable for Palestinians to live in squalor and occupation. Hence, he said:

> I call on the Palestinian people to elect new leaders, leaders not compromised by terror. I call upon them to build a practicing democracy, based on tolerance and liberty. If the Palestinian people actively pursue these goals, America and the world will actively support their efforts. If the Palestinian people meet these goals, they will be able to reach agreement with Israel and Egypt and Jordan on security and other arrangements for independence.

And when the Palestinian people have new leaders, new institutions and new security arrangements with their neighbors, the
United States of America will support the creation of a Palestinian state whose borders and certain aspects of its sovereignty
will be provisional until resolved as part of a final settlement in
the Middle East.

Bush went on to challenge Israel to support the emergence of a
Palestinian state, to withdraw from the occupied territories, and
to stop building settlements:

Israel also has a large stake in the success of a democratic Palestine. Permanent occupation threatens Israel's identity and
democracy. A stable, peaceful Palestinian state is necessary to
achieve the security that Israel longs for. So I challenge Israel to
take concrete steps to support the emergence of a viable, credible Palestinian state.[7]

Even though President Bush was not explicit, it was understood
that the reference to a new Palestinian leadership was a call to
overthrow Yasser Arafat. Colin Powell made this explicit, but
the President did not identify himself with such a demand. In
Egypt President Mubarak also expressed support for Palestinian
reform, but Egyptian leaders refused to name alternative leaders. Although some moderate Palestinians and Israelis welcomed
the speech, Israeli Shimon Peres and others objected that it was
unrealistic to expect the Palestinians to give up Arafat's leadership. They argued that removing Arafat might bring about
further conflict or bring another, even more radical, leader to
power. Right-wing Zionist commentators claimed that the
speech rewarded terror by offering Palestinians the hope of
statehood. Pro-Palestinian analysts called the speech outrageous
and maintained that it called for indefinite continuation of the
occupation.

In August and September 2002, attempts were made to bring about Palestinian cease-fire initiatives but these were opposed by extremist groups. In addition, the killing of Saleh Shehadeh, head of the military wing of Hamas, curtailed negotiations. During this period there was a respite from major suicide attacks, facilitating an Israeli-Palestinian plan to return full Palestinian authority in Gaza and Bethlehem. However, such a scheme was disrupted when violent attacks occurred in Gaza. At the beginning of September, Israeli security forces prevented a number of suicide bombings and detected a truck laden with thirteen hundred pounds of explosives and gas tanks. In the same month, the PLC convened to approve the new cabinet chosen in line with reform. PLC cabinet members refused to ratify the cabinet until Yasser Arafat would allow a Prime Minister to share power. Instead, Arafat agreed to elections in January 2003, despite Israeli occupation.

This period of calm ended with suicide bombings in Umm El Fahm and on a Tel-Aviv bus. In retaliation the Israelis proceeded to attack Gaza, excluding entry into Gaza city and besieging Yasser Arafat and about two hundred others in the Muqata'a compound in Ramallah. Israel demanded that Palestinians give up wanted persons, including Palestinian preventive security boss Tawfiq Tirawi, who had taken refuge there. Arafat was defiant, and Israel destroyed all buildings in the compound except the main one. After a rumour was circulated that Israel was about to blow up the Muqata'a, demonstrations took place in the West Bank and Gaza. The USA then exerted pressure on Israel to stop destroying buildings and withdraw; despite a UN resolution, Israel continued the siege.

The next month the Labour party withdrew from the Israel unity government, and elections were held in January, when Ariel Sharon was re-elected Prime Minister. However, the Palestine–Israeli conflict was eclipsed by events in March 2003 when the United States and Britain attacked Iraq, overthrowing the regime of Saddam Hussein. Prior to this conflict President Bush reiterated his desire for a solution to the Palestinian problem in the Middle East, yet in the Arab world the onslaught against Iraq was widely perceived as a Crusade against Islam. In the view of a number of commentators, it appeared that a new world order had emerged at the beginning of the twenty-first century. As the sole super-power, the United States appeared to have embarked on a policy of world domination and colonization. Deeply suspicious of US intentions, Arab peoples are increasingly coming to see themselves as inevitable victims in this quest.

7

Renewed aggression

In the first part of the year 2003, the United States had expressed their refusal to negotiate with Yasser Arafat, and Mahmoud Abbas began to emerge as a more acceptable figure. As a remaining founding member of Fatah, he was regarded as a credible representative of the Palestinian cause and his candidacy was enhanced by the fact that other leading Palestinians such as Marwan Bargouti were not perceived as suitable. As a pragmatist, he was viewed favourably by the West as well as certain elements of the Palestinian legislature. Eventually pressure was put on Arafat to appoint him as Prime Minister – this took place on 19 March 2003. Initially Arafat sought to undermine the post of Prime Minister, but he was later forced to grant him a degree of power.

Abbas's term as Prime Minister was characterized by various conflicts between him and Arafat regarding the distribution of power. Abbas often indicated that he would resign if he were not allowed to have more control over the PA's administration. In September he confronted the PA parliament over this issue. In addition, Abbas came into conflict with Palestinian militant groups including Islamic Jihad and Hamas over his moderate policies. He pledged not to use force against the militants, an approach which resulted in a pledge from the two groups to honour a unilateral Palestinian cease-fire. Yet the continuing violence and Israeli assaults on known terrorists forced Abbas to initiate a crackdown in order to strengthen the PA's authority. This created a power struggle with Arafat over the control of the Palestinian security services.

In October 2003 Abbas resigned as Prime Minister, citing a lack of support from Israel and the United States as well as internal incitement against his government. Responding to terrorist attacks, Israel launched Operation Rainbow in the Gaza Strip in May 2004; several months later, Operation Days of Penitence was launched in September and October 2004. In November 2004 Yasser Arafat died, and Mahmoud Abbas was elected President in January 2005. During this period, Israel's unilateral disengagement plan, proposed by Israeli Prime Minister Ariel Sharon, was adopted by the government in August 2005 – the aim was to remove the permanent Israeli presence in the Gaza Strip as well as four settlements in the northern West Bank. Civilians were evacuated, and residential buildings demolished. By 12 September 2005 Israel had completed its disengagement and fully withdrew from the Gaza Strip. Ten days later the military disengagement from the northern West Bank was completed.

On 14 April 2006 Ehud Olmert was elected Prime Minister of Israel; previously he had been exercising the powers of the office since they were transferred to him after Ariel Sharon suffered a severe haemorrhagic stroke. A crucial allegation against the PA was that Arafat and Fatah had received billions of dollars in aid from foreign nations and organizations but had never used this money to develop Palestinian society. Instead, it was alleged that the funds were used personally by Arafat. These assertions became increasingly troubling and led to increased support for Hamas which was perceived as both more efficient and honest. Over the years Hamas had created various institutions and social services aimed at improving the life of Palestinians. In opposition to the PA, Hamas stated that it did not recognize Israel's right to exist, nor did it accept the Oslo process or any other peace process with Israel. It openly stated that it encouraged terrorist attacks.

In the January 2006 elections, Fatah and Hamas candidates competed for seats in the Palestinian Legislative Council. Due to widespread dissatisfaction with Fatah, Hamas won a majority of seats and was thereby able to appoint a Prime Minister as well as a number of cabinet posts. Ismail Haniyeh became Prime Minister. Alarmed by these developments, the West branded Hamas a terrorist organization and cut off aid to the Palestinian government in March 2006, insisting that it recognize Israel, renounce violence, and accept the peace process. Like the United States, a number of European countries cut off aid to Hamas and the Palestinian Authority. Israel refused to negotiate with Hamas since it never renounced its conviction that Israel had no right to exist and that the entire State of Israel is an illegal occupation. In June 2006 a war commenced between Israel and Hezbollah when Hezbollah fighters entered Israel and attacked an IDF post and captured several soldiers. In response Israel attacked Hezbollah positions within Lebanon. The result of this conflict was that both sides agreed to a cease-fire, and Lebanon stationed its army along the border with Israel.

During this period of instability, international sanctions against Hamas and the PA resulted in economic and political difficulties for the Palestinian people. On 8 October 2006 Mahmoud Abbas warned Hamas that he would call new legislative elections if it did not accept a coalition government. During November 2006 there were efforts by Mahmoud Abbas to form a unity government with Hamas, but this produced no tangible results. During the same month the PA and Israel declared that they would seek to uphold a cease-fire. On 27 November 2006 Ehud Olmert appealed to the Palestinians to re-enter peace negotiations with the aim of establishing an independent and viable Palestinian state with full sovereignty and defined borders. Since the January elections in which Hamas ousted Fatah, there has been repeated conflict between the two sides. In December 2006 violence between Fatah and Hamas increased, leading to a virtual civil war.

In December 2006 news reports indicated that a number of Palestinians were leaving the Gaza Strip. On 11 December 2006 gunmen killed three sons of Baha Balousheh, an important Palestinian security officer and Fatah loyalist. This event threatened to ignite a Palestinian civil war, and seriously jeopardized Ehud Olmert's efforts to restart the peace talks. Balousheh blamed Hamas for these murders even though the Islamic movement denied responsibility. As the violence increased, Palestinians moved further away from establishing a national unity government. On 19 December 2006 Israel and the US began to strengthen Fatah and explore possibilities of a diplomatic solution. Abbas and Olmert met on 23 December and Olmert promised to release 100 million dollars to the PNA for humanitarian needs. In addition, Israel removed a number of roadblocks and checkpoints in the West Bank. Jordan declared that it would attempt to mediate between Fatah and Hamas, although Egypt sent a shipment of weapons via Israel to forces loyal to Fatah in an effort to support Abbas's position.

In January 2007, fighting continued between Hamas and Fatah. The worst clashes took place in the northern Gaza Strip where Gen Muhammed Gharib, a senior Fatah commander, was killed. The United States announced that it would give 86 million dollars to Fatah, and Abbas and Haniyeh met to discuss ways to stop the fighting. Yet further acts of violence continued and Hamas dominated the West Bank. When Abbas declared that he would outlaw a Hamas security unit and Fatah released a videotape of an abducted Hamas official, Fatah held a rally to demonstrate popular support.

During the same month, the Palestinian Legislative Council was to have its first session, but this was cancelled since some legislators were scheduled to be in Indonesia. To discuss their differences, Abbas met with Khaled Mashaal, the exiled head of Hamas in Syria, but this did not lead to a resolution. By the end of the month, it appeared that a negotiated truce between Fatah and Hamas was beginning to hold. However, new fighting broke out after a few days. Fatah fighters stormed a Hamas-affiliated university in the Gaza Strip. Officers from Abbas's presidential guard engaged in battle with Hamas gunmen, guarding the Hamas-led Interior Ministry.

In February 2007, President Abbas and Prime Minister Haniyeh met in Saudi Arabia to discuss this conflict. It was agreed that Hamas would dissolve the existing government and form a unity coalition with Fatah. This appeared to have the support of both parties and Haniyeh resigned his post in order to form a new government. However, it was unclear whether this agreement would bring about the lifting of sanctions against Hamas and the PA. In fact sanctions continued, resulting in further suffering for the Palestinian population.

During this period, various diplomatic efforts were initiated to bring about a peaceful solution to the Middle East conflict. In early 2007 Amir Peretz and Efraim Sneh of Israel's Labour party announced their own multi-stage plan for a new peace process – this evoked considerable debate, but their plan lacked cred-ibility. In January 2007 US Secretary of State Condoleezza Rice announced on a visit to Egypt that the US would organize a summit between Israel and the Palestinians; in February 2007 a meeting was held in Israel which included Secretary Rice, Prime Minister Olmert, and President Abbas. In March 2007 Japan proposed a peace plan based on common economic development. In late April 2007 the armed wing of Hamas declared that the truce with Israel had ended; Palestinian groups then launched rockets from the Gaza Strip into Israel. On 25 April 2007 Ehud Olmert ruled out a major Gaza offensive, but author-ized the army to carry out limited operations in the Gaza Strip. This led to a new round of Hamas rocket attacks. Israel stated that it would not carry out a major offensive in order for a new truce to begin.

By May 2007 a deal between Hamas and Fatah appeared to be fading and new fighting broke out. Interior Minister Hani Qawasmi, who had been viewed as a moderate civil servant acceptable to both sides, resigned. Fighting continued in the Gaza Strip. In response to rocket fire from the Gaza Strip, Israel launched air strikes against various targets. Hamas spokesman Musa Abu Marzouk declared that Israel and the EU were responsible for the situation. In June 2007 full-scale fighting broke out between factions in several communities, and Hamas won control of the entire Gaza Strip, establishing a separate Gaza Strip government. In response, Israel, the US and other Western countries sought to strengthen Fatah and thereby isolate Hamas. Although Fatah was defeated in Gaza, it retains control of the West Bank.

In the ensuing months, steps were taken to resume the peace process. In November 2007 Israeli and Palestinian leaders agreed to restart peace talks at a Maryland summit, promising further negotiations towards a peace treaty and the development of a Palestinian state. In the same month President Bush pledged his support of Israeli–Palestinian peace efforts. Chief Palestinian negotiator Saeb Erekat stated that the goal was to reach a peace treaty that included a Palestinian state by the end of 2008. By early December 2007 the first Israeli–Palestinian peace talks in seven years got off to a shaky start. At the same time international donors promised to support the embattled Palestinian government of President Abbas, pledging billions of dollars in aid over three years. By the end of the month, a second round of negotiations had taken place between Palestinian and Israeli officials. Yet this event was overshadowed by Palestinian threats not to address substantive issues until Israel agreed to stop settlement construction around Jerusalem – it was revealed that Israel planned to expand two settlements in the occupied West Bank territory in the next year. Thus, as in the past, the treacherous road to peace was beset by hostility and mistrust.

At the Annapolis Conference in November 2007 the idea of a two-state solution was proposed as a means of settling the conflict between Israel and the Palestinians. Subsequently a fragile truce between Hamas and Israel held for over a year. On 19 December 2008 it expired, and Israel and Hamas were unable to agree on conditions for extending the truce. According to Hamas, Israel was responsible for not lifting the Gaza Strip blockade; in addition, Israel was blamed for a raid on a purported tunnel and for crossing the border into the Gaza Strip. Such an incursion was regarded as a breach of the truce. Israel accused Hamas of violating the truce by frequent rocket and mortar attacks on Israeli cities.

The Israeli bombardment of Gaza began with an intense assault on Hamas bases, police training camps, police headquarters and offices. In addition, mosques, houses, medical facilities and schools were also bombarded. Defending these actions, Israel claimed that many of these buildings were used by combatants and also functioned as storage spaces for weapons. In response Hamas intensified its rocket and mortar attacks, hitting such cities as Beersheba and Ashdod. On 3 January 2009 an Israeli ground invasion commenced which resulted in the deaths of more than 1300 Palestinians. Israel claimed that the majority of the dead were Hamas militants, whereas the Palestinian Centre for Human Rights reported that 926 of the 1417 killed had been civilians.

From 2009 the Obama administration continually pressured the Israel government of Prime Minister Netanyahu to freeze the growth of Israeli settlements in the West Bank and restart the peace process. During a speech by President Obama on 4 June 2009 in Cairo, he stressed that the United States does not accept the legitimacy of the Israeli settlements. Following this address, Prime Minister Netanyahu called a special government meeting, and on 14 June 2009 he gave a speech at Bar-Ilan University in which he endorsed the notion of a demilitarized Palestinian state. He argued that Israel would accept a Palestinian state if Jerusalem were to remain the united capital of Israel; the Palestinians would have no army, and would abandon their demand for the right of return. He also claimed the right to the natural growth of existing Israeli settlements in the West Bank, while leaving open the question of their permanent status. Such a proposal was immediately rejected by the Palestinian leadership.

On 25 November 2009 Israel imposed a ten-month construction freeze on all its settlements in the West Bank. According to Netanyahu, this was a painful step, but one that would encourage the peace process, and he urged the Palestinians to respond. The Palestinians, however, were unmoved and refused to enter into negotiations. Eventually on 2 September 2010 the United States launched direct negotiations between Israel and the Palestinian Authority in Washington. Soon afterwards, when the Israeli partial moratorium on settlement construction in the West Bank was about to end, the Palestinian leadership announced that they would leave the negotiations if the moratorium were not renewed. Israel stated that it would not renew this gesture of goodwill and urged the Palestinians to continue negotiations. Later, Israel offered to renew the moratorium in exchange for a Palestinian Authority recognition of Israel as the national homeland of the Jewish people. This request was rejected by the Palestinian leadership.

During September 2011 the Palestinian Authority led a diplomatic campaign aimed at obtaining recognition of the State of Palestine within the 1967 borders, with East Jerusalem as its capital. On 23 September President Mahmoud Abbas submitted a request to the Secretary General of the UN, Ban Ki-moon, to recognize the State of Palestine as the 194th UN member. In the streets of Ramallah, the seat of the Palestinian Authority, the national flag and banners were hung. Loudspeakers blared the Palestinian national anthem and there was dancing and celebration in the city's Yasser Arafat Square, where a large crowd had gathered to listen to the president's speech.

Palestine, he declared, is linked with the United Nations via the resolutions adopted by its various organs and agencies, and via the role of the United Nations Relief and Works Agency for Palestinian Refugees. Hence, the Palestinians seek a greater and more effective role for the United Nations in working to achieve a just and comprehensive peace that ensures the inalienable, legitimate rights of the Palestinian people as defined by the resolutions of international legitimacy of the United Nations.

Referring to the most recent negotiations with Israel, Abbas stated that the Palestinians did not cease in their efforts for initiatives and contacts. Over the past year, he said, the Palestinian negotiators did not leave a door to be knocked, a channel to be tested or a path to be taken. Nor did they ignore any formal or informal party of influence or stature to be addressed. They positively considered the various ideas and proposals and initiatives presented from many countries and parties. Yet the Israeli government dashed the hopes raised by the launch of negotiations. The core issue was that the Israeli government refused to commit to terms of reference for the negotiations that are based on international law and United Nations resolutions. Further, it frantically continues to intensify building settlements on the territory of the State of Palestine. Such actions embody the core of the policy of colonial military occupation of the land, and the brutality of aggression and racial discrimination against the Palestinian people. Such a policy is a breach of international law.

Israel's settlement campaign, he continued, is executed by means of the systematic confiscation of Palestinian lands and the construction of thousands of new settlement units in various areas of the West Bank, particularly in East Jerusalem, as well as the accelerated construction of the annexation Wall that is eating up large tracts of land and dividing it into separate islands and cantons – such a development destroys family life and communities, not to mention the livelihoods of tens of thousands of families. Israel also continues to refuse permits for the Palestinian people to build in occupied East Jerusalem at the same time as it steps up its campaign of demolition and confiscation of homes, actions which have displaced Palestinian owners and residents under a prolonged policy of ethnic cleansing. Further, Israel continues to undertake excavations that threaten holy places, and its military checkpoints prevent Palestinian citizens from getting access to their mosques and churches. It also continues to besiege the Holy City with a ring of settlements imposed to separate Jerusalem from the rest of the Palestinian cities.

Israel, he insisted, seeks to redraw the borders of the land according to what it wants and to impose a fait accompli on the ground that undermines the realistic potential for the existence of the State of Palestine. At the same time, Israel continues to impose its blockade on the Gaza Strip and to target Palestinian civilians by assassinations, air strikes and artillery shelling. Israel also continues its incursions in areas of the Palestine National Authority through raids, arrests and killings at the checkpoints. Such policies and actions destroy the chances of achieving a two-state solution, and also threaten to undermine the structure of the Palestinian National Authority.

In the light of this state of affairs, the president, on behalf of the Palestine Liberation Organization – the sole representative of the Palestinian people – stated the following:

1. The goal of the Palestinian people is the realization of their inalienable national rights in their independent State of Palestine, with East Jerusalem as its capital, on all of the land of the West Bank, including East Jerusalem and the Gaza Strip.
2. The PLO and the Palestinian people adhere to the renouncement of violence and rejection and condemning of terrorism in all its forms especially state terrorism, and adhere to all agreements signed between the Palestine Liberation Organization and Israel.
3. The Palestinian people adhere to the option of negotiating a lasting solution to the conflict in accordance with resolutions of national legitimacy, and the Palestine Liberation Organiza-

tion is ready to return immediately to the negotiating table
on the basis of the adopted terms of reference based on international legitimacy and a complete cessation of settlement
activities.

4. The Palestinian people will continue peaceful resistance to
Israeli occupation and its settlement policies and its construction of the annexation Wall.

5. The Palestinian people will rely on the political and diplomatic option and confirm that they do not seek to take unilateral steps.

On October 2011 a deal was reached between Israel and Hamas,
by which the kidnapped Israeli soldier Gilad Shalit would be
released in exchange for 1027 Palestinians and Arab–Israeli prisoners, 280 of whom had been sentenced to life in prison. On
14 November 2012 Israel began Operation Pillar of Defense in
the Gaza Strip – the aim was to halt rocket attacks and to disrupt
the capabilities of militant organizations. The offensive began
with the killing of Ahmed al-Jabari, chief of the Hamas military
wing. According to the IDF, more than 1500 military sites in
Gaza were targeted including rocket-launching pads, smuggling
tunnels, command centres and weapons manufacturing and storage buildings. Palestinian sources claimed that civilian houses
were hit, and Gaza health officials stated that by 23 November
167 Palestinians had been killed. Palestinian militant groups fired
over 1456 rockets and mortars into Rishon LeZion, Beersheba,
Ashdod, Ashkelon and other centres. Tel Aviv was hit for the
first time since the 1991 Gulf War, and rockets were aimed at
Jerusalem. By 19 November more than 252 Israelis had been
injured in attacks, and Israel's Iron Dome missile defence system
had intercepted more than 400 rockets. Another 142 rockets
fell on Gaza itself, 875 rockets fell in open areas, and 58 hit
urban areas in Israel. On 21 November 2012 a cease-fire was
announced after several days of negotiations.

In 2012 the Palestinian Authority applied for admission to the United Nations as a non-member state, which requires only a vote by the United Nations General Assembly. Hamas backed the motion. The draft resolution was passed on 19 November 2012 by a vote of 138 to 9, with 41 abstentions. Several weeks later, on 29 November, the United Nations General Assembly approved the upgrade of Palestine's status from an observer to an observer state, with 138 in favour, 9 against and 41 abstaining. On 4 January 2013 hundreds of thousands rallied in Gaza in a show of unity between Hamas and Fatah. In February a rocket was fired from the Gaza Strip into Israel, marking the first such attack since a cease-fire was signed in November 2012. This was followed a month later by a visit from Barack Obama, President of the United States, to Israel, the Palestinian territories and Jordan. In July as a goodwill gesture to restart peace talks with the Palestinian Authority, Israel agreed to release 104 Palestinian prisoners, most of whom had been in jail since before the Oslo Accords of 1993. The same month, direct negotiations took place between Israel and the Palestinians following an attempt by United States Secretary of State John Kerry to restart the peace process. These negotiations were scheduled to last nine months, to conclude the Palestine–Israel conflict by mid-2014.

On 29 July 2013 Israeli and Palestinian negotiators met in Washington to discuss renewing peace talks. On 13 August the Palestinian team leaders were Saeb Erekat and Muhammed Sheathe, and their Israeli counterparts were Tzipi Livni and Isaac Molt. The US mediators were Martin Indyk and Frank Lowenstein. On 19 August Mahmoud Abbas called for the US to step up its involvement in the talks. The next day Israel urged the United States to back Egypt's military government. On 22 August, Mahmoud Abbas claimed that no progress had been made in the first four talks. He also declared that the Palestinian right of return would most likely have to be waived in the event of any peace agreement. He also retreated from his earlier statement that he wanted a Palestinian state without a single Israeli. What he meant, he said, was no Israelis who were part of the occupation, but he would have no problem with Jews or Israelis coming into Palestine for business or tourism as long as they were not an occupying force. On 5 September Israel accused the Palestinians of leaking information about the talks, which were supposed to be kept secret. Several weeks later Israel and the Palestinians agreed to intensify peace talks with an increased United States role. On 26 September Mahmoud Abbas spoke in front of the UN Security Council, and welcomed the resumption of peace talks while at the same time criticizing Israel's settlement building. Hamas and Islamic Jihad called for a third intifada, and a spokesman for Hamas's armed wing said that the current peace talks were futile.

On 17 October Mahmoud Abbas reiterated his view that he would not accept any Israeli military presence on Palestinian territory. Several days later, Israel and the Palestinians discussed the issue of water. On 27 October Israel prepared to release another round of Palestinian prisoners to create a positive climate for the talks. The next day Netanyahu categorically rejected the Palestinian right of return and stated that Jerusalem must remain undivided. In November the Israeli negotiators stated that there would not be a state based on the 1967 borders and that the Separation Wall would be a boundary. On 12 November 2013 the Palestinian team left the negotiations, blaming the escalation of settlement building.

On 8 July 2014 an escalation of the Gaza–Israel conflict began when Israel launched Operation Protective Edge in the Gaza Strip. The aim of this campaign was to stop rocket attacks from the Gaza Strip and to destroy tunnels which penetrate from Gaza into Israel. After more than a thousand air strikes had taken place in Gaza, there were attempts to arrange a cease-fire. This conflict is the deadliest military operation to have taken place in Gaza since the Second Intifada. By mid-August 2014 nearly

2000 Gazans had been killed and more than 10,000 wounded. Preliminary reports by the United Nations Office for the Coordination of Humanitarian Affairs (OCHA) estimated that 72 per cent of those who died were civilians, of whom 35 per cent were women or children.

A number of legal issues concerning the conflict arose during the course of the fighting. Various human rights groups argued that both Palestinian rocket attacks and Israel's targeted destruction of homes of Hamas and other militia members violate international human law and international humanitarian laws, and potentially constitute war crimes. Navi Pillay, the United Nations High Commissioner for Human Rights, accused Hamas militants of violating international humanitarian law by locating rockets within schools and hospitals, and launching rockets from densely populated areas. She also criticised Israel's military operation, characterizing the onslaught against Hamas as disproportionate. This latest stage of the Israeli–Palestinian conflict highlights the pressing need for a peaceful solution to this ongoing struggle.

A Palestinian perspective

Dawoud El-Alami

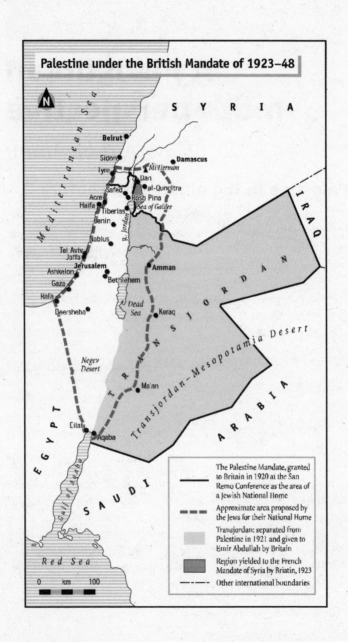

Palestine under the British Mandate of 1923–48

N

SYRIA

Mediterranean Sea

Beirut
Sidon
Tyre
Damascus
Mt Hermon
Dan
al-Quneitra
Safed
Acre
Rosh Pina
Haifa
Tiberias
Sea of Galilee
Jenin
R. Jordan
Nablus
Tel Aviv
Jaffa
Jerusalem
Amman
Ashkelon
Bethlehem
Gaza
Rafa
Dead Sea
Keraq
Beersheba

IRAQ

T R A N S J O R D A N

Transjordan–Mesopotamia Desert

Negev Desert

Ma'an

ARABIA

EGYPT

Eilat
Aqaba

Gulf of Aqaba

SAUDI

Red Sea

0   km   100

	The Palestine Mandate, granted to Britain in 1920 at the San Remo Conference as the area of a Jewish National Home
	Approximate area proposed by the Jews for their National Home
	Transjordan: separated from Palestine in 1921 and given to Emir Abdullah by Britain
	Region yielded to the French Mandate of Syria by Briatin, 1923
	Other international boundaries

8
The origins of modern Palestine

Palestine in the nineteenth century

The modern history of Palestine begins really in the nineteenth century in the dying years of the Ottoman Empire. Palestine, as part of Greater Syria, was under the Ottoman Caliphate for some four hundred years. The Ottomans ran Syria and Palestine as administrative territories, using mainly local people to staff their vast bureaucracy, but did not seek to colonize the land as such, or to settle or assimilate. The main focus of interest for the Ottomans was Jerusalem, but the rest of the country, being for a large part inhospitable, had never been developed and as the Empire fell into economic decline Palestine increasingly became neglected. There was little in the way of infrastructure. In her *Domestic Life in Palestine* (1862) Mary Eliza Rogers records that there were no wheeled carriages in Palestine, 'not so much as a wheelbarrow', and that the condition of the roads was dire.[1]

In the countryside a feudal system was in place which had remained unchanged for generations. Most agricultural land was owned by large-scale landowners and was farmed by poor tenant farmers, or labourers. There was good agriculture along the more fertile coastal plain. In cities such as Jerusalem lived the classes of civil servants who ran the Ottoman bureaucracy, merchants and tradesmen, and here the wealthy landowners began to maintain town houses in addition to the villas on their estates. In the desert areas the Bedouin grazed their animals where possible and conducted whatever trade they could.

Palestine was not, therefore, an empty land. Its inhabitants lived in cities and towns and hundreds of villages. During the late nineteenth century little attention was focused on the presence of Jews in the country. Small Jewish communities existed in Palestine. Some of these were based in the principal cities of religious significance, including Jerusalem, Hebron and Safed. These communities were of long standing and lived peacefully alongside their Arab neighbours. In addition during the nineteenth century there was some small-scale colonization: small Jewish communities had created agricultural colonies in the rural areas of Palestine.

Ottoman administration

The principal administrative divisions of the Ottoman territories were the *Vilayet* or province, and the *Sanjak* (plural *Sanajek*) or district. By 1888 Palestine was divided into three main *Sanajek*. The *Sanjak* of Jerusalem, comprising the southern half of the country was, because of its importance, governed directly by Constantinople. The other two *Sanajek*, Nablus and Akka, were part of the *Vilayet* of Beirut. Jordan constituted a part of the *Vilayet* of Syria, with Damascus as its capital.[2] At this time the population of Palestine in these three districts was approximately six hundred thousand, of whom some ten per cent were Christians, four per cent Jews, and the majority Sunni Muslims. Relations between the different communities were generally peaceful, each following its own way of life.

Ottoman legislation was based on the Shari'a, the Islamic law. In accordance with this, non-Muslim communities were entitled to be governed by their own religious laws where relevant. For Muslims, religious tribunals were constituted under the authority of the Shaykh al-Islam. Matters falling under Islamic religious law were those of personal status, including marriage, divorce and succession. In such matters other religions were allowed to exercise jurisdiction over their own members in accordance with their own traditions. The religious laws of Christians and Jews were therefore recognized and generally had jurisdiction in all religious matters, including the organization and discipline of the clergy, public instruction, poor law and matters of personal status including marriage, dowry, alimony and divorce. The tribunals of certain communities were also allowed to look into matters of inheritance, either by virtue of a specific grant of right by the Sultan or in default of an express act.

Judgements rendered by the religious tribunals within the limits of their jurisdiction were executed by the Ottoman authorities. Other cases of personal status that did not fall under the jurisdiction of the religious tribunals were dealt with by the civil courts, which took into account the certificate issued by the religious authorities of the parties. Cases other than religious matters, such as commercial and criminal cases between Muslims and non-Muslims, or between non-Muslims of different communities, were referred to mixed tribunals. Originally these were composed of a Muslim judge assisted by Muslim and non-Muslim assessors. After 1879 non-Muslims were also admitted as judges. The conditions for giving legal effect to change of religious community were clearly specified, thus emphasizing the importance of religion with regard to the legal status of an individual. A foreigner wishing to become a Muslim would have to do so before the local tribunal in the presence of a representative of his consulate. Before this a foreigner embracing Islam would automatically have become an Ottoman citizen. This now became subject to a nationality law, although in practice a convert would almost automatically acquire Ottoman nationality.

Civil law was essentially of a non-religious character. Its rules were almost entirely drawn from French civil law and were, in so far as they did not conflict with Islamic principles, incorporated in the Ottoman legislation. French models were largely followed in the drafting of the penal code, the codes of civil and criminal procedure, and commercial and maritime law. In civil matters, though family and personal law were left out of the process of codification and continued to be dealt with by the religious courts, the codification of the traditional Shariʻa law in the remaining areas was accomplished according to the scheme and disposition of the French codes. The Civil Code or Majallat al-Ahkam al-Adliyya comprised disposition as to contracts, tort, movable and immovable property, and evidence.

Capitulatory law comprised the body of laws applicable to foreigners in the Ottoman domains, in accordance with the capitulations between the High Court and the respective European powers, not only in matters of religion and personal status but also relating to any commercial or criminal case that could not be tried before the ordinary tribunals but which reverted to the jurisdiction of the consular courts of the state of the party concerned. Where matters arose between foreigners of different religions, or between foreigners and Ottoman citizens, mixed tribunals composed of Ottoman and foreign judges sitting together assumed jurisdiction.

The consular courts applied the laws of their respective states and were in some ways under the control of their metropolitan judicial authorities. The mixed tribunals applied the code and followed a procedure established in agreement with the foreign powers. The privileges of foreigners were not limited to their right to be tried by consular and mixed courts, since even when the jurisdiction of the Ottoman tribunals was admitted, foreigners had the right to be assisted by a representative of their consulate.[3]

Foreign influence and the collapse of the Ottoman Empire

Many general factors were involved in the demise of the Empire as a whole, but two specific elements affected Palestine catalysing a decline in Ottoman authority. The first of these was Napoleon's campaign in Egypt and Palestine, which secured the entry of Europe as a political power into the Middle East and marked the beginning of a long struggle between Britain and France to control the region. Napoleon managed to take Gaza and Jaffa, but was defeated by the British in Egypt.

Napoleon issued a proclamation promising to restore the Jews to Jerusalem and to rebuild the Temple if they helped him to conquer Palestine. This was ignored by the Jews, whose allegiance was to the Ottomans, at that time allies of Great Britain. The proclamation was in itself merely a ploy, comparable to Napoleon's strategy in Egypt when he declared to the Egyptian people that he was at heart a Muslim and had been sent to help the Egyptian people throw off the tyranny of the Mamluks.[4]

The second element was the conflict between Muhammad Ali[5] and the Ottomans. Muhammad Ali succeeded in gaining all of Syria including Palestine in 1833, but the British helped to regain Palestine for the Sultan in 1840. During the short-lived Egyptian occupation of Syria and Palestine, irrevocable damage was caused to Palestine by the opening of the door to European interest in the area. Some historians have referred to this as the 'unarmed crusade', bringing with it every variety of European clergy. Before long (and to the present day) every imaginable denomination had a presence in Jerusalem. Even the Americans, who at that time had no political interest, established missionary educational works. The Greek Orthodox Church, aided by Russia, became active, and the Czar acquired important properties in Jerusalem. The British strengthened their influence in 1838 by establishing a consulate in Jerusalem.

As foreign influence increased during the late nineteenth and early twentieth centuries, economic and social developments left their mark on the infrastructure and the population of Palestine. Palestine, along with the rest of the Syrian region, began to enter the international economic system, both as a supplier of products such as wheat, cotton, olives (olive oil), citrus fruit, etc. and as a market for Western manufactured goods. Foreign investment grew and the cities of Palestine started to grow and develop. A new class of businessmen, traders and middlemen flourished and began to form a significant part of the prosperous middle classes. The elite, the wealthy landowning classes, moved almost permanently to the cities, particularly Jerusalem, visiting their estates only to inspect and to collect revenues. Many landowners lived even further afield, particularly in Lebanon and Syria, having purchased land under new legislation that allowed absentee landownership.[6]

Early Jewish immigration

Throughout the nineteenth century there was small-scale Jewish immigration into Palestine. The Ottomans did nothing at this point to prevent immigration; in fact indirectly they contributed to it by issuing laws that encouraged investment. A law of 1867 gave foreigners the right to own lands in the Ottoman Empire. This had the result of facilitating Zionist acquisition of land in Palestine. The first serious reaction to Jewish immigration occurred as this became more regular and systematic in the last quarter of the nineteenth century. The first civil unrest between Palestinian peasants and Jewish settlers occurred in June 1891.

Representatives of some of the prominent families in Jerusalem sent a letter to Constantinople at this time expressing their concern about the numbers of Jewish immigrants into Palestine and asking the Sultan to control immigration and land purchase. The Christian communities were among the first to become aware of the dangers of growing immigration.[7] The Catholic clergy expressed objection to Zionist activity. Father Henry Lammens wrote an article in *al-Mashriq* in 1899 entitled 'The Jews in Palestine and Their Settlements' in which he mentioned what was being said in the Ottoman press about Jewish colonization in Palestine and asked the Ottoman regime to prevent or restrict this.[8]

At the same time Herzl was trying to persuade the Sultan Abd al-Hamid to treat the aims of the Zionist movement favourably. Abd al-Hamid was the last Ottoman Caliph-Sultan, official head not only of the Ottoman Empire but also of the Muslim Umma. The Ottoman Empire was in economic crisis, the culmination of a long decline compounded by corruption and foreign opportunism. The Empire had a vast national debt. Herzl sought to exploit this weakness by offering to raise financial support to pay the Ottoman debt and thereby release the Empire from foreign domination. In return he asked the Sultan to allow immigration into Palestine, or at least part of Palestine. At one point he asked for the area from Haifa and Akka to the Transjordan and the Dead Sea to be the receptacle of Jewish immigration.

The Sultan refused this but did not cut off the negotiation. There was some indication that a Jewish state under Ottoman authority might be accepted if finance was forthcoming. On his first visit to the Sultan in 1896 Herzl offered 20 million lire for Palestine, to which the Sultan gave his famous response: 'please advise him never to mention this ever. I can not sell one inch of this country – it does not belong to me. It belongs to my people. My people acquired this Ottoman Empire by their blood, and later they fed it with their blood, and we will give our blood before we allow anyone to take it from us. Our men were killed one after the other in Belfana because they all refused to surrender, preferring to die on the battlefield. The Turkish Empire does not belong to me, it belongs to the Turkish people, and I cannot ever give anyone any part of the empire. Let the Jewish people keep their billions. If the Turkish Empire is divided, maybe the Jews will take Palestine for free, but I will never divide it except over my dead body, and I will never accept to carve it up for any reason.'

This answer did not deter Herzl, who asked Kaiser Wilhelm to be a mediator between the Sultan and himself, aware that there was a strong relationship between the Kaiser and the Sultan, particularly with the building of the Berlin–Baghdad railway. The Kaiser did not refuse this. The Zionists had made three main promises to the Germans: 1) to spread German culture; 2) to co-operate with the Germans against the British east of Suez; and 3) to trade only with Germany. The Kaiser related to the Sultan that Herzl wanted to meet him but the Sultan refused his mediation. Herzl persisted in trying to involve the Kaiser, but eventually the Kaiser's advisers persuaded him not to pursue the subject with the Sultan, since it posed a risk to the good relationship between Germany and the Ottomans. Herzl's memoirs mention speeches that he delivered before the Kaiser in Jerusalem in which Herzl states that the Zionists intended to form a company to purchase land in Syria and Palestine, and that they wished this company to be under the protection of the Kaiser. The Kaiser answered briefly that he supported the idea. He spoke about the need for clean water and medical facilities in Palestine, and the meeting ended without any firm encouragement having been held out to the Zionists.[9]

Herzl's efforts even included attempts to communicate with some prominent Palestinians, including a former member of the Ottoman Parliament, Yusuf Dia al-Din al-Khalidi, who was teaching oriental languages at the University of Vienna. Herzl corresponded with Khalidi and put it to him that there was no Zionist agenda to colonize Palestine but only to develop the Holy Land and to live there alongside the Palestinian Arabs. He indicated that if this were rejected, Palestine would lose the benefit of Jewish wealth, which would be turned to some other part of the world.[10] The negotiation between Herzl and the Sultan consisted of five meetings, all of which ended in failure except the last, at which there was an offer to the Jewish people to settle in the Ottoman Empire generally, but not at the cost of detriment to any other people of the Empire. They would receive Ottoman citizenship and would have the rights and duties of any other citizen. In 1900, however, the Sultan issued a proclamation prohibiting the permanent settlement of Jews in the Holy Land.

The decline of the Ottoman Empire

The nineteenth century saw shifting alliances and interests. For a large part of the century Britain had pursued a policy first put forward by William Pitt[11] at the end of the eighteenth century – that the Ottoman Empire should be preserved and supported because if it disintegrated parts of it might fall into Russian hands.

This was the reason for the British and French defence of Turkey against Russia in the Crimean War (1855), and for British policy at the Congress of Berlin in 1878, where with the aid of Bismarck the Czar was persuaded to grant better terms to Turkey than in previous treaties. At the same time, however, the Sultan was persuaded to allow Britain to occupy Cyprus in return for an undertaking by Britain to defend Asia Minor against further Russian aggression.

In the late nineteenth and early twentieth centuries the Western powers established certain great enterprises in the Middle East, e.g. the Baghdad Railway, Suez Canal, the oil industry in Iran. Although beneficial, these began to be regarded with suspicion by local people and governments as instruments of foreign economic and political influence. Towards the end of the nineteenth century Germany began to court the Sultan. The Ottoman Empire had lost the Crimea and parts of the Caucasus to Russia, Cyprus and Egypt to Britain, Algeria and Tunisia to France, and Bosnia and Herzegovina to Austria. Only Germany had taken no Ottoman territory. Germany took over the training of the Ottoman army and started the construction of the railway eastwards from Constantinople – the Baghdad Railway. When the German railway company secured an extension of its concession into the Persian Gulf, the British government became conscious of the threat to its interests in the Gulf. This induced Britain to join Russia, which was weakened by war with Japan and internal revolution, in the 1907 agreement about Iran and to ally itself with Russia in the First World War.

Britain and France had been colonial rivals for years. Russia's colonial activity was ultimately curtailed by the Bolshevik revolution. By the beginning of the twentieth century the competition was focused on the Middle East. For Britain a major concern was to secure the routes to its colonies in India, and the Middle East was vital to this. The British had long held footholds in the Arabian Peninsula and the Gulf. In the nineteenth century they occupied Aden and many of the small principalities in the Gulf (now the United Arab Emirates), Kuwait, Bahrain and some strongholds on the Persian side of the Gulf. By the end of the nineteenth century the new threat in Arabia and the Gulf was Germany. Britain and France now felt that it was in their common interest to resist Germany. The British made it clear that their interests in the Gulf were so vital that if these were threatened it would be deemed to be an act of war against the British Empire.

These fears led Britain to make a number of treaties with the key powers in the Arabian Peninsula, the first being in 1865 with the Shuyukh of the Al Saud, rulers of the Najd in the heart of the peninsula. The treaties generally required that the signatories should recognize and respect all other territories in the area that were under British protection, meaning that the Al Saud should not attempt to invade or attack these territories, nor should they sell to, invite or deal with any foreign power that might endanger good relations between the British government and the Al Saud. At the same time the British government offered military protection and financial aid to Al Saud. Syria was also important to Britain, both because of the religious significance of the Holy Land, which was part of Syria at the time, and as part of Britain's preservation of the route to India.

In addition to the economic problems of the Ottoman Empire already referred to, there were breakaway movements all over the Empire seeking liberation. Many political parties were formed in Constantinople and the Arab capitals. This led the Ottomans to make promises on many sides which they were unable to keep. Different trends of opinion among the Arabs were in favour of either fighting for their independence from Ottoman oppression, or supporting the Caliphate as a unified resistance to foreign influence and interference, and pressing for full participation therein. At this point, however, all of this was overtaken by the Young Turks movement, whose aim was to depose Sultan Abd al-Hamid and his dictatorship. The Young Turks rejected the concept of a religious empire with a spiritual leader as the head of state and looked to the ideals of the French Revolution and democratic government as their model. They quickly realized, however, that if true democracy were established they would be outnumbered and outvoted by the non-Turkish elements of the Empire, and specifically the Arabs, the largest remaining group under Turkish rule.

Even in Turkey itself the Turks were dependent on people of other races (Greeks, Bulgarians and Arabs) to run government offices. The modern concept of self-determination for subject races had permeated the Empire, the Greeks, Serbs, Bulgars and Persians had already broken away and a nationalist spirit was growing in the Arab world. The Turkish reaction to this was the adoption of a strong nationalist stance, the formation of a Turkish brotherhood, and a policy of 'Turkification'. The idea was that Turkey should rule over a subject empire, rather than being the central state of a religious empire dominated by the Qur'an and the Arabic language. The Arabic script in which Turkish had been written was replaced with Latin script, and the Qur'an was translated into Turkish. Sherif Hussein and his family were sent back to Makka.

When the Armenians rebelled, the Turks crushed them, killing large numbers, but the Arabs were a more daunting prospect, being more numerous. The Turks began to suppress any movement in the Arab world towards independence, or even equal partnership. Arab members of the Turkish parliament were scattered, Arab political society was suppressed and public use of the Arabic language was forbidden except for purely religious purposes.

All over the Empire any talk of Arab self-government was put down and as a result secret societies began to form of a more violently revolutionary kind. One of these, the Syrian Society, was numerous and well organized and kept its secrecy so well that although the Turks had suspicions they could find no clear evidence of its activities, leadership or membership. Another society was composed almost entirely of Arab officers serving in the Turkish armies, who were sworn to turn against the Turks as soon as the chance arose. This society was founded in Iraq and was so fanatically pro-Arab that its leadership refused to deal with the British, French and Russians who might otherwise have been their allies, in the belief that if they accepted any European help they would not be allowed to keep any freedom they might win.

The Syrian Society, however, was less rigid in its outlook. Some Syrian revolutionaries were found to have been appealing to the French for help in their campaign for freedom and this provided an excuse for the Turks to put them down without mercy. Arab Muslims and Christians were crowded into the same prisons and many were executed. By the end of 1915 the whole of Syria was united against Turkish oppression. The Turks made an alliance with Germany against Britain and France. They were now convinced, however, that in order to win the war they should use the religious element that the Young Turks had ignored as the key to uniting all the subjects of the crumbling Ottoman Empire.[12]

The First World War and the Arab revolt

Up until the outbreak of the First World War British government policy had aimed to control what parts it could of the collapsing Ottoman Empire. There had been an attempt by Sherif Hussein of Makka, who was a descendant of the Prophet and a religious figurehead with responsibility for the shrines at Makka and Madina, through his sons Abdullah and Faisal, to approach the British High Commissioner in Egypt for military and political support, or at least to find out what the British position would be if the Arabs started to rebel against Turkish rule in the Arabian Peninsula. The British did not give a satisfactory response and indicated reluctance to become involved. The issue remained dormant for some time but matters came to a head when Turkey declared its support for Germany against Britain and France. This prompted Britain to support the Arabs and any group working against Turkey. Several separate sets of secret negotiations were conducted by the British during this period, including negotiations between Sherif Hussein and McMahon, the British High Commissioner in Egypt, conducted by correspondence.

One of the major obstacles to the British in fighting the Turks was that historically the Ottoman Sultan was the Khalifa or Caliph, Defender of the Faith, the overall spiritual head of the Islamic faith. To the masses in the Empire the Caliph represented Islam and an attack on him by an external force was an attack on the faith, even if they were suffering from Ottoman oppression. It was fortunate for the British that they found Sherif Hussein ready to stand against the Ottomans. The advantage held by the Sherif of Makka over the Caliph was that he was a descendant of the Prophet rather than an Ottoman Turk.

The Sherif was at first hesitant, fearing that the balance might swing towards the Turkish side and he might be left to face the consequences. As an initial step he ceased mentioning the name of the Caliph in the Friday prayer. News from the battlefields was encouraging, however, when reports were received that the British were preparing an attack at Gallipoli. It was thought that this would be the decisive battle and that the Allies would enter Constantinople. This gave the Arab forces motivation to become involved in the war. Gallipoli ended in Allied defeat, however, and there was fear that the Turks were approaching Egypt, but they were defeated and stopped. At this point the Arabs started to negotiate with the Allies, represented by McMahon. They needed to know what the outcome would be if they stood with the Allies against the Ottomans. The Sherif Hussein wanted an Arab Kingdom that would unify Syria, Iraq and the Arabian Peninsula. The negotiation was protracted especially with regard to the precise status of Palestine.

At a later point, Faisal insisted that Palestine, which had never been a separate or independent state, should be included in Greater Syria. The British insisted that it should not and would have a special status. The Arab forces managed to push back the Turkish armies from the Arabian Peninsula into what is now Jordan. The decisive battle was at al-Aqaba, where the Turks were driven out of Palestine by Arab forces led out of the Hejaz by T.E. Lawrence. Meanwhile British troops under

General Allenby occupied Jerusalem, and Syria and Palestine were then free of the Turks.

Secret agreements and broken promises

Freed from Turkish oppression, the Arabs believed they were on the point of self-determination, and questions of the agreement between the British and the Arabs began to come to the fore. The Arabs had come so far, however, only to be disappointed and disillusioned. The secret Sykes–Picot agreement, between the French and British, regarding control of the area, shared out the whole region between the victors, France and Britain. The French had strong interests in Palestine dating back to an Ottoman treaty that gave France responsibility for all pilgrims in Palestine, and they therefore felt that they had a historical connection with Palestine. The British insisted that Palestine was excluded from the negotiations and that it would have a special position. Britain had also promised that Syria would be part of the Arab Kingdom. Arab nationalism had been simmering for some time in Syria and Lebanon. We should be careful to note, however, that this was a political movement, not specifically religious, and not Islamic. In fact some of the main players were Christians.

Faisal entered Syria with his armies and declared himself King. The French mobilized against him and demanded that he withdraw his Bedouin forces from Damascus. The British intervened to avoid bloodshed and took Faisal to Iraq, which was to be under the British Mandate, and he was later installed there as King. The French in Syria held part of the interior and some of the ports such as Sidon and Beirut, the mountains of Lebanon and Damascus. Thus, Syria, having freed itself from the Ottomans, found itself again under foreign domination.

The French insisted that their aim was to improve the situation in Syria.

Until this point there had been conferences to discuss the status of Palestine. The principal aims of the Versailles Conference were the dismemberment of what was left of the Ottoman and Austro-Hungarian Empires and measures against Germany. The Arabs sent delegations to Versailles to speak for their causes and aspirations, but they were ignored.[13]

The Balfour Declaration

The greatest shock to the Arabs was the Balfour Declaration, which was issued before the end of the war. This was the outcome of negotiations between the Zionists and the British government and stated that the British government was committed to assisting the Jews in acquiring a homeland and that this homeland would be in Palestine.

On what basis did the British believe that they were entitled to promise to the Zionists a land that belonged to others? This question lies at the core of the Palestinian position. The British, uncertain of the outcome of the war, had made conflicting undertakings in an attempt to keep all potentially friendly elements on the side of the Allies. It has been argued that the Declaration had a proviso that the interests of the indigenous population should not be prejudiced. This, however, does not lessen the fundamental injustice of such an undertaking. At the beginning of a century in which native populations were beginning to throw off the oppression of foreign colonial influence, the most calculated scheme for the artificial settlement of an incoming population was being hatched.

There are legal arguments that insist that the Balfour Declaration was of no legal substance so long as it was not integrated into legislation. The fact was, however, that as the spoils of the First World War were distributed among the victors, Palestine fell to the British and came under their 'protection'. The Declaration was incorporated into the Mandate and was given substance in a White Paper (known as the Churchill Memorandum). The Mandatory power established a commission that was to determine the way Palestine would be run. The task of this commission was to facilitate Jewish immigration, while ensuring that this would not be to the detriment of the local population.[14]

9
Palestinians, Jews and the British

By the end of the First World War the Arabs in general and the Palestinians specifically were shocked by the realization that there was to be no independence or Arab Kingdom. On the contrary the whole area was to be divided between the Great Powers, the victors. The greatest blow to the Arab world was the removal of Palestine from the international negotiations because of its special nature. The much-quoted Balfour Declaration was not as significant at the time it was issued as it was later to become, since the British government was giving promises to any power that might offer help in winning the war, and, in fact, did not have sovereignty over the area to allow it to give it away. What made the Balfour Declaration an important element in the creation of the State of Israel was its subsequent incorporation in the British Mandate. The great irony is that in the 'new order', the mandatory powers were supposed to be trustees with regard to the countries for which they took responsibility. They were not to be occupying powers. As far as Palestine was concerned, when the British Mandate was confirmed by the League of Nations, the Preamble to the text of the mandate stated,[1]

The Council of the League of Nations

Whereas the principal Allied Powers have agreed, for the purpose of giving effect to the provisions of Article 22 of the Covenant of the League of Nations, to entrust to a Mandatory,

selected by the said Powers, the administration of the territory
of Palestine, which formerly belonged to the Turkish Empire,
within such boundaries as may be fixed by them; and whereas
the principal Allied Powers have also agreed that the Mandatory
should be responsible for putting into effect the declaration originally made on 2nd November, 1917 by the Government of His
Britannic Majesty, and adopted by the said Powers, in favour of
the establishment in Palestine of a national home for the Jewish
people, it being clearly understood that nothing should be done
which might prejudice the civil and religious rights of existing
non-Jewish communities in Palestine, or the rights and political
status enjoyed by Jews in any other country.[2]

It was at this point that the Balfour declaration became a legal
document recognized by the international community.

Early Palestinian reaction

The first Palestinian conference, including delegates from many
Arab villages and major towns representing Muslim and Christian communities, was convened in early 1919 in Jerusalem. The
primary focus of the conference was the question of Zionism
and the political future of Palestine. The conference expressed
the wish to see a unified and fully independent Palestine as
South Syria. At the same time Dr Howard Bliss, President of the
American University in Beirut, wrote to President Wilson that
the people of Syria were relying on his principles of self-determination, and wanted a fair opportunity to express their political
aspirations. Bliss suggested an American commission should be
sent to the area to carry out a fact-finding mission.

President Wilson put forward this proposal to the Supreme
Council of the League of Nations on 20 March 1919. At this
point the British and French withdrew from participation, but

an American commission, the King-Crane Commission, was appointed and spent some six weeks in Palestine and Syria. The Commission interviewed a large number of delegations from some forty towns and rural areas, and received more than eighteen hundred petitions. One of the initial conclusions of the Commission was that Syria, as a whole, should be put under American or British mandate with a monarchy under the Emir Faisal.

Those opposed to the Zionist movement claimed that there was a Zionist plan to displace the indigenous Palestinian population by land purchase and military mobilization in order to enforce mass Jewish immigration. The Commission echoed this view and warned against it on the grounds that the enforcement of such a scheme against the will of nine-tenths of the existing population, and in effect ignoring their existence, would be a gross violation of the principles of self-determination that were such an important element of the Wilson government policy that was being promoted at the time.

The final report did not offer any useful recommendations. Its proposals were self-contradictory. It proposed that the US should hold a mandate, but there was no indication that the US was prepared to do so. It proposed that there should be local self-determination, but the US was not in a position to offer this. In addition, Wilson had expressed full support for the Balfour Declaration.[3] The British were the second choice of the Commission as mandatory authority, but the Balfour Declaration was integral to the British policy in accepting the Mandate for Palestine.

The upshot of this fact-finding commission was a further disappointment for the Palestinian people. This led to the first civil unrest in Jerusalem in the spring of 1920 during the annual Palestinian festival of al-Nabi Musa (Prophet Moses – a Muslim and Christian festival). The unrest erupted into demonstrations against both the British and Jewish immigration. At the same time another blow to the Palestinians came in the form of the French suppression of the Syrian nationalist movement in Damascus, and Faisal's departure from Syria. This movement had been one of the last hopes of the Palestinians and they now found themselves severed from the main body of Syrian political activity.

A third conference[4] was held in Haifa in 1920, headed by Musa Kazem al-Husseini. At this conference an executive committee was elected to monitor the situation and to advise as necessary. The Palestinian leadership attempted to contact Churchill during a visit to Cairo, to try to persuade him to change British policy. The failure of these negotiations led to a further uprising in Jaffa, resulting in more than two hundred casualties, mostly Jewish.

The British Mandatory authority appointed a commission of investigation known as the Haycroft Commission (Haycroft being the Lord Chief Justice at the time). The Commission found that the aim of the Zionist movement in Palestine was permanent settlement, and that the promotion of this by the Balfour Declaration had provoked the Arab reaction. During the same year, 1920, the Palestinians held their fourth conference in Jerusalem, headed by Musa Kazem al-Husseini and attended by hundreds of delegates from all over Palestine. The conference resolved to send a delegation to Europe to explain the Palestinian situation. The chairman of this delegation was Musa Kazem al-Husseini, and the other members were Tawfiq Hammad, Amin al-Tamimi, Mu'in al-Madi, Shibli al-Jamal and Ibrahim Shammas.

The High Commissioner in Palestine, Sir Herbert Samuel, permitted this delegation to travel as individuals, but refused them permission to travel with the status of a body representing the Palestinians. The delegation travelled first to Cairo, then to Rome, where they had an audience with the Pope, then to Britain, where Parliament was in its summer recess and there was therefore no meaningful interaction, and then to Geneva. Returning to the UK they published a pamphlet entitled *The Holy Land: The Muslim and Christian Case against the Zionist Aggression*. They initiated a propaganda campaign and gained some support particularly from Conservative members of the House of Lords.

Organized pressure was used to try to persuade the Colonial Office to change its pro-Zionist stance. The Colonial Office advised the Arab delegation that they should meet the Zionist leaders in London and try to reach a negotiated agreement, rather than simply antagonize the government. The Palestinian delegation agreed to meet the Zionist leaders on neutral ground. The parties met in the Middle East section of the Colonial Office. The Palestinian delegation met Dr Chaim Weizmann but no agreement was reached. The Palestinians wanted the draft of the Mandate to be amended to include a provision for a legislative council in Palestine with powers that would enable the existing majority of Palestinians to prevent the Mandatory power from carrying into effect the policy of creating a Jewish National Home. The British government expressed readiness to modify the terms of the Mandate, but refused to consider any change to the policy of the Balfour Declaration. The legal advisers to the British government drafted a proposal for an administrative organization for Palestine which would comprise the British High Commissioner, an official Executive Council, and a partly elected legislative council. Under this constitution no ordinance that was repugnant to the Mandate could be enacted, and the High Commissioner retained a power of veto.

The legislature was to consist of the High Commissioner, ten officials and twelve elected members. One member was to be elected by the Chamber of Commerce, and two were to be nominated by the High Commissioner. Ten members would constitute a quorum. The Palestinian delegation refused this proposal outright. They agreed to consider the terms of a constitution if the British government denounced the Balfour Declaration, halted immigration and offered Palestine self-determination. Negotiations between the Palestinians and the British government lasted almost a year. The British government was disappointed by the failure to reach agreement with the Palestinian leadership. All of this, however, took place before the actual enactment of the Mandate. The delegation returned to Palestine having failed in its mission.[5]

The 'Churchill White Paper'

In 1922 the British government issued the White Paper that came to be known as the 'Churchill White Paper' but which had originally been drafted as a memorandum entitled 'British Policy in Palestine'. An advance draft of this memorandum was communicated to the Palestinian delegation in May 1922 and discussions began on 1 June with Sir Herbert Samuel and a representative of the Colonial Office. The Palestinian delegation indicated no change of opinion or policy. On 3 June the draft was communicated officially to the Zionist Organisation. The statement included a paragraph that put on record the British Government's official denial of the claim by the Palestinian delegation that Palestine west of the River Jordan was included in the pledge made to the Sherif Hussein by Sir Henry McMahon.

The following are the most significant paragraphs of the Churchill White Paper:

Unauthorised statements have been made to the effect that the purpose in view is to create a wholly Jewish Palestine. Phrases have been used such as that Palestine is to become 'as Jewish as England is English'.

His Majesty's Government regard any such expectation as impracticable and have no such aim in view. Nor have they at any time contemplated, as appears to be feared by the Arab Delegation, the disappearance or the subordination of the Arabic population, language or culture in Palestine. They would draw attention to the fact that the terms of the declaration referred to do not contemplate that Palestine as a whole should be converted into a Jewish National Home, but that such a Home should be founded in Palestine.

It is also necessary to point out that the Zionist Commission in Palestine, now termed the Palestine Zionist Executive, has not desired to possess, and does not possess, any share in the general administration of the country. Nor does the special position assigned to the Zionist Organisation in Article IV of the Draft Mandate for Palestine imply any such functions. That special position relates to the measures to be taken in Palestine affecting the Jewish population, and contemplates that the Organisation may exist in the general development of the country, but does not entitle it to share in any degree in its Government.

So far as the Jewish population of Palestine are concerned, it appears that some among them are apprehensive that His Majesty's Government may depart from the policy embodied in the Declaration of 1917. It is necessary, therefore, once more to affirm that these fears are unfounded, and that the Declaration, re-affirmed by the Conference of the Principal Allied Powers at San Remo and again in the Treaty of Sevres, is not susceptible of change.

During the last two or three generations the Jews have recreated in Palestine a community, now numbering 80,000, of whom about one-fourth are farmers or workers upon the land. This community has its own political organs; an elected assembly for the direction of its domestic concerns; elected councils in the towns; and an organisation for the control of its schools. It has an elected Chief Rabbinate and Rabbinical Council for the direction of its religious affairs. Its business is conducted in

Hebrew as a vernacular language, and a Hebrew press serves its needs. It has its distinctive intellectual life and displays considerable economic activity. This community, then, with its town and country population, its political, religious and social organisations, its own language, its own customs, its own life, has in fact 'national' characteristics. When it is asked what is meant by the development of the Jewish National Home in Palestine, it may be answered that it is not the imposition of a Jewish nationality upon the inhabitants of Palestine as a whole, but the further development of the existing Jewish community; with the assistance of Jews in other parts of the world, in order that it may become a centre in which the Jewish people as a whole may take, on grounds of religion and race, an interest and a pride. But in order that this community should have the best prospect of free development and provide a full opportunity for the Jewish people to display its capacities, it is essential that it should know that it is in Palestine as of right and not on sufferance. That is the reason why it is necessary that the existence of a Jewish National Home in Palestine should be internationally guaranteed, and that it should be formally recognised to rest upon ancient historic connection. For the fulfilment of this policy it is necessary that the Jewish community in Palestine should be able to increase its numbers by immigration. This immigration cannot be so great in volume as to exceed whatever may be the economic capacity of the country at the time to absorb new arrivals. It is essential to ensure that the immigrants should not be a burden upon the people of Palestine as a whole, and that they should not deprive any section of the present population of their employment. Hitherto the immigration had fulfilled these conditions.

It is the intention of His Majesty's Government to foster the establishment of a full measure of self-government in Palestine, but they are of opinion that, in the special circumstances of that country, this should be accomplished by gradual stages and not suddenly. The first step was taken when, on the institution of a civil Administration, the nominated Advisory Council, which now exists, was established. It was stated at the time by the High Commissioner, that this was the first step in the development of self-governing institutions and it is now proposed to take a second step by the establishment of a Legislative Council containing a large proportion of members elected on a wide franchise . . . After a few years the situation will be again reviewed, and if the experience of the working of the constitution now to be established so warranted, a larger share of authority would then be extended to the elected representatives of the people.

In effect, the main principles were, as outlined in the Government's official summary, as follows:

1. His Majesty's Government affirms the declaration of November 1917, which is not susceptible of change.
2. A Jewish National Home will be founded in Palestine. The Jewish people will be in Palestine as of right not on sufferance, but His Majesty's Government has no such aim in view as that Palestine should become as Jewish as England is English.
3. Nor do His Majesty's Government contemplate disappearance or subordination of Arab population, language or culture.
4. Status of all citizens of Palestine will be Palestinian. No section of population will have any other status in the eyes of the Law.
5. His Majesty's Government intended to foster the establishment of full measures of self-government in Palestine and as the next step a legislative council with the majority of elected members will be set up immediately.
6. Special position of the Zionist executive does not entitle it to share in any degree in government of the country.

7. Immigration will not exceed economic capacity of the country at the time to absorb new arrivals.
8. Committee of elected members of legislative council will confer with administration upon matters relating to regulation of immigration.
9. Any religious community or considerable section of population claiming that terms of Mandate are not being fulfilled will have right of appeal to the League of Nations.[6]

The policies and promises of the times have been analysed and discussed over the years, but the enduring impression is that the Balfour Declaration and the White Paper were exercises in attempting to satisfy, or at least pacify, all the parties to which the government had made commitments. A promise had been made to the Jews that the British government was in favour of the creation of a Jewish National Home, but this had not been defined in any real or tangible terms. Promises that had been made in similarly general terms to the Arabs were now fading, to be replaced only by an undertaking that the indigenous population would not suffer detriment. The White Paper echoed the same policies, apparently offering something, but really offering nothing at all. Meanwhile, in today's terminology, facts were being created on the ground. While the Arabs were protesting against the Balfour Declaration and the White Paper and demanding the withdrawal of these almost meaningless statements, the Jews were steadily buying land, promoting agriculture, building schools and developing social organization.

The Mandate

When the Mandate was approved, the British government accepted its responsibility to implement the policy spelled out in the White Paper. The High Commissioner, Sir Herbert Samuel, promoted the issue of the legislative council in an effort to appease some of the Arab objections. The intention was to reduce the number of appointed members and to establish an advisory committee on immigration. On their return from London the Palestinian delegates held their fifth conference in Nablus in 1922, the outcome being to reject the legislative council. This did not deter Samuels in his aim to involve the Arab population and gain their co-operation. Samuels suspended the legislative council, replacing it with a representative council comprising eight Muslims, two Christians and two Jews.

The Arabs, however, continued the boycott on the basis that this form of resistance would ultimately be successful. Pressure was exerted on the members of the council to refuse to serve. The British offered a compromise by assuring the Arabs that service on the council would not be deemed approval of the Palestinian Constitution. This was also rejected by the Executive Committee, however, and at this point the British more or less gave up the idea of involving the local population in the representative council.

As a final attempt to gain the co-operation of the Arab population, the British proposed the establishment of an Arab Agency, on the model of the Jewish Agency. This body would be responsible for administration of social affairs for the non-Jewish population, and it would be consulted with regard to immigration, particularly in so far as this was likely to be detrimental to the non-Jewish population. The difference between these two bodies was that whereas the Arab Agency represented only the interests of the indigenous Arab population, the Jewish Agency represented the ambitions of the worldwide Jewish community in Palestine. Moreover, the Arab Agency was to be appointed by the High Commissioner, whereas the Jewish Agency was a democratic organization. In any case, the Arab Executive rejected the Arab Agency within the framework of the Mandate. At this point the Colonial Office instructed the High

Commissioner to terminate the negotiations with the Arabs and to administer the country with the help of an advisory council composed of British officials. This was initiated in late 1923.

The Palestinians sent a delegation to Lausanne in October 1922 to attend the conference convened with the intention of modifying the terms of the Treaty of Sevres, which had been signed in Paris in August 1920. *En route* to Lausanne, the delegation visited Turkey for preliminary discussions with the Turkish authorities with the aim of gaining Turkish support for the modification of Article 95, which endorsed the Balfour Declaration. This was rejected by the Turks on the grounds that the loss of their Arab territories was a major factor in the collapse of the Ottoman Empire and Turkish defeat in the World War. The Palestinian delegation achieved nothing at the Lausanne conference.

The Sixth Palestinian Arab Congress was held in Jaffa in June 1923. Among its most important goals was the reform of the national movement. While the conference was taking place Sherif Hussein wrote to Musa Kazem, the Chairman of the Congress, indicating that he had concluded a treaty with the British government, the effects of which were British recognition of Arab independence throughout the Arabian Peninsula except for Aden. The British response was to deny this claim, while giving assurance that the government had no intention of taking any steps that would affect the civil and religious rights of the Arab population. The Palestinian Arab Congress made the decision to reject this treaty, to boycott any loans entered into in the name of Palestine and to exclude from the Palestinian Executive any Palestinian individual who accepted the terms of this treaty. It was felt that despite the failure of negotiations with the British to reach an acceptable solution, it might still be possible to reach a negotiated solution.

The Congress elected a delegation to travel to London to observe the negotiations between Sherif Hussein's representative and the Foreign Office. The negotiations failed because of the fact that Palestine was not included in the treaty. The British government offered two different options. One of these was to include Palestine in the treaty on the basis that the Sherif accept the Balfour Declaration and the British would issue an interpretation of the Declaration to the effect that it was not intended to lead to the creation of a Jewish state. The alternative was that Palestine would be taken out of the equation on the basis that there would be unity between Iraq, Transjordan and the Hejaz. The negotiation was severed abruptly by the abdication of the Sherif in favour of his son Ali and his departure from Makka after it was occupied, along with Ta'if, by the Wahabis.

Two important events in the year or so before Samuel completed his term of office were of great significance. The first of these was the inauguration of the Hebrew University on the Mount of Olives. The attendance of Lord Balfour at this inauguration added insult to injury in the eyes of the Palestinians. The Executive Committee issued a call to all Palestinians to refuse to have anything to do with this visit and to boycott the celebrations and organize what was in effect a national strike. The second was the visit of Emery, the Minister for the Colonies. The Executive Committee was to meet Emery, but the National Party, which opposed the Executive Committee, insisted on a separate meeting, thereby presenting a divided front. A fundamental source of weakness amongst the Palestinians at this time, in contrast to the Jews, was their lack of unity and their inability to set aside their differences for the common good. Competing parties and factions emerged which essentially mirrored rivalries between the prominent families, in particular the Husseinis and Nashashibis.

From the time of the White Paper until 1929 there were no major impediments to Jewish development of the country. The limitations specified relating to economic absorptive capacity did not prevent immigration on a fairly large scale. By 1927, however, emigration began, for a short time, to exceed immigration, mainly owing to external economic factors and the effects of the worldwide depression, compounded by a series of natural disasters, including a drought in 1926, an earthquake in 1927 and a plague of locusts in 1928. Overall, however, this was a successful decade for the Zionist ambition, and when Samuel came to the end of his term of office in 1925 he was praised in the Report of the Executive to the Fourteenth Zionist Congress as follows:

> Sir Herbert has, by common consent, acquitted himself of his historic task with dignity and distinction, and he carried with him in his retirement the enduring gratitude of the Zionist Organisation and of the Jewish world at large. The contrast between the Palestine of 1920 and the Palestine of 1925 speaks for itself. Political unrest has subsided; a stable and efficient Administration has been built up; and there has been a marked and general quickening of economic life. Not only have the past five years brought Palestine peace, order and good government, but they have witnessed the successful completion of the first and most difficult stage in the establishment of the Jewish National Home.[7]

Samuel was replaced as High Commissioner in August 1925 by Lord Plumer, who served until 1928. Plumer's main tasks were to improve security in Palestine, to reduce the weaponry held by the Jewish settlers (although the momentum of immigration was maintained) and to improve the agriculture and economy of the country. There was no significant change in British policy, but the Palestinian Executive was recognized for the first time as the representative of the Palestinian people.

The Seventh Palestinian Arab Congress was held in Jerusalem on 20–7 June 1927 and was attended by 250 delegates representing all Palestinians. The outcome of this was the formation of a new Executive Committee comprising forty-eight members, and the dissolution of all other local committees. The new Executive Committee started to meet on a regular basis and was the official representative of the Palestinian people until the death of Musa Kazem al-Husseini in 1934. The procedure for election to the Executive Committee began with the election of two members by each local association. This resulted in the election of thirty-six Muslim delegates representing eighteen districts, and the nomination of twelve Christian delegates representing the Christian population but according to overall numbers, not local distribution. As usual the Chairman of the Congress and the Executive Committee was Musa Kazem al-Husseini. It was agreed that the Executive Committee should be convened monthly and that one-third (sixteen delegates) would be required for a quorum. The main issues before the Congress included the tithes, the agricultural bank and agricultural loans, nationality and immigration, the concession for the Dead Sea project (which was given to a foreign company), and the demand for democratic representative government.[8]

The Dead Sea concession was granted by the Palestinian government (the Mandate power) on 1 January 1930 to Palestinian Potash Ltd, for the extraction of minerals and salts from the Dead Sea. This firm was established by Moses Novomeysky, a mining engineer from Serbia. Although the company was formed by Jewish initiative, there was strong British representation on the board of directors. The company employed both Jews and Palestinian Arabs and there were good working relationships between the two. No change was made at this point to the tithe system, a leftover from the Ottoman administration.[9]

The Wailing Wall crisis

In 1929 civil unrest took place known as the 'Wailing Wall crisis' (*Thawrat al-Buraq*). The Wailing Wall, considered by Jews to be one of the last vestiges of the Temple of Solomon, forms part of the vast platform on which the Aqsa Mosque and the Dome of the Rock stand.[10] Moreover, the Wailing Wall is considered by Muslims to be the location of the gate through which the Prophet was carried by the mythical creature Buraq. The site is therefore of great significance to both communities. The Wailing Wall was at the time surrounded by the 'Moroccan Quarter', where most of the property was owned by a religious endowment, 'Waqf Abu Middayn', established at the time of the Ayyubids. Part of this property had been converted into a hospice. Jews were allowed to visit the Wailing Wall to perform their prayers and religious observance. Immediately before Yom Kippur in 1928 a screen for the segregation of women was installed on the pavement beside the wall.

The Palestinians voiced their objection to the British authorities, who ordered the removal of the screen, the installation of fixtures at religious sites being prohibited under Mandate law. This was seen to be an attempt to discredit the holy day, and the local and international Jewish lobbies expressed their indignation, claiming that the British authorities and the Arabs were denying them their religious freedom. Lobbying on both sides continued, involving posters and protests. The British government, in an attempt to keep the peace, agreed that only such fixtures as had been permitted under Ottoman rule should be allowed at the Wailing Wall. This was unsatisfactory, since the Ottomans had not regulated such matters in an effective manner.

In August 1929 violence erupted in Jerusalem and spread all over Palestine during the following few days. The British brought in troops from Egypt and Malta to subdue the inter-communal fighting. In the wake of this, on 13 September 1929, Lord Passfield, Secretary of State for the Colonies in the new Labour government, sent a commission under former Chief Justice Walter Shaw to investigate and analyse the causes of this disturbance.

The report of the commission appeared in March 1930 and held that the outbreak in Jerusalem on 23 August was from the beginning an attack by the Arabs on Jews, for which no excuse in the form of earlier murders by Jews had been established. The attacks were vicious and were accompanied by wanton destruction of Jewish property. In a few instances Jews assaulted Arabs and destroyed Arab property, but these attacks, though inexcusable, were in most cases in retaliation for wrongs already committed by Arabs in the neighbourhood in which the Jewish attacks occurred.[11]

In the meantime the General Muslim Conference convened in Jerusalem on 1 November 1929 under the leadership of Hajj Amin al-Husseini. The Conference demanded that the integrity of the Muslim holy site should be protected from any infringement. At the same time the Supreme Muslim Council, over which Hajj Amin also presided, began development in the vicinity of the Wailing Wall. Sir John Hope-Simpson was appointed on 6 May 1930 to carry out a report on the economic condition of Palestine. He was a retired India Civil Service official and a member of the League of Nations Commission for the Resettlement of Greek Refugees. Hope-Simpson reached Palestine on 20 May 1930, to spend two months studying reports and visiting Arab villages and Jewish settlements.

1932 marked the beginning of a new phase in the crisis among the Palestinians themselves. The nationalist movement was failing, the Executive Committee was weak and its decision making was ineffective, and an Islamic Congress had little impact. The Shaw and Simpson reports on which the White Paper was based indicated between the lines that both land sales and immigration should be restricted. The Prime Minister, however, immediately ruled out such suggestions. A series of events in the early 1930s, beginning with the Wailing Wall incident, marked a political gain on the part of the Mufti but

with little practical effect on the main issues. There was nothing, however, to give the Palestinians any form of hope, since
immigration continued and the existing population were feeling gradually overwhelmed by this alien invasion. There was
no possibility of negotiation with the Mandatory power.

The outcome of this was an expression of popular unrest in
1936 triggered by an attack by three Palestinian Arabs on a Jewish convoy near Nablus, resulting in two dead and one injured.
The following day two Palestinians were killed in reprisal, and
when news of these events reached Jaffa there were civil disturbances, resulting in a twenty-four-hour curfew issued by the
High Commissioner on Jaffa and Tel Aviv. The following day
there was a general strike in Jaffa. The only action taken by the
political leaders, however, was to meet representatives of the
British government and to denounce the violence. It can be seen
as a general pattern that the only really effective action in the
history of the Palestinian struggle up to the present day has been
spontaneous popular uprising.

The first political support for the uprising in Jaffa came from
Nablus. There was a public meeting at which it was agreed that
Nablus should lead the general struggle on a national rather
than a party basis and would be responsible for liaising with
other cities and organizations. The consensus was that the primary enemy should be identified, that is, the British who were
responsible for the mass Zionist immigration, rather than the
Zionists themselves. It was agreed that the struggle should not
cease until Palestinian demands were met, and that there should
be no co-operation with commissions and inquiries and no delegations sent to London. The main aim of this movement was to
halt Jewish immigration that was endangering the livelihood of
the inhabitants of Palestine. At this point the Palestinian leadership realized that it would have to unify itself with this movement, and the eventual outcome of this was the formation of the
Arab Supreme Committee.

Shortly after the strikes there was a general call for the withholding of taxes on the principle of 'no taxation without representation'. The movement was by this point, however, turning towards military struggle. The British took strong action against this in the form of imprisonment, exile and demanding compensation for damage caused in the unrest.

In 1936 a number of letters were received from the Arab kings and princes pressing for the Palestinians to cease their actions against the British. The Arab Supreme Committee agreed. The Palestinians had understood that immigration would be restricted but in the event they felt that nothing had been done to change the situation.

A Royal Commission under Lord Peel arrived in Palestine in November 1936 and held both public and private sessions. In contrast to previous commissions, carefully prepared memoranda were submitted by both the British and the Jewish Agency on specific areas of the problem. The Palestinians boycotted the Royal Commission. Shortly before the completion of the inquiry, the Palestinians changed their policy, again following persuasion by the Arab princes, and began to co-operate with the inquiry, which was completed in January 1937.

The position of the Jewish Agency can be summarized more or less as follows:

1. That the interests of the Jews and Arabs were inherently reconcilable.
2. That they accepted the Churchill White Paper supporting the position of the Balfour Declaration that the interests, language, religion and culture of the Arab population should not be prejudiced.
3. That they were determined to live with the Arab population in terms of concord and mutual respect, and to work for the development of the country for the benefit of all its population.

The Arab spokesmen, however, took a completely different line, strongly denouncing the Jewish National Home. Their objections focused on issues of loss of land, lack of development in the countryside, increased cost of living, loss of jobs and discrimination against Arabs in employment. Arab demands were summarized as the withdrawal of the Jewish National Home policy and the establishment of an Arab state (in accordance with the original British promise) in which the majority would determine the place of the Jewish population.

The conclusions of the Royal Commission were that the recent disturbances could be attributed to two key factors; the desire for Arab national independence, and fear of the establishment of a Jewish National Home. The report went on to say that all other elements were secondary, contributing to the unrest or triggering specific outbreaks. The report held that the Jewish National Home which had been a dream was now a going concern; in response to the Arab position it indicated that according to all statistical measures the condition of the Arab population was now, under the British administration, better than it had ever been under Ottoman rule.

The recommendations of the report were divided into two main sections:

1. Pacification measures. These included restriction of Jewish immigration to twelve thousand per year, restrictions on the sale of land by Arabs to Jews, and secondary measures including the creation of an Arab Agency (reviving the rejected 1923 recommendation), the assurance of greater public security in Palestine, and improvement of relations between Arabs and Jews through modification of the educational system.
2. The proposal for partition. The Royal Commission indicated that, whatever partial measures were taken, ultimately it would not be possible to satisfy both sides. In view of the

strength of feeling in the Arab world against the National Home, it would not be reasonable to hand over four hundred thousand Jews to Arab rule, nor would it be fair if the Jews became a majority and were given authority over one million or so Palestinian Arabs. A proposal was therefore made to divide Palestine into independent Jewish and Palestinian areas, with the Mandatory authority retaining part of the territory.

The report stated,

> Considering the attitude which both the Arab and the Jewish representatives adopted in giving evidence before us, we think it improbable that either party will be satisfied at first sight with the proposals we have submitted for the adjustment of their rival claims. For Partition means that neither will get all it wants. It means that the Arabs must acquiesce in the exclusion from their sovereignty of a piece of territory, long occupied and once ruled by them. It means that the Jews must be content with less than the Land of Israel they once ruled and have hoped to rule again. But it seems to us possible that on reflection both parties will come to realise that the drawbacks of Partition are outweighed by its advantages. For, if it offers neither party all it wants, it offers each what it wants most, namely freedom and security.

The first proposals for partition

One proposal for division of the country involved a form of canton system whereby Jewish land acquisition and settlement would be encouraged in certain areas, and others would be reserved for the Arab population. The government of each canton would be autonomous in matters such as public works, health, education and general administrative matters such as immigration and determining the official language, and the Mandate would have overall control of areas such as foreign relations, defence, customs, transport and communications infrastructure, etc. This plan would not, however, fulfil the nationalist ambitions of either community. The Peel Commission therefore proposed a full partition of Palestine.

The Royal Commission submitted an outline division as a basis for consideration, according to which Palestine and Transjordan would be split into three regions: 1) a Jewish state including the coastal region from a point between Gaza and Jaffa to Megiddo in the Valley of Esdraelon, there turning east to include the Valley and Galilee to the northern boundaries between Palestine and Syria; 2) an Arab state comprising the remainder of Palestine south and east of the Jewish state and the whole of Transjordan; 3) a British enclave, under permanent Mandate, which would include Jerusalem and Bethlehem as Christian sites, and Lydda and Ramleh with a corridor to the sea at Jaffa for military and economic reasons.

Among the theoretical difficulties involved in this were the logistics of population exchange between the areas. The relocation of the Jewish population from the Arab area would not have posed a serious problem, since they numbered only 1250 and their land amounted to only one hundred thousand dunums (one dunum is roughly equivalent to one quarter of an acre). The Arab population of the area to be designated as Jewish would, however, have posed more serious problems, since this area included almost half of the total Palestinian population, some three hundred thousand people, whose lands amounted to 3.25 million dunums.

At this point the Palestinians found themselves trapped in a situation in which they could not win; their future was to be controlled by the British Mandate and/or the Jewish state, and Arab politics, specifically those of the Amir Abdullah of

Transjordan. The Palestinian Arabs refused the partition plan and sent delegations to all Arab countries to express their objections. An Arab Summit was called at Bludaan in Syria and made five main resolutions:

1. That Palestine is an integral and indivisible part of the Arab world.
2. That the proposed partition of Palestine and creation of a Jewish National Home should be opposed.
3. That the Mandate and the Balfour Declaration should be voided and that a treaty should be made with the British government to give the Palestinians their independence and sovereignty over Palestine. Moreover, that Palestine should have a constitutional government in accordance with the principles of which the rights of minorities would be identical to those of the majority.
4. That the demand for restriction of Jewish immigration be reaffirmed, and that there should be legislation preventing the transfer of lands from Arab to Jewish ownership.
5. That the continuation of the long-standing relationship between the British and Arab peoples was dependent upon the fulfilment of the aforementioned conditions, and that failing this the Arabs would be forced to take a different position. Also that the desired co-operation or integration between the Arab and Jewish communities would not be achieved by the implementation of a partition.

The Palestinian leaders started to intensify their negotiations with the Arab regimes in an effort to rally support for their cause. In 1937 Hajj Amin al-Husseini made official visits to Syria, and to Saudi Arabia in conjunction with performance of the pilgrimage. During this period the British authorities attempted to root out the ringleaders of the Palestinian resistance by detention and deportation. They focused on Hajj Amin al-Husseini, who was removed from his post and at one point forced to take refuge in the Aqsa Mosque, where he remained for three months. The British authorities were unable to enter to remove him owing to the religious significance of the mosque, and eventually prepared to send in Muslim soldiers from their colonies in India.

Forewarned, Hajj Amin escaped to Syria, where there was a newly elected national government and where he believed he would find support. The ship on which he was travelling to Syria was, however, intercepted by the Lebanese coastguard (at the time under French authority) and he was taken to the French High Commission in Beirut, where the Commissioner refused to allow him to enter Syria but offered to send him to Paris. Hajj Amin refused and was supported in his refusal by popular demonstrations. He spent the next two years until the outbreak of the Second World War under house arrest in the mountains of Lebanon.

The growing problems in Europe now began to be reflected in the affairs of the Middle East. By 1938 it was becoming obvious that war between Britain and Germany was inevitable. Threatened at home, Britain feared losing its influence abroad in the process. Seeing no prospect of their aspirations being satisfied by the British, the Palestinians had entered into talks with Germany. Britain was aware of this and deeply concerned, and as a consequence began to offer concessions to the Palestinians. A Palestinian and a Jewish delegation, along with Egyptian, Saudi, Yemeni, Iraqi and Jordanian monitors, were invited to London for negotiations held at St James's Palace in 1939. The British were adamant in excluding Hajj Amin, and Jamal al-Husseini was nominated in his place as head of the Palestinian delegation. The conference took place on 7 February 1939. The Arab demands were that Palestine should be independent, the Mandate abolished and the concept of the National Home abandoned. Britain rejected these demands, offering only to restrict immigration to eighty thousand to one hundred thousand over a period of ten years, to be reviewed thereafter and subject to Arab approval.

The 1939 White Paper

The new British policy was formulated in the 1939 White Paper, which started by reiterating the obligations of the Mandate to secure the establishment of a National Home for the Jewish people, to safeguard the religious and civil rights of all Palestineinhabitants and to place the country under workable political, administrative and economic conditions. The new policy was set out in the White Paper under three main headings:

1. Constitution
2. Immigration
3. Land

Constitution

The White Paper acknowledged that previous statements might have caused confusion and concern, and stated that 'His Majesty's Government, therefore, now declare unequivocally that it is not part of their policy that Palestine should become a Jewish State.' At the same time, however, the British government adhered to the view 'that the whole of Palestine, west of the Jordan, was excluded from Sir Henry McMahon's pledge and they, therefore, cannot agree that the McMahon correspondence forms a just basis for the claim that Palestine should be converted into an Arab state'. It was indicated that the spirit and the letter of the Mandate were not aimed at maintaining the Mandate indefinitely but, ultimately, at establishing self-government in a similar manner to that in neighbouring countries, but self-government to be shared between the co-existing communities.

Immigration

It was proposed that immigration should be limited for a period of five years, after which it would be stopped, unless the Arab population acquiesced to further immigration.

Land

It was stated that the High Commissioner would be given powers to prohibit further land transfers, as of the date of the 1939 White Paper. These powers would be retained until the establishment of the Palestine government as planned.

The White Paper was rejected vehemently by both Arabs and Jews. Among the Arabs a minority saw potential in the White Paper but were not in a position to voice their views for fear of victimization. At this point certain Palestinian leaders began to explore the possibility of opening relations with Germany, among them Awni Abd al-Hadi, who actually visited Germany, and Musa Alami. They came to the conclusion, however, that Germany could not be relied on to support the Palestinians in their aspirations. Hajj Amin al-Husseini left Lebanon for Iraq in October1939 and became involved in internal politics in Iraq following the change of government and during an atmosphere of uncertainty as to whether Iraq should throw in its lot with Germany or with Britain.

When in May 1940 the British government became aware of negotiations between the Kilani government in Iraq, Hajj Amin and the German government, they considered the Iraqi government unfriendly to Britain and the influence of Hajj Amin to be opposed at all costs. For a year Britain put political and economic pressure on Iraq in a plan to bring down the government. British troops entered Baghdad in 1941, securing it against

German influence, established a new government under the Crown Prince and drove Hajj Amin out. Hajj Amin then spent the remaining war years between Germany and Italy.

In Palestine scattered armed resistance took place during this time against the British and the Zionists, but there was no unified front or concerted effort. By the outbreak of the Second World War, however, this had more or less ceased.

10

Towards the establishment of a Jewish state

The Second World War

Immediately before the war Jewish opinion was divided as to whether support should be given to the British against Germany. Jewish communities in Europe declared their support, but anger about the 1939 White Paper and restriction of Jewish immigration into Palestine meant that there was resistance to the British authorities by the Jews in Palestine. When war was declared on 3 September 1939 the Jewish Agency at Jerusalem issued a statement, part of which read as follows:

> His Majesty's Government has today declared war against the Germany of Hitler. At this fateful moment, the Jewish community has a threefold concern: the protection of the Jewish homeland, the welfare of the Jewish people, the victory of the British Empire. The White Paper of May, 1939, was a grave blow to us. As heretofore we shall defend to the utmost of our ability the right of the Jewish people in its National Home. Our opposition to the White Paper was, however, never directed against Great Britain or the British Empire.
>
> The war which has now been forced upon Great Britain by Nazi Germany is our war, and all the assistance that we shall be able and permitted to give to the British Army and the British People we shall render wholeheartedly.

On the same day registration of both male and female volunteers began for service during the emergency. The volunteers were recruited for two purposes: to serve the needs of the Jewish community in economic endeavour, security and other public requirements, and to be at the disposal of the British military authorities in Palestine. Of the 136,043 persons who registered, 85,781 were men and 50,262 were women. These recruits eventually formed the basis of the Israeli armed forces.

During the Second World War the Jewish community in effect had two secret armies. The first of these was the Haganah, which followed the Zionist ideal and originated from the settlers armed by Jabotinsky during the Palestinian uprising of 1920. Jabotinsky was also the moving force behind the Irgun, the aim of which at the time of its establishment was the expulsion of the British from Palestine. Jabotinsky was born in Russia in 1880. He was a supporter of liberalism on the British model, but also adopted Garibaldi's treaties as his own personal model. During the First World War he had founded the Jewish Legion to help the British to fight the Turks in the Middle East. He favoured democracy and secularism, seeking a powerful Zionism, rather than social or cultural Zionism.

In 1940 the Jewish Agency asked the British Mandatory authority to be allowed to form an independent Jewish force. This was refused repeatedly, until the point that German and Italian forces reached El-Alamein and the threat to the area was grave. Permission then was given for the formation of a joint force to include both Jewish and Arab volunteers in equal numbers. A secret treaty was established between the British military forces in the Middle East and the Haganah, which was to work as an underground force in the case of invasion by the Germans and Italians. On this basis the British armed and trained the Haganah, and in addition armed a further fifteen thousand individuals as protection for the settlements. Some twenty-seven thousand Jews living in Palestine also signed up with the British Army.

Throughout the war international Jewish agencies sought to persuade the British government to allow the formation of a Jewish Brigade to fight the Nazis. On 20 September 1944, after long negotiations in both Houses of Parliament, this was agreed. A strong recruitment drive took place in both Palestine and the UK. In October the government agreed that the Brigade should fight under its own emblem, which is now the national flag of Israel. The Brigade was on active duty in Italy from March 1945, attached to the British Eighth Army.

There is a stark contrast here between the degrees of Jewish and Arab organization. The Jewish movement had international financial and organizational backing; the immigrants into Palestine came from developed societies with a more sophisticated level of general education even at the lower end of the scale, and with large numbers of highly educated or highly skilled people with a driving motivation. In contrast, although there was a level of political awareness among an educated and privileged elite, the majority of the Arab population of Palestine, and indeed of the region, languished in the state of inertia to which they were conditioned by centuries of subjugation by the Ottoman Empire, and the feudal system, culture and mentality which that involved, followed by the Western colonial authority that replaced it. The Jewish immigrants were in Palestine because they had chosen to go there in pursuit of an ideal; the Palestinian Arabs, however, lived there because they and countless generations before them were born there, and therefore did not have the same political awareness and pioneering motivation.[1]

Jewish acquisition of land

By 1947 two million dunums[2] out of a total of seven million were under Jewish ownership. This land was acquired in the following ways: four hundred thousand dunums were purchased

from Palestinian and non-Palestinian landowners under Ottoman rule. These were mostly in Jaffa and Haifa. Roughly three
hundred thousand dunums were rented to Jews by the Ottoman
Empire and remained in their hands following the Ottoman
defeat. Some eight hundred thousand dunums were sold by
non-Palestinian landowners. These had previously been acquired
by absentee landlords, including Syrians, Lebanese and others in
auctions of lands repossessed by the Ottoman government for
non-payment of rents and tithes.

Lands sold by Arab Palestinians from 1917 to 1947 amounted
to approximately five hundred thousand dunums. It was not,
however, the masses of the Palestinian population who sold
this land, but rather a few large-scale landowners. It has been
suggested that the notion that the Palestinians sold their lands
was propaganda promoted by the British and the Zionists to
undermine support and sympathy for the Palestinians from their
Arab neighbours.

Arab unity

From the 1940s there was among the intellectual elite in the
Arab world a movement towards Arab unity. The only solid
outcome of this was the Arab League, which was formed with
British support. The League was promoted by Egypt and the
first preparatory meetings were held in Alexandria in 1944.
The Covenant of the League of Arab States was proclaimed in
Cairo on 22 March 1945. To many the Arab League had little
credibility in view of the fact that the majority of the signatories
were either subject to some form of British military or colonial
authority, or allied with Britain in some way. It was therefore
seen by some as a puppet organization, whose establishment as
an Arab institution for resolving the Palestine question was a
faE7ade for the imposition of Western influence.

Palestine had no official representation at the preliminary conference of the Arab League. The Mufti was discredited, as was his successor Jamal al-Husseini, who was known to have assisted him in organizing the pro-German *coup* in Iraq in 1940. The role of representative was eventually assumed by Musa al-Alami, a British-educated lawyer acceptable to Britain and to Palestinian society, who had served for long in the British administration in Palestine.[3]

At the outset Musa al-Alami had no official status and was not given an official reception by the Egyptians. After a meeting with Clayton, head of British intelligence in the Middle East, Musa al-Alami received a letter indicating British approval of his role as representative of the Palestinians. On this basis he was given official recognition at the preliminary conference. At the conference in September 1944 Musa al-Alami described the situation in Palestine to the dismay of many delegates who were unaware of the full extent of the crisis. He proposed that an Arab fund should be established for the restitution of lands in Palestine.

The conference issued a declaration, known as the 'Alexandria Protocol', announcing the formation of the League of Arab States. The section on Palestine stressed the importance of Palestine as an integral part of the Arab world and indicated that the British undertaking to curtail Jewish immigration, preserve Arab lands and support the independence of Palestine was in fulfilment of firm Arab rights. The conference expressed its support for the Arabs of Palestine, and declared that though it was pained by the atrocities suffered by the Jews of Europe, this problem should not be confused with the ambitions of Zionism, and that there would be no greater injustice than to solve the problem by perpetrating another injustice against the Arabs of Palestine, irrespective of religion.

The Charter of the League of Arab States was issued the following spring. The Charter gave the Council authority to nominate the Palestinian representatives in the League, since Palestine, not being an independent state, was not a full member. A decision on Palestinian representation was delayed because of infighting, but eventually four representatives were chosen: Jamal al-Husseini, Amil al-Ghouri, Husayn al-Khalidi and Ahmad Hilmi Abd al-Baqi.

The policy of the League with regard to Palestine took four main directions: continued pressure on Britain to restrict immigration and land purchase, the boycotting of Zionist products, the saving of Palestinian lands by the establishment of a development fund, and the establishment of representative offices in capitals worldwide. The establishment of representative offices was not finalized at this time, since the countries that initially voiced their support were less forthcoming when it came to providing the financial means, claiming that the facilities of their diplomatic missions could be used for the purpose of representation.

A conference was held in London in September 1946. The outcome of this was the confirmation of certain main points, primarily that Britain (with the backing of the USA) was still the main player in matters affecting Palestine, that one hundred thousand Jews would be allowed to settle in Palestine within two years and that thereafter immigration would be limited by economic considerations, and that if the Jews and Palestinians were unable to come to a negotiated agreement the matter would be handed over to the United Nations.

In February 1947, Alexander Caddington, Head of the British Delegation to the United Nations, met the Secretary General to discuss the formation of a committee comprising both Palestinian and Zionist representation to prepare the Palestine issue for presentation to the General Assembly at its next session. The United Nations Special Committee on Palestine, known by the acronym UNSCOP, was established to examine the entire situation and all the factors involved. Eleven countries were represented in this committee, including Canada, Czechoslovakia, Guatemala, India, Peru, Sweden, Uruguay, Yugoslavia, The Netherlands and Iran. The Arab Higher Committee boycotted UNSCOP on the basis that it was confusing the Jewish refugee crisis with the Palestine question, and that the continual flow of committees of inquiry was a violation of the Palestinians' rights as the indigenous population of the land.

The UNSCOP findings were as follows:

1. That the Mandate should be terminated and Palestine given independence.
2. That in the interim Palestine should be put under UN supervision.
3. That the European refugee problem should be connected with the Palestine issue, inasmuch as the resolution of the latter would make resolution of the former easier.
4. That the religious significance of all the Holy Places should be preserved.

The majority of the Committee were of the opinion that Palestine should be divided into a Jewish and an Arab sector. The Jewish sector should include agricultural areas and the commercial cities. A minority proposed that there should be a federal state with Jerusalem as its capital. The federal government would have authority for overall policy in matters such as defence, foreign affairs, immigration, monetary policy and general taxation, and the local governments would have authority in matters such as education, internal migration, local taxation and local security. The federal government would comprise a president and two councils, one legislative and one executive, and a federal court. Representation would be in proportion to population in one council, and equal in the other.

The Arab states represented at the Arab League rejected this report. A decision was made that all borders with Palestine should be reinforced in case of war, and one million pounds was granted as aid to Palestinian defence and was to be paid by member countries. The primary importance of the report, however, is that it established the foundation for the partition plan.

In September 1947 the General Assembly formed a special committee for Palestine and appointed the Prime Minister of Australia as its head. Palestinian and Jewish representatives were invited to attend the discussions that went on from 26 September to 21 October. The Arab delegation rejected proposals for partition and demanded independence and the end of the Mandate. By 29 November 1947 the General Assembly agreed the plan for the partition of Palestine. The plan included the termination of the Mandate and withdrawal of British forces after August 1948.

The Arabs felt that the partition plan constituted a gross injustice, in that it would give Arab lands to an incoming people, that it would uproot a settled population, that it would create a foreign state in the middle of the Arab world, that it would divide one Arab state from another and that it would put key economic areas under Jewish control. The plan gave the prime agricultural land to the Jews, leaving the Palestinians with the less hospitable desert, stony lands and barren hills. Placing Jerusalem under the UN was a way of removing this Arab city from Arab hands. Throughout the Arab world there were popular demonstrations, but nowhere was there any real political action to support the Palestinians in their plight.

Jewish terrorist organizations had fought the British since the 1930s but had showed restraint during the war. After the war, however, there was a wave of Jewish terrorist activity against Palestinians and even more so against the British. On 9 April 1948 a branch of the Irgun led by Menachem Begin carried out a massacre of men, women and children in the village of Deir Yassin. The calculated intention of this was to cause mass panic in the surrounding areas and in this aim it was entirely successful. Entire villages fled in fear that they would suffer the same fate.[4] The two most notorious acts of Jewish terrorism against the British were the hanging of two British officers and the bombing of the King David Hotel in Jerusalem. These were the final events leading to the British decision to give up the Mandate and withdraw their forces.

The declaration of the state of Israel

The day following the final withdrawal, 14 May 1948, Ben-Gurion declared the foundation of the State of Israel. The United States was the first to recognize the newly created state, followed by the Soviet Union. The Israeli state had the advantage of vastly superior organization, combined with the financial backing of world Jewry. There was Palestinian paramilitary resistance. The Arab states came to the Palestinians' aid and on 15 May entered the territories allocated to Palestine under the partition plan.

The Arab forces that entered Palestine at this point comprised six thousand Jordanians, nine thousand Iraqis, five thousand Egyptians, one thousand Syrians, three thousand Saudis and some three thousand volunteers from other Arab countries. On the borders were a further four thousand Jordanians, one thousand Iraqis, eight thousand Egyptians, fifteen hundred Syrians, eighteen hundred Lebanese and 3500 volunteers from other Arab countries. The Arab forces amounted to some forty-six thousand in total.

The Israeli forces in Palestine comprised seventeen thousand mobile attack troops, eighteen thousand semi-mobile attack troops, fifty thousand regular defence troops, twelve thousand members of the Irgun and somewhere between four hundred and eight hundred members of the Stern Gang, constituting a total Israeli fighting force of some 97,800.

According to a Reuters report at the time, the British Foreign Office declared that so long as the Arab forces were entering Arab territories, not then subject to a recognized Arab government, then there was no action to be taken, but if they entered the areas claimed by the State of Israel the UN would have to intervene.

Musa al-Alami described the military situation as follows:

> In the first instance, the principal weakness in the Arab forces was that we were not prepared, although we were not taken by surprise, while the Jewish forces were fully prepared. We conducted the battle in the manner of the previous disturbances, while the Jews conducted it as a full-scale war. We approached it in an ad hoc manner, with no unity, no comprehensive strategy and no overall leadership. Our defence was piecemeal and we were in chaos. Each country was fighting alone. Only those in the areas in close proximity to the Jews entered the battle. The Jews conducted the war with a unified strategy, unified leadership and general conscription. Our weapons were poor and defective, while those of the enemy were good and powerful. Our aims in the battle were confused and diverse. The aim of the Jews was to win the battle.[5]

On 22 May the British proposed at the UN Security Council that the two sides should be given thirty-six hours to cease hostilities without prejudice to the claims of either side. The delegates of the Arab states at the UN asked for more time. On 25 May Egypt stated that it was unable to agree to a cease-fire, since it was not at war with a sovereign state but rather was acting to defend a vulnerable population from the aggression of a terrorist organization. The Political Committee of the Arab League issued a declaration in similar terms on 27 May, demanding UN action to resolve the crisis caused by Jewish terrorist action aimed at creating a *fait accompli*, by the massacre of large numbers of Palestinians in key cities, and by driving people from their homes. Within three months of the outbreak of hostilities, over a quarter of a million Palestinians were living as refugees in neighbouring Arab countries.

On 29 May the UN Security Council resolved that there should be a cease-fire for a period of four weeks commencing on 11 July. This was incorporated, along with conditions for the cease-fire, in a memorandum issued on 7 July by Count Folke Bernadotte, a member of the Swedish royal family appointed by the UN as a special envoy. Following the implementation of the cease-fire, the Political Committee of the Arab League met in Cairo to discuss the situation. On 27 July, Bernadotte put forward proposals, based on his findings, for a permanent solution to the problem. This was to involve an Arab and a Jewish state. The Arab sector would include Transjordan, Jerusalem and part of the Negev; western Galilee and most of the existing Jewish areas were to be included in the Israeli area, and there was to be an independent Jewish municipality in Jerusalem. The port of Haifa, including the oil terminal, was to be a free zone, as was the airport at Lydda. The issue of immigration was to be left to the individual states, who were also to decide whether or not they wished to form a confederation. Bernadotte's proposals led to him and his French aide being shot dead in Jerusalem on 17 September 1948. The Stern Gang subsequently claimed responsibility for the killing.

Both the Arab League and the Jews refused the Bernadotte proposal and the Arabs presented an alternative plan: the formation of an interim Palestinian government in which the population would be represented in a proportional manner. This would set up a founding committee to draw up an electoral register. The interim government would perform all the legislative functions and would be responsible to the founding committee. The following principles were to be observed and were to form the basis of a constitution:

1. Palestine is a united sovereign state.
2. The Palestinian government should be a democratic government, responsible to a legislative council.

3. There should be constitutionally guaranteed security for religious areas and minorities and freedom of worship for all.
4. There should be respect for basic freedoms without prejudice on the basis of religion, national or ethnic origin, or language.
5. All religious minorities would be entitled to form organizations, which would ultimately be subject to the authority of the government.
6. The constitution would recognize the Hebrew language in the Jewish areas.
7. Any person seeking naturalization would have to be a legal-resident and to have lived in the country for a period to be specified by the government.

This proposal was never implemented. Bernadotte asked the Security Council to put pressure on the Arabs to extend the cease-fire, but the Arabs refused and hostilities resumed on 9 July. At this time Israeli military forces were growing. According to newspaper reports, they had some seventy-five training camps in Europe. On completing their basic training, recruits sailed for Palestine from French and Italian ports.

During the first few days of fighting, the Arab forces appeared to be achieving some success, but this changed suddenly. The Jordanian and Iraqi forces withdrew from strategic areas such as Lydda and Ramla, although there was no imminent danger in those areas from the Israeli forces and no immediately apparent reason why they should withdraw. Israeli planes bombed Cairo and Damascus to demonstrate to other Arab countries the capability of their air power.

The Israeli Cabinet was adamant in its intention to annex the Negev area. It feared the presence of Egyptian forces in such proximity to Israel's borders. Ben-Gurion ordered that whatever forces were necessary should be deployed to take the Negev from Egypt. The battle for the Negev was fought from 11 June 1948 to 6 January 1949, when it was seized from the Egyptians.

Immediately Egypt began negotiations for an armistice agreement with the Israelis and signed an agreement on 24 February
1949. This was to form the basis for a later peace agreement.
The borders were drawn along the lines marking the existing
positions of the armies. Lebanon, Jordan and Syria followed suit
and signed armistice treaties the same year.

The main problem to be dealt with was the refugee problem.
A reconciliation committee was formed and Arab and Israeli
delegates were invited to Lausanne to discuss the most important issues, particularly the refugee problem. The Arabs stated
that the return of the refugees would be the basis for establishing peace in the area. The Israelis felt that this issue should be
suspended until a final peace agreement was made. The Israeli
delegate agreed, however, to support a protocol comprising
three main principles:

1. respect for the boundaries agreed in the partition plan, with
   any modifications required for technical reasons;
2. consent to Jerusalem becoming an international city,
3. the return of the refugees and the restoration of their
   property.

The Arab parties agreed to these terms and signed the protocol on 12 May 1949; on the same day Israel was accepted as
a member of the UN. By this time, however, the number of
Palestinians living as refugees in neighbouring countries was
approaching one million.

11
Arabs and Jews

Peace with Israel

Making peace with Israel has been a long process in the short history of the Arab–Israeli conflict. At the armistice talks between Egypt and Israel which took place under UN auspices in Rhodes in 1949, Mahmoud Riad, a member of the Egyptian delegation later to become Egypt's Foreign Minister and Secretary General of the Arab League, was asked by an Israeli delegate, 'Why cannot Egypt and Israel have peace right now? Why do we need this transitional period? We are ready to make peace along the cease-fire lines, to be the permanent boundaries between us.' Mahmoud Riad answered, 'No, we cannot accept you. An armistice, that is one thing, but to make peace with you would mean that we have to accept that you are here to stay. We are not ready. This situation in our country and in the Arab world will not permit it. We cannot yet live in peace with you.'

Further efforts were made in 1952 after the Egyptian Revolution. An Egyptian diplomat stationed in Paris sent a report to Egypt indicating that in 1951 he had been approached by an Israeli diplomat offering to open a channel for peace talks between Egypt and Israel. By this time the Free Officers were in control of Egypt. Nasser encouraged the contact and talks started. Nasser insisted, however, that the talks should remain secret until the signing of an agreement appeared possible.

The Israeli agenda focused on the mutual acceptance of armistice lines as permanent borders, an immediate non-aggression pact, an agreement on the future of the Gaza Strip, efforts to solve the refugee problem in the Gaza Strip, efforts to obtain military and economic aid from the US and other sources, co-operation in regional security, co-ordination of Israel's position and activities in the UN, and establishment of commercial ties between the two countries. Israel's priority was to secure safe passage for Israeli shipping through the Suez Canal. Egypt's priority was to rid Egypt of British forces. The Egyptians indicated to Israel that, although these two issues were not directly related, Israel's help in getting the British out of Egypt would encourage Egypt to look favourably at Israel's request.

Over two years of negotiation there were signs of goodwill. Physical hostilities between the two countries ceased, but attacks from other Arab countries persisted. In October 1953 Palestinian commandos attacked a Jewish village near Tel-Aviv, killing a woman and her two children. In reprisal Israel launched a retaliatory commando raid on the village of Qibya in Jordan, killing sixty-nine people. This set back the negotiations. The Israeli representation at the secret negotiations claimed that this disproportionate reprisal was the work of the Israeli hardliners in the government.

In 1959 agreement was reached between the British and the Egyptians on British withdrawal from Egypt. Some Israeli hardliners were deeply concerned that the Suez Canal was left under Egyptian control, and that the military buffer zone between Egypt and Israel was removed. A plan was devised, sanctioned by the Israeli Defence Minister, Pinhas Lavor, and with the knowledge of Prime Minister Sharrett, to implement sabotage operations in Cairo against American targets in order to damage US–Egyptian relations and thereby delay the British troop withdrawal.

The operation was uncovered by the Egyptian authorities and the Israeli spy ring was captured. This was a blow to Sharrett. Nasser told his negotiators that Sharrett was part of the moderate tendency in Israel seeking peace but that Egypt should continue with the secret negotiations until the moderates found a solution to their own internal problems.

Transjordan, and later Jordan, had been involved in negotiations with the Jewish Agency as early as the 1930s. In 1946 Prince Abdullah offered to agree to the partition plan in return for Jewish financial aid. In 1947 Abdullah offered to agree to the plan and to recognize an independent Jewish state in part of Palestine in return for US recognition of Jordan as a kingdom and himself as King. This led to direct negotiation between Abdullah and Golda Meir, who was acting head of the Jewish Agency's political department. The King had agreed to the establishment of a Jewish state in parts of Palestine already occupied by Jews, but in November of the same year the UN General Assembly adopted the partition plan. As a result, Jordanian forces entered Palestine to replace the British forces as they withdrew from Palestine in the area designated for the Arabs.

Correspondence was maintained between Abdullah and the Jews up to 1948, when Golda Meir visited Amman. This was shortly after the Deir Yassin massacre, and the King told Meir that he had to go along with the rest of the Arab League. Heikal gives details of this in his *The Secret Channels*:

> After the conquest, the Arab world was divided and Israel became a state of 8000 square miles, one third larger than the UN Resolution of 1947 had intended. Israel was not, however, the only winner of the 1948–49 war. The other was Abdullah, whose secret deal with Golda Meir brought most of the spoils he had wanted.[1]

Fatah and the PLO

In 1958, an organization called Fatah was founded by Yasser Arafat and others. 'Fatah' was a reverse mnemonic for 'Hizb al-Tahrir al-Filastini' (the Palestinian Liberation Party). It was headed by a general secretariat under Arafat's leadership and had its own democratic institutions, of which the largest and most representative was the Fatah Congress with twelve hundred members.[2] The founders managed to establish a base for Fatah in most of the Arab countries. The first training camp was in Algeria and was a base for one hundred fighters.

In the same year Nasser summoned the Arab leaders to a summit in Cairo to discuss Israel's action to divert water from the River Jordan, by pipeline, to the Negev desert. The main concern was that Israel's action would strengthen its capacity to absorb large numbers of new immigrants.

The summit did not reach any definite solutions, except that Nasser agreed to support a plan to establish an institution to represent the Palestinians. The Arab leaders delegated a Palestinian leader, Ahmad al-Shukairy,[3] to explore ways of setting up a representative body for all Palestinians, and this ultimately became the Palestine Liberation Organization.

This act was considered to be the first attempt to bring the Palestinian issue back into the international political arena. Shukairy toured the Arab world and discussed with Palestinians the proposal of elections to a national assembly to be convened in East Jerusalem. He also put forward the idea of a Palestine Liberation Army to give the organization military support. The assembly was held in Jerusalem at the Ambassador Hotel. Palestinians from all over the world attended. There was a silent struggle between the younger generation represented in the Fatah movement, and the older generation represented in the PLO. The young people felt that the Palestinian Liberation Army might become a puppet of the Arab regimes and that recruitment for the armed struggle would as a consequence be reduced. The Fatah movement opened channels with the PLO and asked it to give secret support to Fatah in attacking Israel. They wanted a relationship similar to that between the Jewish

Agency's mainstream Haganah forces and irregular terrorist groups such as Irgun and the Stern Gang. This proposal was rejected on the basis that it might injure the relationship between the PLO and the Arab governments. Relations between the two organizations subsequently deteriorated.

The leadership of the Fatah movement wanted to demonstrate its strength. One group proposed to launch immediate attacks on Israeli targets, but the lack of funds and of arms put this task somewhat out of their reach. Egypt wanted restraint, but Syria accepted and encouraged the idea of immediate attacks on Israel and even opened training camps. The members of Fatah were divided on the question of attacks. Those not in favour of them based their argument on the fact that they were not ready. Arafat's side won on a basis of compromise. Fatah would start its attacks, but under another name 'al-Asifa' (the Storm). If al-Asifa succeeded, Fatah would then endorse the armed struggle. If al-Asifa did not succeed, then it and not the main movement would take the responsibility for failure.

Many members of Fatah and the fighters still did not believe that Arafat was serious in launching attacks on Israel. The first operation was to attack an Israeli phosphate plant with a home-made bomb. When challenged that a single bomb attack would not really help the armed struggle, Arafat answered that 'when the fuse of this bomb goes off, it will cause an explosion not only in the phosphate factory but all over the Middle East'.

The Fatah movement launched a few operations. These were not very effective in a military sense, but they were used as a way to demonstrate to the Arab world that there was an armed struggle. This had consequences for raising financial support from Kuwait, Qatar and Saudi Arabia. In 1966 the Saudi government began discreetly supplying Fatah with arms. Most of the Arab countries bordering Israel were, however, reluctant to encourage these raids. The Egyptian government was extremely cautious about al-Asifa.

The real outcome of the Fatah raids on Israel was to drive the Arab countries to war with Israel. One of the consequences of the raids was Israeli retaliation in the form of attacks on Syria and Jordan. The PLO was too weak to make any impact on the situation, but Shukairy is reported to have said at the end of May 1967 that the Arab states would crush Israel if war broke out.[4]

Egyptian involvement

At this time, Arab politics were in disarray. The Egyptians were involved in Yemen and Syrian–Egyptian relations were, at best, cool. The West had condemned Egypt as a puppet of the USSR. In late 1965 Nasser was still trying to improve his relations with the USA. Certain factors, however, started to push Egyptian policy towards revolutionary struggle, including co-operation between Saudi Arabia and Iran, the Islamic summit, the sale of US arms to Saudi Arabia and the arms race in the Middle East, not just between the Arab states and Israel, but also between the different Arab regimes.

The political focus of the new regime in Syria was Arab unity in the struggle for Palestine. The result of all of this was to put the whole region into a war mood similar to that which had prevailed in 1956. By the end of October 1966, Syria had given its full support to Fatah, but Egypt was not involved. The Palestinians and Syrians wanted Egyptian support, but Egypt continued to hold back. On 4 November, however, Egypt signed a new defence alliance with Syria. Egypt was now committed to the liberation of Palestine, but was still deeply involved in Yemen. It has been suggested that the reason for Nasser's new alliance with Syria was more as a show of strength and solidarity in an attempt to stabilize the situation without war. A full-scale war against Israel could not, in any case, be conducted without Jordanian involvement.

Egypt had not intended to go to war, but was preparing for this eventuality. On 13 November, Israel carried out a reprisal raid against the Jordanian village of Sammu, near Hebron, with tanks, artillery and aircraft, razing it to the ground. The raid led to riots in Palestinian towns of the West Bank. By early 1967 both Egypt and Israel were accusing each other of troop build-up on the Syrian front. On 7 April exchange of fire occurred between the Israelis and the Syrians. The battle included jet fighters, heavy artillery and tanks. Syria lost six jet fighters. Jordan accused Egypt of failing to protect Syria. Nasser's response was given on 16 May. The Egyptian Chief of Staff requested the withdrawal of the UN Emergency Forces (UNEF) contingent separating Israeli and Egyptian troops along their common border, including the fortifications of Sharm al-Shaykh overlooking the Straits of Tiran. Within hours of the request, Nasser confirmed his intention to close the straits to Israeli shipping. The UN complied with Egypt's request over the following weeks, but Israel considered Egypt's action an act of war.

A few weeks before the war, the position of the USSR was uncertain. The Soviets informed a parliamentary delegation led by Sadat on a state visit to Moscow in May 1967, after Nasser had closed the Straits of Tiran, that an Israeli invasion of Syria was imminent. Nasser sent a delegation to Moscow headed by the War Minister to discuss co-operation between the USSR and Egypt. The intention was to tell the Soviets that Egypt wanted to have first strike against Israel. The Russians were reluctant to help and made clear that they could not support the aggressor, which Egypt would be if it were to attack. They would, however, intervene in the war in support of Egypt if the United States were to become involved.

On 2 June, Nasser met his army commanders and informed them that Egypt could not strike first, since Moscow would not help. The commander of the air force said that losing first strike would be a disaster and would tip the balance of war in Israel's favour. Amer, the chief of the armed forces, replied that Egypt was not willing to fight the United States. Ironically, the United States was actually involved in the field of battle and this was one of the factors that led to the Arabs losing the Six-Day War. Material assistance was deployed on behalf of Israel on 23 May. The United States President authorized an emergency air shipment of armoured personnel carriers, tanks, spare parts for the Hawk-missile air-defence systems, bomb fuses, artillery ammunition and gas masks. These weapons were sent to Israel before the 6 June war. These shipments of military hardware were sent before the President imposed an embargo on all military hardware going to the Middle East.

The US provided aerial reconnaissance to Israel from a US base in West Germany. This was the Thirty-Eighth Tactical Reconnaissance Squadron of the Twenty-Sixth Tactical Reconnaissance Wing of the US Air Force. The pilots, technicians and much of the equipment were supplied by the RAF at Upper Heyford. The identifying marks of the RAF were painted over with a white Star of David on a blue ground on the rear fuselage. New tail numbers were painted on the aircraft corresponding to actual inventory numbers in the Israeli Air Force. The American aerial reconnaissance assistance was a vital aid to Israel.

The war started on 5 June 1967 with surprise Israeli air strikes on all Egyptian airfields. These destroyed a large part of the Egyptian Air Force on the ground. This was intended to enable the ground forces to move into Sinai, to reach Sharm al-Shaykh and open the Straits of Tiran to Israeli shipping. The Israeli ground forces continued to push into Sinai, contrary to Dayan's instructions to keep ten kilometres distant from the Suez Canal. The ground commanders advanced until they reached the east bank of the Suez Canal. The political and military command in Egypt realized that the situation was hopeless and decided to withdraw their troops. Nasser had given

King Hussein of Jordan something less than the whole picture of the situation on the Egyptian front. The Israelis sent a clear message to King Hussein through the UN truce supervisor that if he did not engage in the war Jordan would not be attacked. Jordan could not do this, however, since half its population was Palestinian. For Hussein there was no option but to be a national hero and lose the war, if he was not to be seen as a traitor.

The Israelis destroyed all Jordan's air bases and the Jordanian forces withdrew. Over a period of four days Egypt and Jordan lost Sinai and the West Bank, including Jerusalem. There was debate within the Israeli government about taking the Golan Heights. The Americans thought that Israel should take the Heights, especially since the Syrians were the cause of much killing before the war.

One opinion was that to continue the push towards the Golan Heights would encourage the Russians to enter the war on the side of Syria. The prevailing opinion, however, was that the attack should go ahead. There was a period of great tension between the USA and the Soviet Union. The Soviets used the hotline between Moscow and Washington to try to defuse the crisis. The Soviets deployed their forces on alert to stop the Israeli advance towards Damascus, and the Americans sent the Sixth Fleet to the region, where it took up position fifty miles off the Syrian coast. All sides were relying on the UN to reach a solution, and on 10 June 1967 at 6.30 p.m. a cease-fire came into effect.

After the Six-Day War

In Egypt, President Nasser declared that he assumed full responsibility and offered his resignation from public life. He asked Zakariyya Mohieddin to take over the presidency, but there were mass public demonstrations insisting that he should stay and therefore he withdrew his resignation. The outcome of the war was that Israel became the dominant military power in the region. Israel's troops were stationed on the Suez Canal, the Red Sea and the River Jordan and held a line on Syria only thirty miles from Damascus. They controlled the whole of Palestine, including the West Bank of the Jordan and Jerusalem, along with one million Palestinians in the West Bank and Gaza Strip, and they occupied the Sinai Peninsula and a thousand square miles of Syrian territory on the Golan Heights. Furthermore, one million Arabs were displaced. Some 350,000 Palestinians fled from the West Bank to the East Bank of the Jordan. For at least 150,000 of these, this was the second time that they had been made refugees. A further 116,000 people were refugees in Syria from the villages and farms of the Golan Heights.[5]

The war of attrition from mid-1967 to October 1973

The Egyptian reaction shortly after the cease-fire was to launch new tactics against Israel – not a full-scale war but a long, low-intensity campaign of attacks aimed at bolstering flagging Arab morale and at making Israel feel the emptiness of victory without peace.

On the Egyptian front there was a struggle over points in the Sinai Peninsula that the Israelis had failed to occupy in their rush to the canal on 8 June. After a famous battle for a position called Ras El-Esh in the early days of July, the fighting settled into Eilat. Israel retaliated by shelling the towns of Suez, Isma'iliyya and Port Said, which became virtually hostages to Israel because of their proximity to the front.

At a Fatah meeting in Damascus after the war, twenty Palestinians, representing their compatriots all over the world, discussed what the next step should be. The more cautious of them thought that to continue the fight would be madness. The argument was put forward that the insistence on launching armed struggle back in 1964 had caused the problems that the Arabs now faced following the Six-Day War. Yasser Arafat was convinced that the struggle must go on, and it was his opinion that prevailed.

Many trips were made to the West Bank to promote the Palestinian armed struggle. Security was low key at first and Arafat used to come and go relatively easily as he organized the basis of the struggle. Fatah's attempt to create an armed revolution in the West Bank was ineffective, however, because the inhabitants of the West Bank, after two decades of Jordanian rule, were still looking to Jordan as their guardian. There was also a severe shortage of funds and weapons. These factors did not deter the leaders of Fatah, who, with their limited resources, launched attacks on Israel. The Israelis, however, possessed intelligence files left behind by the Jordanians and arrested hundreds of political activists. They smashed cells of activity and dynamited the houses of those suspected of sheltering activists. In December 1967 the Israelis announced that since June they had killed sixty commandos and imprisoned three hundred.

The different Palestinian movements failed to unite under one main group, and the PLO was discredited in the eyes of the Palestinians and other Arabs. Most Palestinians rejected Shukairy and the old guard. Some members of the PLO approached Arafat to see if he could help in shaping the PLO to meet the new challenge. Among these was Abdulmajid Shoman, Chairman of the Arab Bank. Shoman had maintained close ties with a growing network of wealthy businessmen in the Palestinian diaspora, using them to good effect in his role as Chairman of the Palestine National Fund. He approached Arafat after 1967 and asked him to help revive and improve the PLO.

Matters were developing rapidly. In December 1967 seven of Shukairy's colleagues on the executive committee demanded his resignation. When he refused, funding to the PLO was cut. Shukairy appealed to President Nasser, but Nasser refused to intervene. There was a need for new blood to look after the affairs of the PLO. Shukairy's replacement as PLO Chairman was a lawyer who was to act as a caretaker, with the job of preparing for the guerrilla takeover. Eventually Fatah and several other smaller groups combined and took control of the PLO under a committee headed by the Fatah leader Yasser Arafat. The Fatah movement was the dominant group in military and political affairs. Other strong groups included the PFLP (Popular Front for the Liberation of Palestine) led by George Habash.

The Palestine National Council meeting in Cairo 1969 endorsed the leadership of the PLO. The new policy of the PLO was to establish a democratic secular system in Palestine, but to achieve such a political entity would require the continuation of the armed struggle. The PLO organized militarily, and subsequently recruited militants, and managed to control the Palestinians under the Arab states. Furthermore they needed to challenge Israeli control over the Palestinians in the West Bank and Gaza by all means, including commando attacks and material, political and economic support of the representatives of the Palestinian people everywhere.

In 1968 the Palestinian guerrillas belonging to Fatah and other groups had established bases across the border in Jordan, and launched attacks against Israeli targets. This culminated in confrontation between Palestinian guerrilla fighters and Israeli armed forces at al-Karameh.

The Palestinians were operating in the Jordan Valley under the blessing of the Jordanian army. The Israelis sent in their troops on 21 March 1968, but before this Israeli aircraft dropped leaflets urging the Palestinian fighters to surrender. When the army crossed the Jordanian border the fighting was almost hand to hand. The Jordanian army became involved, fighting along-side the Palestinians. The Israelis suffered an unanticipated level of casualties: twenty-eight dead, sixty-nine injured and thirty-four tanks hit. Palestinian losses were ninety-eight killed out of four hundred freedom fighters. The support of the Jordanian army was crucial in this victory. Without it the Palestinians would have been crushed. This battle did, however, become the symbol of the Fatah movement.

One effect of al-Karameh was to impress upon Israel the reality of Palestinian armed resistance. Volunteers now poured into Jordan to join Fatah and the other movements. Another breakthrough was the co-operation between Egypt and Fatah. Nasser was at first reluctant, but then opened Egypt up to Fatah for training and helped Fatah to meet the Soviets. This support helped Fatah to become the focus of the struggle for the Palestinian people and gained it recognition from the rest of the Arab world. Through the Algerians, Fatah was allowed by President de Gaulle to set up its first European mission in Paris in 1968.

On 3 February 1969 Arafat was elected as Chairman of the Executive Committee of the PLO. At the Arab Summit in Morocco, Arafat asked the Arab states for the equivalent of some forty million US dollars. Not all Palestinian groups were happy about the Fatah takeover, however, and the main leftist group led by Habash refused to recognize Fatah and boycotted the National Council in protest. Severe difficulties were awaiting the PLO in Jordan, the only front for the armed struggle against Israel. The various Palestinian factions in Jordan became more powerful and began to act as a state within a state. Within the PLO there was a difference of opinion as to how to deal with Jordan. At one extreme was the pseudo- Marxist Popular Front for the Liberation of Palestine, led by George Habash. He called for a revolution not only against the Jews in Palestine, but also against reactionary Arab leaders such as King Hussein. There was no co-ordination between the Palestinian factions.

In the summer of 1968 three members of the PFLP hijacked
an Israeli plane *en route* from Rome to Tel Aviv and forced
it to divert to Algiers, demanding in exchange for the Israeli
passengers and crew the release of Palestinians held in Israeli
gaols. Algeria released the plane and passengers and two days
later Israel released sixteen Palestinians. This made a powerful
impression on the public of the strength of the Palestinian armed
struggle, but played into the hands of its enemies.

Relations between the Jordanian authorities and the different Palestinian factions deteriorated from 1968 until 1970.
The authority of the Jordanian army and police force was
undermined as the Palestinians became a law unto themselves.
Palestinian refugee camps in Jordan became no-go areas. King
Hussein's authority was challenged. In 1969 Hussein proposed
an agreement between the PLO and himself to co-operate and
promote non-aggression between the two sides, but the attitude
of the Palestinians was to reject any form of external control.
They formed their own police, built roadblocks and imposed
paramilitary rule.

There was chaos, and all sides committed atrocities during
this time. One result of this situation was that the Palestinians
lost much of their support among the other Arab countries and
even began to lose the goodwill of Egypt.[6]

In 1969 the American administration proposed a peace settlement. The Secretary of State, William Rogers, put forward
a plan for an agreement between Israel on one side, and Egypt
and Jordan on the other. The proposal included Israeli withdrawal as part of a package settlement, cessation of the state of
war, secure and recognized borders, demilitarized zones and
special arrangements in Gaza and Sharm al-Shaykh, freedom
of navigation through the Straits of Tiran, that Egypt should
allow Israel to use the Suez Canal, a just settlement of the refugee problem, and mutual respect for sovereignty. Lastly it was
proposed that the agreement should be deposited with the UN,

endorsed by the Security Council, and mutually binding. There was also to be a parallel Israeli–Jordanian agreement that was to address most aspects of the Palestinian problem.

The Soviets rejected the plan, and the Egyptians abstained, but by July 1970 the Egyptians agreed in principle on a US revised peace agreement. Here the Palestinians made a grave mistake. Impatient to see the Egyptian response to the Rogers plans, the Palestinians unleashed a storm of protest among the resistance organization in Jordan. Arafat and Fatah attacked Nasser by name and threatened in a radio broadcast to use bullets to quash any attempt to impose a political solution. Nasser's response was to close down PLO broadcasting stations in Cairo and to expel many radical Palestinians from the country. At this point the Palestinians in Amman realized that the movement had damaged itself. After several attempts, Nasser agreed to meet the Palestinians in Alexandria. He delivered a clear message that they should not try to oust King Hussein, saying, 'Don't give me heroic speeches about resistance. I want to keep Hussein. I am not asking for your secrets, but I tell you: don't try to do such a thing.'

The situation in Jordan worsened during August and September. King Hussein warned the Palestinian forces that he would not tolerate any challenge to his authority. This caused more civil unrest in Amman, including an assassination attempt on Hussein. The Palestinians called for a general strike to protest against Hussein's co-operation with American peace plans, but it was now clear that something had to be done to bring the Palestinians under control.[7]

Black September

Arab mediators advised the PLO to compromise with Hussein, but the latter was already making plans. On 16 September 1970

Hussein declared martial law and announced that he was setting up a military government to restore law and order and security. Within twenty-four hours, bloody fighting had broken out in Amman as the army closed in on the Palestinian military personnel. Arafat tried to talk to the King, but he was 'unavailable'. The expectation had been that within forty-eight hours the situation would be brought under control, but Palestinian reaction was underestimated and the fighting escalated.

The Palestinians managed to take the city of Irbid, north of Amman, and declared it a Palestinian republic. Fighting intensified between the Palestinians and the Jordanian army. The Arab League sent a delegation to try to stop the fighting. This included President Numeiri of the Sudan and the Crown Prince of Kuwait. Their mission was to locate Arafat in Amman and present a strong request from Nasser that Arafat should accompany them to Cairo. They managed to smuggle Arafat out of Amman disguised as a Kuwaiti official. The eventual outcome was a fourteen-point agreement, including a cease-fire and the withdrawal of all forces from Amman and their regrouping in agreed areas suitable for guerrilla attacks on Israel. The agreement was sealed with a handshake between Arafat and Hussein.

Arafat estimated the Palestinian casualties at twenty thousand, but according to the Red Cross the figure was probably around three thousand. Matters did not proceed as the Palestinians had anticipated, however, because Nasser, exhausted from the strain of the previous weeks, died of a heart attack on 28 September 1970. Neither Jordan nor the Palestinians seriously intended to carry out the agreement signed in Cairo. Hussein wanted all the Palestinian fighters out of Jordan. In a secret negotiation between Jordan and Israel he had promised to stop all Palestinian attacks against Israel from Jordanian soil. Talks between Jordan and the Palestinians were back to square one. Jordan now had a new hardline Prime Minister, Wasfi al-Tal, who suppressed the Palestinian military resistance. Arafat's life was again in danger. The Kuwaiti

Ambassador in Amman and a Palestinian minister tried to take him to meet the King, but during the car journey he asked to be taken to the Syrian border. This was the end of the Palestinian military presence in Jordan. Egypt now had a new President, Anwar Sadat, whose focus was more Egyptian than Arab nationalist and Egypt did not come to the rescue this time.

The irony is that only Israel gained immediate benefit from the conflict between the Jordanians and Palestinians. One of the side effects of the crushing of the Palestinians in Jordan, however, was to take the conflict abroad, resulting in a series of terrorist attacks on civilian targets.

The Black September movement, which formed shortly afterwards and which was named after the month of the massacre of Palestinians in Jordan, was a Palestinian response to the shelling of the refugee camps in Amman, which killed men, women and children indiscriminately. Unjustifiably, but unsurprisingly, many civil targets were hit. The Israelis suffered civilian casualties, and the killing of Israeli athletes at the Munich Olympics shocked the world. Wasfi al-Tal was assassinated in Cairo. The Israelis and some Arab regimes retaliated against Black September. There was a hate campaign against Arabs in general and the Palestinians in particular.

The Palestinian poet Mahmoud Darwish attempted to explain the feelings of desperation that drove the acts of terrorism:

The one who has turned me into a refugee has made a bomb
   of me,
I know that I will die
I know that I am venturing into a lost battle today, because it
   is the battle for the future.
I know that Palestine on the map is far away from me
I know that you have forgotten its name and that you use a
   new name for it
I know all that

That is why I carry it to your streets, your homes, and your
    bedrooms
Palestine is not a land, gentlemen of the jury
Palestine has become bodies that move
They move to the streets of the world, singing the song of
    death
Because the New Christ has given up his cross and gone out
    of Palestine.

12

Towards liberation

The October War

When the Palestinian freedom fighters left Jordan, some sought asylum in Israel rather than risk falling into Jordanian hands. It was becoming apparent to the Palestinians that in addition to the Israelis they were also facing Arab hostility. They felt that all they could do was to attempt to set up a state on any area of liberated Palestinian soil. Fatah hardliners were against the concept of the mini-state, fearing that this might be the end of the road. Furthermore, there was the problem of the refugees, and the Jordanian plans to create a new united Arab Kingdom including the West Bank and Gaza after Israeli withdrawal. Meanwhile, the Israelis were making efforts to demonstrate by staging municipal elections that the Palestinians in the occupied territories had settled down under occupation. The PLO reaction was a series of assassinations of those whom it considered had collaborated with either the Israelis or the Jordanians and thereby undermined the Palestinians in the West Bank.

At a meeting of the Palestinian National Council in September 1972, President Sadat of Egypt urged the Palestinians to form a government in exile. It was a plan for the Palestinians to make a break from the past, to denounce terrorist acts, and to define their aims. However, Sadat warned the PLO that a government in exile might end in the same manner as, twenty years previously, the All-Palestine movement, sponsored by the Arab League, had failed. At the same time Jordan was putting pressure on the PLO in the West Bank. On 10 April 1973, Israeli commandos stormed an apartment occupied by three

PLO senior officials in Beirut, killing all of them. The Lebanese authorities in the area did nothing to stop the killings. The Palestinians suspected that the Lebanese Christian leadership had helped the Israelis. Less than six months later the Egyptians and Syrians launched a full-scale war against Israel, the October War. Sadat had tried to approach the Americans for a peaceful settlement, but the Americans and Israelis had not responded and he felt that he had to do something to move the Israelis. The no peace, no war situation had to change in order for things to go forward.[1]

The October War took the Israelis by surprise. In ninety minutes the Egyptian forces created a bridgehead through the Suez Canal and kept their advantage the next day up to a point five kilometres east of the canal, putting Israel's fortifications on the canal's east bank fully in Egyptian hands. Heikal notes that the Soviets informed Sadat that the Syrians had asked them to arrange for a cease-fire on the Syrian front. Sadat felt that this put the Egyptian forces in a compromising situation. After correspondence with President Asad, the latter informed Sadat that Syria had not asked the Soviets for a cease-fire but had declared that any cessation of hostilities must be connected to a return of lands. He insisted that the Syrian forces were doing well and inflicting heavy casualties on the Israelis. Heikal notes,

> What lay behind this incident was that Sadat, whether he knew it or not, had begun to prepare himself psychologically for loosening his alliance with Syria and was looking for a pretext. What he most wanted was the freedom to act alone, independently of Syria, if his contacts with Kissinger bore fruit. The fear that Syria might reject US proposals which Egypt would be prepared to accept was high in mind.

Following the October War, the UN General Assembly agreed on Resolution 238 and negotiations began between Israel and

Egypt to disengage their forces. The Americans were the sponsors of these negotiations and were represented by Henry Kissinger. This was the first time that the two highest military officers of Israel and Egypt had sat face to face. These negotiations were the beginning of the peace process.

Sadat opened a channel of communication.[2] On 7 November 1977 in the Egyptian Parliament in an open session, Sadat announced that he was ready to go to the end of the world, even to the Knesset, in search of peace. Chairman Yasser Arafat was present, and there was Arab disbelief at what Sadat had said. Some thought it was a political manoeuvre. To put all minds at rest, Sadat met the editors of all of the important newspapers to clarify his real intentions. He confirmed that the ball was now in Israel's court.

On 17 November, with the help of the American administration, Sadat received a formal invitation to talks from the Israeli Prime Minister. Sadat went to Syria to meet President Asad and to persuade him not to object to his move until he saw the outcome. If it were successful then Syria should follow suit. After a long meeting between the two presidents, Syria refused Sadat's plan. On his way back to Egypt, Sadat authorized his administration to go ahead with his planned visit to Israel and on 20 November he delivered a speech in the Knesset:[3]

> I come to you today on solid ground to shape a new life and to establish peace. Any life that is lost in a war constitutes a huge wall between us, which you tried to build up, but it was destroyed in 1973. Conceive with me a peace agreement in Geneva that we can herald to a world thirsting for peace, a peace agreement based on the following points: ending the occupation of the Arab territories occupied in 1967, achievement of the fundamental rights of the Palestinian people and their right to self determination, including their right to establish their own state. The right of all states in the area to live in

peace . . . commitment in the region to administer the relations amongst them in accordance with the objectives and principles of the UN Charter, particularly the principles concerning the non-use of force and a solution of difference among them by peaceful means.

You, sorrowing mother, you, widowed wife, you the son who lost a brother or a father, all the victims of wars, fill the air and space with recitals of peace, fill bosoms and hearts with aspirations of peace.

The Israeli Cabinet met Sadat in Jerusalem and offered a partial withdrawal from Sinai and limited self-rule for the Palestinians. Sadat was angry because he felt that nothing had been achieved. Another meeting, in Britain, failed, following which President Carter invited Begin and Sadat to Camp David, the Presidential retreat, on 30 July 1978. After laboured negotiations, on 26 March 1979 a peace treaty was signed on the White House lawn between the Egyptians and Israelis.

The Camp David talks were more about Egypt and Israel than about Palestine. The reduction in tension between the two caused a rift in Arab relations in general and set back the Palestinian cause. The Arabs had lost the core of Arab unity, which had been represented by Egypt for many years. The peace treaty was merely a bilateral agreement between Israel and Egypt and the talk about Palestinian self-determination was completely spurious.[4]

The Arab reaction was to cut all diplomatic and economic ties with Egypt, move the Arab League from Cairo to Tunis and suspend Egypt's membership. Syria now became the main player in Arab–Israeli politics and began to adopt all the different Palestinian liberation organizations. The new enemy was Egypt. Certain Palestinian factions carried out attacks against Egyptian targets. The Arab world was simmering with anger. Lebanon was entering its fifth year of civil war between the Muslims and Christians.

The Palestinians and Lebanon

After the exodus of the Palestinian freedom fighters from Jordan in 1970, they took refuge in the south of Lebanon. This was not to be their permanent base, however, and a series of factors led to their eventual expulsion. These factors included the loss of Egyptian support of the Palestinian cause as a consequence of the Egyptian–Israeli peace treaty. The PLO tried to compensate for this by making moves towards the new Iranian religious state, but this proved a short-lived friendship.

In the mid-1970s the PLO and other Palestinian organizations effectively controlled Lebanon. Dormant inter-religious and inter-ethnic tensions that existed in Lebanon were aroused by the introduction of this new element and exacerbated by the economic gap between rich and poor. The different fighting forces in Lebanon changed their allegiances by the day. Meanwhile the Syrians monitored the situation, eventually deciding to enter Lebanon on the pretext that they did not want a new power on their doorstep. Syria gained control of most of the country, but heavy fighting in Beirut resulted in many civilian casualties among the Palestinian refugees. The Syrians' primary concern at first was to support the Christians. After twenty months of fighting, the PLO was dominant in the border area and West Beirut and the Christians were dominant in northern Lebanon and East Beirut. The Syrians kept the balance between the two.

However, the Christians fell out with the Syrians and looked for help from the Israelis. At first Israel supplied the Christians with arms on condition that the latter had to fight the war themselves, but matters changed when Ariel Sharon became Defence Minister in 1981. His aim was to drive the Palestinians out of south Lebanon – to stop the shelling of Israeli settlements – and to crush the PLO headquarters in Beirut once and for all.

The Israelis had two possible plans for intervention. The first was that Israel would go thirty miles into south Lebanon to secure their settlements. The second was to make a full-scale invasion of Lebanon as far as Beirut to finish off the Palestinians. The Christian old guard refused these proposals on the grounds that Lebanon still constituted part of the Arab world and they could not fight alongside the Israelis. At the same time, Bashir Gemayel[5] tried to negotiate with the Palestinians by telling them to leave Lebanon and in return he would stop the Israeli invasion.

Israel was looking for a justification to enter Lebanon. The chance came when the Israeli Ambassador to London was shot and injured in the head. The Israeli Cabinet met during the night of 4 June 1982. The attempt on the life of the Ambassador was the trigger for the Israelis' full-scale invasion of Lebanon. The assassins were not, however, connected to the PLO but to a different faction, the organization controlled by Abu Nidal (Sabri al-Banna). Security chief Shalom, Prime Minister Begin's adviser on war against terrorism, suggested that Begin should tell the Cabinet about the Abu Nidal organization. He wanted the ministers to know that Abu Nidal was not close to the PLO and that Arafat could not control Abu Nidal. This information could not stop the invasion, however. To Begin, all Palestinians were PLO and were to be punished.

The invasion

When all the information indicated that an Israeli invasion of Lebanon was imminent, Egypt was out of the picture. In 1980, Sadat asked Said Kamal, the PLO representative in Cairo, to attend a meeting. This was unusual, especially since the PLO had been anti-Sadat after the peace treaty with Israel. The purpose of the meeting was to encourage the PLO to start talking to the Israelis and try to reach a solution. Sadat suggested that any talks should not be directly with the Israelis or through the American government, but through the Jewish lobby, especially in the US. Stephen Cohen, director of an American academic institute dealing with Middle East studies and having links with all the major Zionist and Jewish organizations in the US, was named specifically as a contact. Sadat felt that Cohen was best placed to put the PLO in touch with appropriate Jewish contacts who were not members of the Israeli Government.

After some initial correspondence with the PLO headquarters in Beirut, it was agreed that Kamal would meet Cohen in his private capacity, not as an official of the PLO. The PLO dismissed him tactically to free him to attend the New York Congress, an academic meeting between Arabs and Israelis, in a private capacity. In 1981, the Americans informed Sadat that Israeli patience was reaching its limits and that an invasion of Lebanon was likely at any time. Sadat summoned Kamal and asked him to convey an urgent message to Arafat that the PLO was surrounded by hostile Israeli, Syrian and Christian forces and would be squeezed between them.

On 6 October 1981 Sadat was assassinated during a military parade to mark the October War. A few months after Sadat's assassination, Stephen Cohen arrived in Cairo for a meeting with Kamal to discuss 'an important matter'. When they met, Cohen asked to see Arafat. The Egyptians offered a plane to take Cohen and Kamal to Beirut. It must be noted that, to Kamal's surprise, Cohen already had contacts with Abu Jihad, then Arafat's deputy. Kamal asked what would be the purpose of a meeting with Arafat and Abu Jihad? Cohen replied that if Sharon attacked Lebanon and pressed as far as Beirut, the PLO would be able to offer little resistance.

At a meeting in Arafat's place of hiding in Beirut, Cohen asked Arafat and Salah Khalaf[6] how long the PLO could resist the kind of attack anticipated. They indicated that they would be able to resist for six months, not counting the Arab reaction. Cohen said that the Israelis were not concerned about the regional reaction. He ended the meeting saying that he doubted that the PLO could withstand the predicted attack.

On 28 May 1982 Hosni Mubarak, the new Egyptian President, sent a further warning to Arafat that the Israelis were going ahead with their planned invasion as far as Beirut, not just the thirty-kilometre zone in the south of the country. He stated, 'Maybe you would find it best to avert the attack now by making a political move . . . the time has come to put your sword in its sheath before it is too late.' The PLO took no notice.

Another message came to Arafat from King Hussein, who sent his Foreign Minister to warn of imminent Israeli invasion. Arafat's response was that the PLO was ready. On 6 June 1982 the Israeli forces pushed across Lebanon's southern border, supported by air and naval units. Some forty thousand Israeli troops in hundreds of armoured personnel carriers crossed the border and continued moving northwards, beyond the thirty-kilometre zone. Within eight days Sharon's forces reached West Beirut, home to half a million Lebanese and Palestinians plus the Eighty-Fifth Syrian Brigade, and laid siege for more than two months.

Sharon continued shelling the city with the sole aim of driving out the Palestinians and the Syrians. The Americans sent Habib to act as a mediator between the Lebanese government and the Israelis. The outcome was the exodus of the Palestinian freedom fighters. Arafat gave a written commitment and in twelve days the Palestinians were out. The problem then was to find somewhere to go. The Egyptians and Syrians refused to take them in. The Jordanians took in those who carried Jordanian citizenship. Some of the remainder went to Southern Yemen, Sudan, Iraq and Algeria. Arafat and his commanders went to Tunis. This was the third exile for the Palestinians – a great loss of hope as they contemplated fighting for Palestine from a distance of fifteen hundred miles. No armed Palestinians remained in Lebanon, only the refugees in the camps.

The President elect of Lebanon, Bashir Gemayel, was invited to meet Prime Minister Begin in Nahariyya in northern Israel but was assassinated by a bomb at the Phalange party headquarters before he even took office. His followers sought revenge and in September 150 Christian Phalangists entered the Palestinian camps of Sabra and Shatila. They were allowed in by the Israeli forces that were controlling movement in and out of the camps. The militia massacred between seven hundred and one thousand people (some reports say two thousand). The majority of the refugees in the camps were civilians: old men, women and children. There were certainly no armed Palestinians. There was international outcry and in February 1983 Sharon was forced out of office. Six months later Begin resigned. As a result of the Israeli invasion a total of approximately forty thousand Palestinians and Lebanese were killed, one hundred thousand were injured and half a million made homeless. The major Palestinian political and social institutions were destroyed.[7]

The new hope

The Palestinian political and armed freedom fighters were dispersed into the Arab world, and the head of the PLO, Yasser Arafat, found refuge in Tunisia. The Arabs blamed Arafat for his shortsightedness. The Israelis were content that their mission had ended in the elimination of the Palestinians from Lebanon. Meanwhile, however, world media attention was focused on the Iran–Iraq war and on the situation in Afghanistan, and the Palestinian situation became less prominent. By this time much of the Arab world had developed an anti-Palestinian attitude, blaming the Palestinians for the lack of development in the Arab world and labelling them as troublemakers, or at least a burden. The refugee camps, particularly those in Lebanon, represented the depths of human misery and degradation, and their occupants were still treated as prisoners and prevented from working to earn a living. No building materials were allowed into the camps and the refugees had to carry ID cards, which were renewed by the Lebanese authorities. There was no freedom of travel, and violation of any administrative order would result in deportation or imprisonment.

The situation in the occupied territories was even worse. A whole generation had now been brought up under Israeli occupation, a life governed by barbed wire and an armed occupying force, military orders, restriction of movement, house demolitions, land confiscations, detention, deportation and other methods of systematic degradation and demoralization aimed at wiping out Palestinian identity and rights. New settlements were being built in the West Bank and Gaza and Jewish immigrants were pouring into the country from all over the world. The occupying force paid no attention to infrastructure in the Palestinian areas. Ironically, Palestinian workers, unable to support their families in any other way, were forced to work for Israeli contractors building settlements for Jewish immigrants, at rates of pay that would have been unacceptable to Israeli workers. They were not allowed to form or join unions and at the slightest incident of protest or resistance Gaza and the West Bank were closed, preventing inhabitants from travelling to work. By blatant use of military force and economic leverage the Israelis kept the upper hand. Human rights abuses by the Israeli government were widespread but largely ignored by the rest of the world. There was, and remains, a reluctance to accuse the Israeli state of such violations because such accusation, however legitimate, attracts counter-accusation of anti-Semitism.

In 1982 Sinai was returned to Egypt, and East Jerusalem and the Golan Heights were formally annexed by Israel. The Israelis insisted on referring to the West Bank as Judea and Samaria. Camp David offered little hope, being primarily concerned with the relationship between Israel and Egypt, rather than Palestinian issues. The situation was one of frustration and desperation.

The *Intifada*

By the mid-1980s the mood in the occupied territories was one of simmering frustration. New peace proposals involving Jordan, Egypt and Israel were not promising. The US Secretary of State visited the Middle East with the aim of meeting some prominent Palestinians, but pressure from the street prevented this. At this point, Palestinian anger and frustration boiled over and the *Intifada* was born. A community materially and morally subjugated realized it had nothing left to lose. This was an uprising of the people, armed only with stones and crude petrol bombs, against one of the most sophisticated and well-resourced armies in the world. Young boys with stones confronted Israeli soldiers with automatic weapons, like David standing in the face of Goliath. The momentum of the *Intifada* was maintained and proved problematic to the Israelis. Suddenly an issue that had been almost dead was back in the headlines. The Israelis tried to target the leaders of the *Intifada*, but the solidarity and organization at street level protected their identities. The Israelis inflicted heavy casualties on the Palestinians and committed abuses towards young Palestinians, but this only served to fuel Palestinian rage. As film of young boys confronting armed soldiers began to appear on television screens worldwide, Israel's friends began to question the legality of Israel's actions. Israel began to lose some of the moral high ground in the propaganda war.

The Israelis kept trying to find ways to stop the *Intifada*. Domestic politics required some kind of military success against the uprising, and the most effective way they could devise was to kill one of the leaders of the PLO. It was said that Khalil al-Wazir, Arafat's deputy, had great influence in the towns of the West Bank and that his word was law. In March 1988, Yitzhak Rabin, as Defence Minister, took the decision to assassinate al-Wazir in Tunisia. On 16 April several Boeing 707s took off from a military base south of Tel Aviv. One of these carried Rabin and other senior Israeli officers and was in constant communication with the team of assassins in another aircraft. Two more 707s acted as fuel tankers, thus eliminating the need to land *en route*. Early on 16 April a ground team located al-Wazir at his villa. They killed his driver and his two armed guards, entered the house, found him in his office, shot him twice in the head and twice in the heart and left.

The killing of al-Wazir was a loss for the PLO, but did not affect the *Intifada*. At first the Palestinians in Tunis were not aware who had initiated the *Intifada*, nor did they have any idea how long it would last. Some eight months after its initial eruption, Arafat realized that he could use it to revive the Palestinian cause after the setback of Lebanon. Edward Said[8] describes how the momentum of the *Intifada* and its success in creating a clear civil alternative to the Israeli occupation regime necessitated a definitive statement of support by the Palestine National Council (PNC) for the *Intifada* as an end to occupation and a relatively non-violent movement. This required an unambiguous claim for Palestinian sovereignty on whatever Palestinian territories were to be vacated by the occupation, with any settlement between the Palestinians and Israelis being based on UN resolutions. The main issue was that the PLO should change its aim from that of a liberation movement to that of an independence movement, especially in the light of Jordan's withdrawal of all claims to the West Bank in 1988 to break legal and administrative ties.

The *Intifada* brought about more radical change within the PLO. The time had come for the PLO to change its policy. It was the time to grasp the chance or lose it. At the nineteenth session of the Palestine National Council, which took place on 12–15 November 1988 in Algeria, known as the '*Intifada* Meeting', Arafat proclaimed the creation of the State of Palestine with the holy city of Jerusalem as its capital, and accepting Resolutions 242 and 338. Up to this point the PLO had denied the right of Israel to exist, but pressure was on them to accept the two resolutions. By accepting the right of Israel to exist, Arafat put the ball in the American court. This was not enough, however, to persuade the Americans to engage in discussion with the PLO. In order to start negotiations, the Americans required one further condition: that the PLO should renounce terrorism.

When Arafat met the Swedish Foreign Minister, Sten Andersson, the latter presented him with a letter from the US Secretary of State, George Schultz, indicating that if the PLO issued a statement renouncing terrorism, this would open the door for talks between the US and the PLO. Arafat answered that he would take their offer to the UN General Assembly, which was to be held in New York on 13 December. However, the US refused Arafat an entry visa, and the whole General Assembly was therefore moved to Geneva for this specific purpose.

Schultz set out exactly what Arafat had to say and made it clear that any deviation would make the US offer void. This put the PLO in a difficult position, since it considered itself a nationalist resistance movement rather than a terrorist movement, and preferred to 'denounce' rather than 'renounce' terrorism. The Americans would not consider the slightest alteration, however. On 7 December 1988 Schultz received a signed statement, which read, 'The Executive Committee of the PLO condemns individual, group and state terrorism in all its forms and will not resort to it.' Arafat indicated that he would make a speech at Geneva saying exactly the same thing.

Arafat gave his speech at the UN General Assembly in Geneva and did not change the words but transposed them in such a way as to make the statement ambiguous. He thought he could get away with this, but Schultz noted the changes and reported them to President Reagan.

The Swedish Foreign Minister informed Arafat that the Americans were not satisfied and that they would have to find an alternative occasion for Arafat to deliver what the Americans dictated. Anderson suggested that Arafat should hold a press conference and make the declaration that the Americans demanded. Arafat remained reluctant, but at a dinner with the Egyptian Ambassador, Musa, later Foreign Minister, it was agreed that Arafat should go ahead with the declaration. The press conference took place, but Arafat gave it a theatrical ending by looking into the camera and asking, 'Do you want me to do a striptease now?'

The PLO had met the requirements for talks with the US, and these started on 16 December 1988 in Tunis. They were suspended shortly afterwards, however, because a group linked with Abul-Abbas, leader of the Palestinian Liberation Front (PLF), carried out an attack on the beach in Tel Aviv in May 1989. The US used this as an excuse to break off talks on the grounds that the raid had violated the conditions on which they were based.

The Second Gulf War

By August 1988 a cease-fire had been implemented in the war between Iran and Iraq. Saddam Hussein was portraying this as an Iraqi victory, but the country was seriously damaged and depleted and in need of funds to rebuild its infrastructure. Iraq's main source of income was oil, but oil prices on the world market were depressed owing to massive overproduction. Iraq and some of the OPEC countries tried to press for a reduction in production but Kuwait refused. Both Kuwait and Saudi Arabia had provided financial support to Iraq throughout the Gulf War, but Saddam Hussein was now hostile to the good relationships that appeared to prevail between Kuwait and the US and resented the apparent lack of appreciation of Iraq's sacrifice in preventing radical Iranian rule from spreading to the rest of the region. Iraq asked America what its reaction would be if Iraq were to annex Kuwait. As late as July 1990, the US Ambassador to Baghdad, April Gilespie, told Saddam Hussein that the USA 'had no opinion' about the border dispute between Iraq and Kuwait.

On 2 August 1990 the US issued an ultimatum to Baghdad to withdraw their forces from Kuwait. The whole world, including most Arab countries, realized that the American ultimatum was serious, especially since it was now obvious that America was the only remaining superpower, the USSR being in the final stages of its collapse. Arafat made a dangerous mistake by appearing to throw in his lot with Saddam Hussein. He believed that America would not attack and that the crisis would be resolved through negotiation between the Arab countries. When the Iraqi forces were defeated in April 1991, Arafat and the PLO were left, along with Jordan and Yemen, separated from the majority of Arab countries that had been against the Iraqi invasion. The PLO lost the financial support of Saudi Arabia and Kuwait. Large numbers of Palestinians had been working in Saudi Arabia and Kuwait, and the majority, particularly in Kuwait, had their contracts terminated. There were many reports of revenge attacks against Palestinians in Kuwait, including torture, beatings and killings. Large numbers of Palestinians were forced out of Kuwait and Saudi Arabia, many of them settling in Jordan. Jordan was struggling to cope

at this point, since this influx was combined with refugees
fleeing Iraq.

A further blow to the PLO came with the assassination of
two key leaders by the Abu Nidal group on 14 January 1991.
No one wanted anything to do with Arafat or the PLO, but
at the same time the Arab masses observed that the USA was
imposing a double standard. Iraq's violation of international law
was punished without mercy and UN resolutions were imposed
by force, but Israel's breaching of UN resolutions which had
made a mockery of the United Nations since 1949 was ignored.
Israel had been illegally occupying territory, annexing lands and
defying the UN for decades, but no punitive sanctions were
imposed against it. Moreover it has had a nuclear capability
that has not been subject to the same investigation by weapons
inspectors as have Iraq's military programmes.

This goes some way towards explaining the rise of militant
factions in the Arab world and the call for changes in the Arab
regimes which would allow a holy war to be carried out against
Israel. The rise of Islamic movements in the occupied territories
was one of the main factors that undermined the PLO. In 1987
when the *Intifada* erupted, many groups, including the Muslim
Brotherhood and the PLO, claimed that they were responsible.
The *Intifada* was, however, an explosion of the anger of the
real Palestinian population, the masses living under occupation.
Nevertheless, as a result of the *Intifada* the Muslim Brotherhood
held a meeting in Gaza in December 1987 with prominent
Muslim leaders. Six of these formed the first Hamas leadership,
which established committees in the political, security, military
and information spheres. There was no definable point where
a decision was made to form the Hamas movement, rather it
emerged over time. Hamas is led by a consultative body whose
members live inside and outside the occupied territories.

Another Islamic movement has also come into the equation.
Islamic Jihad is a splinter group of the Muslim Brotherhood.

The founders of the movement were very much aware of the militant trends. Many of them had studied in Egypt and been exposed to militant Islamic groups such as the Salih Sirriyya group, affiliated with the Islamic Liberation Party which in 1974 attacked the Egyptian Military Technical Academy. Salih Sirriyya was considered to be one of the founders of Islamic Jihad, which was established officially in 1980. The theory put forward by Islamic Jihad was that Palestine had been lost because of corrupt and opportunistic, non-Islamic Arab leadership, and that the Arab nationalist movements were the product of Western influence against the Islamic nation. The relationship of Islamic Jihad with the PLO was somewhat ambiguous.

Madrid, Oslo and beyond

The surge in the number and diversity of players in this turbulent area gave the Americans a sense of urgency, making it imperative that they do something or risk losing their influence in the Middle East, especially after the showdown with Iraq. On 6 March 1991, President Bush stated, 'A comprehensive peace must be grounded in Resolutions 242 and 338 and in the principle of territory for peace.' This principle had to be elaborated, and at the same time the legitimate political rights of the Palestinian people had to be provided for. If the US administration had applied these more vigorously from the outset, Arafat might not have been driven into the arms of Saddam Hussein.

In October of the same year, James Baker met with a group of prominent Palestinians in the occupied territories, including Hanan Ashrawi and Faisal al-Husseini, aware of their links with the PLO. One of the main difficulties was to find a way to make Palestinians and Israelis meet together. The Israelis refused outright to talk to the PLO. An agreement was reached whereby the Palestinians would be represented by a Jordanian–

Palestinian delegation and the PLO would be excluded. As a compromise, however, the PLO was to be allowed to choose the members of the Palestinian delegation, and Israel was to have no veto. But the Israelis still refused to meet certain members of the Palestinian delegation. The sponsors sent a letter of invitation to Israel, the Jordanian–Palestinian delegation, Syria, Lebanon and Egypt, as well as to the European Community, the Gulf Cooperation Council and the UN, who were invited to send observers.

The aim of these talks was to reach an agreement within a year on arrangements for a five-year interim period during which negotiations were to begin about permanent status on the basis of Resolutions 242 and 338.

Faisal al-Husseini stated that the Palestinian position in agreeing to the exclusion of the PLO did not affect the status of the organization as the sole representative of the Palestinians involved at every stage of the process. Help was offered to the Palestinians from many sides, especially from Egypt, which was able to give advice based on the experience of Camp David and which provided training in how to handle the Israeli style of negotiation. Many members of the European Community also gave valuable advice.

The Madrid Conference was attended by the Palestinian delegation, a number of prominent Arab leaders, President Bush and the Israeli Prime Minister, Shamir. At the first session, Dr Saeb Erkat nearly caused a diplomatic crisis by insisting on wearing the *kufia* (the distinctive Palestinian head-dress). Arafat, based in Tunis, curtailed the issue by asking the delegation to exclude Erkat from the conference. Arafat used to fly the delegates daily from Madrid to Tunis on the basis that if he could not attend the conference the delegates would have to come to him.

The achievement of the Madrid Conference was that Arabs and Israelis sat together at the same negotiating table. Madrid established a two-track system that was to become the pattern in subsequent negotiations. The first track was the multilateral negotiations in which Israel, the Palestinians, the Arab states and other interested parties outside the region could join in discussion of a number of key Middle East problems, including water, the environment, arms control, refugees and economic development. These multilateral talks initiated at the Madrid Conference resumed in earnest in Moscow in 1992.

The second track was the bilateral track in which Israel negotiated in Washington with each of its Arab neighbours: Syria, Lebanon, Jordan and the Palestinians.

When the Washington talks began, a kind of 'corridor diplomacy' took place, involving the exchange of memos between parties in separate rooms. The situation was one of continual change. In 1992, during the general election in Israel, Yitzhak Rabin, leader of the Labour Party, made a pre-election promise to talk directly with the PLO and Arafat. In this context the joint delegation in Madrid was a strategic necessity for the Palestinians. After the announcement of the election results and the defeat of Likud after fifteen years in power, Prime Minister Yitzhak Shamir declared that he was retiring from politics. The PLO began to talk through informal channels to the new administration in Israel. In spite of the change of government, in order to maintain some continuity, the Israeli negotiating delegation did not change. Within a year of the beginning of the negotiation, eight rounds had taken place but nothing had been achieved.

On 17 December 1992, Israel deported 415 Palestinian members of Hamas across the border into Lebanon. This incident overshadowed the negotiations. Following a great deal of effort by the Arabs and PLO, the Security Council adopted Resolution 799 regarding the return of the men who had been deported to Lebanon. The negotiations were not making any progress until Shimon Peres sent two of his officers to contact the PLO representative in London. The PLO had a number of working groups that met in Europe, the USA, Canada and Japan. They handled different issues, such as water, refugees, economic development, environment, security and arms control.

It was the Norwegians who succeeding in creating the appropriate atmosphere for negotiations, not only by their attempts to reconcile the viewpoints of both sides, but also by creating a friendly climate. On 11 February 1993 the Israeli delegation presented a draft which the Palestinians accepted in principle. The newly elected President Clinton was keen to keep the negotiations on track. On the other hand the Palestinians also wanted the Washington talks to carry on, for fear that if they stopped, the momentum of the Palestinian effort would be lost.

The informal talks in Washington and Oslo had reached a crucial point − at which the parties might withdraw or real progress might be made. The main problem for the Israelis was still recognition of the PLO. Peres and Rabin were opposed to this step, but they continued talks without actually recognizing the PLO. On 19 August an agreement was reached between the government of Israel and the Palestinian team in the Jordanian–Palestinian delegation to the Middle East peace conference. The Israelis felt they had to inform the Americans of the breakthrough in Oslo. The Israeli Prime Minister asked Shimon Peres to go to the US, accompanied by the Foreign Minister of Norway and the team that had conducted the agreement. In America the news was received with joy and it was suggested that it should be made public. On 9 September 1993, Arafat sent a letter to Prime Minister Rabin confirming that the PLO recognized the State of Israel, was committed to the peace process and renounced the use of terrorism and other acts of violence. Furthermore, he affirmed that those Articles of the Palestinian covenant that denied Israel's right to exist were inoperative and no longer valid. Rabin responded in a letter to Arafat, outlining that the government of Israel had decided to recognize the PLO as the representative of the Palestinian people and that it would commence negotiation with the PLO within the Middle East peace process.

Before the ceremony for the signing of the Oslo agreement, a problem arose because the agreement in Oslo had been made before Israel had officially recognized the PLO. As a result the wording of the agreement stated that it had been made with the government of Israel but did not mention the PLO. Arafat insisted on having the words 'Palestine Liberation Organization' inserted in the documents to be signed or he would not go ahead. After the intervention of the Americans and the efforts of Peres, the Israelis agreed to alter the documents to indicate that the agreement was between the 'Government of the State of Israel' and the 'Palestine Liberation Organization'. The signing of the Declaration of Principles and the famous handshake between Arafat and Rabin took place on the White House lawn. Both parties expressed their wish that the bloodshed should end and a new age should begin in which they would work towards peace.

As Edward Said continues to emphasize, this left the Palestinians very much the subordinates with Israel still in charge of East Jerusalem, the settlements, sovereignty and the economy. The peace plan raised many questions and was unclear in its details. Israel agreed to allow limited autonomy in the Gaza Strip and Jericho. Palestinians would be allowed to handle health, internal security, education, the postal services and tourism, but the Israeli army would be deployed around the main cities and Israel would control the land, water, overall security and foreign affairs as they affected the 'autonomous' areas. For an unspecified future period, Israel would dominate the West Bank, including the corridor between Gaza and Jericho, the Allenby Bridge to Jordan and all the water and land, a good part of which had already been taken.

In August 1995, negotiations were under way in Eilat in an attempt to reach another deal. In September 1995 the Oslo II agreement was signed in Washington. Israeli forces began to withdraw from six major West Bank cities, although the rede-ployment of forces around Hebron did not take place until three months later. In reality Oslo II offered the Palestinians nothing, but restricted Palestinian residents and separated them from each other and from Israel. The issue of land and settlements still had not been discussed. Only a few months later, Rabin was shot and killed by a right-wing Israeli extremist at a rally for peace in Tel Aviv.

The Palestinian leaders feared that Peres might not be able to enforce the agreement for Palestinian self-rule if he succeeded Rabin as Prime Minister. The great shock came, however, when Likud won the Israeli elections under an extreme right-wing leader, Benjamin Netanyahu. Israel rejected the legacy of Rabin, and the hopes of the Palestinians of creating an independent Palestinian state in the West Bank and Gaza were shattered. The concessions offered by the Labour Party were small and achieved with difficulty, but Netanyahu was not in favour even of these. His policies damaged the fragile peace process and caused anger among the Palestinians and other Arabs. He allowed further expansion of the settlements and supported the opening of a second entrance to an archaeological tunnel in Jerusalem which ran along the western foundation of the Aqsa Mosque. Later he sent a team of assassins into Amman to assassinate the leader of Hamas. This attempt failed and Netanyahu was forced to apologize to Jordan for this blatant violation of its sovereignty. Netanyahu also changed the plans for withdrawal from Hebron in a manner contradicting the Oslo agreements.

President Clinton stepped in to save the peace process. The Palestinians and Israelis were invited to the Wye River Conference Centre in Maryland to try to reach an agreement. After nine days of negotiations, Clinton invited Arafat and

Netanyahu to the White House to sign an agreement and King Hussein was invited too as a long-term major player in helping to secure the agreement. He left the Mayo Clinic where he was receiving treatment for cancer to attend the ceremony.[9]

The essence of the treaty was the strengthening of Israeli security, expansion of the area of Palestinian control in the West Bank, and enhancement of the opportunities for Israeli and Palestinian people alike. This agreement continues the progress made towards bringing a lasting peace to the Middle East, including the following:

1. A comprehensive security agreement designed to stop violence in the region and strengthen Israeli security.
2. Redeployment of Israeli troops from an additional thirteen per cent of the West Bank.
3. Transfer of an additional 14.2 per cent of jointly controlled territory to Palestinian control.
4. Reaffirmation of changes in the Palestinian Charter to delete language calling for the destruction of Israel.
5. The release of 750 Palestinian prisoners.
6. The opening of an airport in Gaza and an industrial zone.
7. The opening of corridors of safe passage between Gaza and the West Bank.
8. Discussion on the opening of a sea port in Gaza
9. Israeli approval of additional reunification of Palestinian families.
10. Permission for students in Gaza to travel to the West Bank and vice versa.

The question that might be asked is 'What have these agreements meant for Palestinians?' In reality the Palestinians have achieved little. The Palestinian National Authority (PNA) has the trappings but not the substance of government. New issues have arisen, including human rights abuses by the PNA itself and misuse of funds provided by Western donor countries for the building of infrastructure such as the airport (which is in any case largely controlled by the Israelis). The Palestinians in the diaspora have been excluded to a great extent from the entire process and this is a source of deep resentment.

Despite the agreements, the Israelis remained all too ready at any time to react to words or actions by stopping the negotiations or by closing the Palestinian territories, demonstrating the farcical nature of negotiation between unequal parties, one of which can exert its overall control of the situation at any point.

Nothing moved until the summer of 1999 when the discredited government of Netanyahu fell and Ehud Barak and the Labour Party were elected. This gave fresh hope that the peace process would come back on track. Since the election, new negotiations have been conducted in which Egypt has played go-between. On 4 September 1999 an agreement was signed by the Prime Minister of Israel and Arafat in the presence of Egypt and Jordan to implement the Wye River agreement.

The Sharm al-Shaykh agreement was signed on 5 September 1999 and dealt with the following:[10]

1. The Israeli withdrawal from the Palestinian area would take place in three stages on 13 September 1999, 15 November 1999 and 20 January 2000, respectively. There was also a verbal promise to withdraw from specific areas yet to be designated. This differs from the Wye River agreement, which was supposed to comprise two phases on 2 October 1999 and 15 November 99.
2. Palestinian prisoners. The Sharm al-Shaykh agreement provided for the release of 350 prisoners in two groups, whereas the Wye agreement provided for the release of only 102.
3. Final settlement. There would be continued negotiation in two phases, the first being up to February 2000, and the

second final agreement to take place within a year of the beginning of the negotiations.

4. Port of Gaza. Construction of this was agreed to commence in October 1999. The Wye River agreement had appointed a committee to conclude the agreement for the port.

5. Bypass roads. The southern bypass road was to be opened on 1 October 1999 and the northern passage four months later when the Israelis had designated the control points. [These 'bypasses', actually highways with controlled entry and exit points, allow Israeli traffic to cross the country without passing through Palestinian towns. It might reasonably be suggested that they serve mainly to entrench the Israeli siege mentality.]

6. Martyrs Road in Hebron was to be opened in two phases. The wholesale market was to become a trade market, and a committee was to be activated to organize community prayer at the Ibrahimi Mosque in Hebron.

7. Security. The Palestinians' obligation undertaken at Wye River was to be implemented, that is, the Palestinian police would be responsible for arresting anyone wanted by the Israelis. A plan was put forward for the collection of all weapons, and a list of the Palestinian police force was to be compiled.

8. Economy. A committee was to discuss a range of issues including car theft, Palestinian debts and Israeli purchase tax.

Jordan secured a peace treaty with Israel in 1994. This treaty contained a preamble, thirty articles and five appendices dealing with land, borders, water, security and other issues. At the time of the Madrid Conference and during the following year, the Israelis began to show some willingness to return the Golan Heights to Syria, but the assassination of Rabin and the installation of Likud sent the negotiations with Syria into deadlock. With the Labour Party back in power, the negotiations have started again, albeit in slow motion.

13

The wall

Like a giant scar across the landscape, brutal concrete eight metres high stretching as far as the eye can see, is the latest addition to the architecture of occupation. Israel's wall is the ultimate symbol of the intractability of the situation. Euphemistically termed 'the Separation Fence', this monstrosity, electrified and surrounded with trenches, razor wire and electronic surveillance and with control towers every three hundred metres and permanent patrols, will, when completed, be some 350km long. Everywhere in Israel and the Occupied Territories there are walls, fences, checkpoints, barricades; the whole of Gaza is surrounded by an electrified fence, but there is nothing like this. Reminiscent of the Berlin wall, only on a larger scale, it is a blunt instrument by which Israel can enforce its control of the West Bank. By imprisoning and sometimes dividing communities and controlling entry and exit between Israel and the West Bank it reinforces the siege mentality of the Israeli population and blatantly asserts Israel's military and logistical superiority. The wall does not even follow the Green Line (the line of the pre-1967 border) but sweeps across Palestinian land in the West Bank, effectively annexing large areas of some of the most productive agricultural land. Many villages have been separated from agricultural lands that they own and on which they are dependent for their livelihoods. The building of the wall has progressed rapidly since its commencement in June 2002 and the process has led to confiscation of land, destruction of crops and uprooting of olive and citrus trees, and destruction of houses and property. Nothing that stands in the path of the wall is spared.[1]

How did the situation reach this stage?

Throughout 1999 and into 2000 negotiations on the implementation of the 'land for peace' proposals of the Wye agreements failed repeatedly and by the middle of 2000 it was becoming obvious that no acceptable solution was going to come out of the negotiations. How could a just solution be reached without equality between the parties? Israel, as the occupying power, has continued to dictate terms to the Palestinians; it has pretended to offer magnanimous concessions whilst in reality offering nothing. The obstacle to peace is the Occupation and the primary manifestation of the Occupation has always been the settlements in the Occupied Territories. The settlements are Jewish communities of varying size, some being full-sized towns, built on occupied land. These are illegal in international law, as is the Occupation itself, but they are one of Israel's 'facts on the ground'. In Gaza they draw a grossly disproportionate amount of the available groundwater, providing settlers with ample running water to fill their swimming pools whilst leaving Palestinian towns and refugee camps with intermittent and often foul water supplies. In the name of 'self-defence' (against the people whose land they occupy illegally) settlers are allowed to carry firearms, including semi-automatic weapons. In the early nineties, before the beginning of the Oslo talks, settlement building was rife and unchecked. In fact it was actively encouraged by Ariel Sharon who, when he was Minister for Construction and settlement, urged settlers to 'take every hilltop'. Successive Israeli governments of all parties have allowed and even condoned continued settlement building. Some, such as that of Benjamin Netanyahu, have not disguised their support for settlers, but settlement building under Netanyahu was not as high as under Ehud Barak, who paid lip-service to the Declaration of Principles, claiming to have frozen settlement or limited settlement building to natural growth whilst in reality authorizing or turning a blind eye to massive expansion. In an act of blatant deception Israel claimed that in the Wye River negotiations Barak had generously offered huge concessions to the Palestinians, including sovereignty over the West Bank, and that Arafat had rejected this most reasonable proposition out of sheer intransigence. In reality the PNA would have had no territorial integrity and only limited authority over parts of the West Bank, which was subject to the overall control of Israel, and in any case could exercise no real authority over territories scattered with heavily fortified settlements and criss-crossed with 'by-pass' roads, newly built highways which may only be used by settlers and Israelis to travel to and between the settlements and between the settlements and Israel. These roads cut swathes across the countryside, clearing vast tracts of land in their path with no consideration for local populations and their agricultural land or buildings. They are closed to non-Jews and patrolled by the IDF. Where ordinary roads cross them, Palestinian traffic has to wait, sometimes for hours, while settlers pass. A hundred Palestinian vehicles, sometimes including ambulances, children going to school, or perishable goods, may be kept waiting at a crossing while a single settler vehicle passes. IDF patrols radio ahead to crossing controls, which may close the crossings even when such a settler vehicle is still miles away.

On 28 September 2000, in what looked to the Palestinians like a calculated provocative gesture, Ariel Sharon, who at this point was a Member of the Knesset and had not yet been elected Prime Minister, visited al-Haram al-Sharif accompanied by a 'small party' of around one thousand armed police and soldiers. Ehud Barak had refused to ban the visit, seeing it as an internal political challenge to him personally. Sharon presented his visit as a symbolic gesture, exercising his right as a Jew to visit the Temple Mount. Barak knew that if he opposed this he would be playing into Sharon's hands and so authorized the one-thousand-strong escort.

The visit took place on a Thursday, so although there were demonstrators there was not much more than the ordinary daily bustle of people, but the visit was guaranteed to provoke an angry reaction the following day when, as usual, tens of thousands of Muslim Palestinians gathered for the Friday Noon congregational prayer. The Haram is a vast raised paved platform on which are sited the two great mosques, al-Aqsa and the Dome of the Rock. Both are of great significance to Muslim Palestinians, but the magnificent Dome of the Rock with its great golden dome, visible from all the hills that surround the city, is an icon that is found in a range of representative forms in the homes of Palestinians around the world.

The crowds at Friday prayer the following day voiced their anger at this arrogant gesture. In the violence that followed, several Palestinians were killed and dozens injured. It was not seen, as some have suggested, as a defiling of a sacred place by the presence of non-Muslims. It was seen as a display of power in a deliberate affront by a hawk who has never hidden his hatred for the Palestinians and who has never cared what the world thinks about him. Ariel Sharon has a fifty-year record of atrocities against the Palestinians going back to the massacre of villagers in their homes at al-Qibya in the West Bank in 1953 when he led the elite 101 Commando Unit. It was Ariel Sharon who launched the invasion of Lebanon with the aim of driving out and destroying the PLO, leading to the deaths of thousands of Palestinian and Lebanese civilians, PLO fighters and over a thousand Israeli soldiers, and it was he who allowed the Lebanese Christian Phalange militias into the Sabra and Shatila refugee camps where, in a killing spree lasting a day and a half, they massacred at least seven hundred, and some estimates say as many as two thousand, Palestinian refugees, many of them women, children and elderly people. The mood of Palestinians was already one of simmering anger at the hopelessness of the situation and despair of there ever being a just solution. For this old enemy to march on to the Haram was then the simple adding of insult to injury, the deliberate sabotaging of the last hopes of peace, and this was the trigger that led to the explosion of rage.

Like the first Intifada, this uprising of the Palestinian people was a spontaneous reaction. In small acts of defiance, ordinary Palestinians expressed their frustration in the form of demonstrations, strikes and episodes of the now symbolic stone-throwing by gangs of youths facing one of the most highly funded and sophisticated armies in the world. For months the state of hostility continued. The Israelis maintained their iron grip on the Territories, defending the illegally built settlements and the bypass roads while demolishing houses built by Palestinians on their own land without permits. They responded to sporadic attacks with collective punishments by demolishing the homes of those accused of terrorism and leaving families homeless, by arrests and assassinations, and by the 'closures'. This is the word used for the sealing off of the Territories so that those who, in the ultimate humiliation, depend for their livelihood on work inside Israel, are prevented from working and thereby forced into the ever-descending spiral of poverty. Suicide bombings heightened the state of tension still further and in early 2001 Israeli voters, having lost any confidence they might have had in the possibility of a peaceful settlement, elected the only man they felt could take the hard line they believed was necessary. Ironically this was the man who had triggered the Intifada. In a bizarre distortion of the great Wye River deception, the Israeli electorate was persuaded that Barak had offered too much to the Palestinians, negotiated too far and compromised the security of Israel. This was a somewhat far-fetched accusation of a military man who had seen his share of active service, including directing the commando squad that in 1998 assassinated Abu Jihad[2] in his villa in Tunisia. Prime Minister Sharon proceeded to assume the responsibilities of the Minister of Defence and the 'peace process' was now officially dead. Sharon has never negotiated or compromised and the mood of the Israeli public was not to do so now.

The Intifada continued through the summer. The Israeli Government line over the last few years had been to propagate the claim that Yasser Arafat actively promotes terrorist groups, and to hold him responsible for all acts of violence against Israel, including the actions of Hamas – a claim that is patently ludicrous. This has been used to pressurize the PNA security into clamping down on Palestinian activists, thereby effectively doing the Israelis' 'dirty work' for them, and to justify the targeting of the PNA when they fail to do so. In this way they have attempted to discredit Arafat and the PNA as negotiating partners and thereby rule out any chance of meaningful negotiation.

In September 2001 the attacks on the World Trade Center towers and the Pentagon changed everything. Far from rejoicing, as has been claimed, thinking Palestinians knew only too well that they would be damaged by association, real or imagined. Osama Bin Laden's primary achievement in this horrific and psychopathic act has been to confirm anti-Arab and Islamophobic prejudices and stereotypes of Arabs and Muslims as murderous fanatics. There are fundamental issues to be dealt with in reconciling the pre- and post-September 11 worlds but these are not within the scope of this text. A side effect has been, however, to increase sympathy for Israel as a 'victim' of terrorism and to provide it with moral ammunition against the Palestinians. The Israeli claim to have intercepted a shipment of arms allegedly destined for the PNA in January 2002 was the clinching factor justifying the onslaught that ensued.

Increased repression under Sharon had led, predictably, to a spate of suicide bombings and this in turn brought down the full force of the IDF on the West Bank and Gaza. Attacks were launched on several West Bank towns in late March and April 2002 using tanks and attack helicopters. Arafat himself was besieged in his compound in Ramallah as the IDF shelled the buildings around his office, leaving him without water or electricity. Another siege was in progress in Bethlehem, where alleged militants had sought refuge in the Church of the Nativity. Houses were shelled, bulldozed and burnt on the pretext of rooting out 'terrorists' and large numbers of civilians including women and children were killed and injured. The worst of the carnage was at the Jenin refugee camp. Israel claims that 'only' about fifty people were killed and that these were mostly terrorists, but eyewitness accounts and the footage that was not shown on Western television news suggests that the reality was much more horrific. Many people remain unaccounted for. Many bodies and body parts were unidentifiable. Ordinary civilians, including children, found themselves picking up and handing in pieces of dismembered corpses. Some were buried hurriedly in mass graves, primarily to avoid the risk of disease but also out of customary respect for the dead, which requires that bodies be interred before they suffer the degradation of deterioration, but where this was not possible they lay and putrefied where they fell. Many remained under the rubble of their demolished houses. Some died because they were denied access to medical assistance as the Israelis prevented medical teams from entering for nine days. People of all ages were shot indiscriminately by IDF snipers, including some attempting to save the lives of the injured. During and immediately following the attack on Jenin the Israelis prevented independent observers from entering the camp and have refused to date to allow a full independent investigation. Unless and until such an investigation takes place it will be impossible to confirm or rule out the allegation that the Israelis removed and disposed of bodies in order to evade charges of war crimes.

In mid-April, Arab members of the Security Council at the UN called for a multilateral peacekeeping force to defend the Palestinians from Israeli aggression, and a full inquiry into crimes of the Occupation. To obstruct this, the US proposed a milder resolution calling for a fact-finding mission into the events at Jenin, and this was passed unanimously on April 19. Not only did this fail to investigate the attack on Jenin in any depth, restricting its main criticisms to the prevention of access to rescue workers and medical teams, but also by limiting it to Jenin and disregarding the invasions of other West Bank towns it obstructed the investigation of violations of International Law by the occupying power.

By May the Israelis had withdrawn, or been redeployed, but made further incursions in June, at which point the building of the 'Separation Fence' commenced. Subsequent events were overshadowed by the war on Iraq.

In the context of recent events, Israel's claim that it is prepared to support the establishment of a Palestinian state now stretches the limits of credibility. It is equally difficult to interpret President George W. Bush's statements supporting the establishment of a Palestinian state as anything more than empty words, just enough correct formula to allow him to claim to be a peacemaker whilst waging war on Iraq.

Imagine a middle eastern country which has for years been armed by and enjoyed the patronage of the West, which is governed by an ageing war criminal known to have committed crimes against humanity over several decades, which has aggressively seized territory and dispossessed and repressed its inhabitants, which has attacked civilians and destroyed their homes and livelihoods, whose officers have by their own admission and with impunity executed prisoners, which carries out torture and sends out assassination squads to murder its enemies within its borders and in other sovereign states, which has a propaganda machine that disseminates fabrications and gross distortions of the truth, which has over decades consistently and purposefully disregarded and defied UN Resolutions. What should be the international response to such a country? The alternatives are to strangle it with sanctions for twelve years, destroy its economy and watch while its people suffer and its children die from starvation and lack of basic healthcare, then when it is at its weakest launch a massive military campaign against it and expect it to be grateful for its salvation, or reward it year after year with billions of dollars of aid and armaments to protect it from its own wretched victims. It all depends on the name of the country.

14
The legacy of the old guard

The last five years have seen the end of an era with the fall of two of the most prominent of the 'old guard', and the end of an ancient enmity. The personal conflict between Sharon and Arafat lasted more than four decades, taking with it the lives of thousands and wasting the prospects of generations of Palestinians and Israelis. After living under siege in his compound in Ramallah for months, Arafat's health collapsed and he died after a relatively short illness in a Paris hospital in 2004. Sharon, on the other hand, lingers in a coma following a stroke in April 2006.

More than any other leaders these two personified the conflict. With his military uniform and black and white Palestinian head-dress, Arafat was an icon of the Palestinian cause from the early 1960s until his death. Until the 1990s he was known as the man who never slept in the same place twice. To the Palestinians he was an uncompromising freedom fighter who brought the Palestinian cause to the attention of the world. He asserted the Palestinian identity as a people dispossessed in the face of a deliberate and cynical propaganda campaign by the Israelis to deny their existence and dismiss them as merely a refugee problem, generic Arabs for whom the Arab states should take responsibility. To the Israelis he was a terrorist and the greatest threat to their existence. Sharon's unapologetic, uncompromising, hardline ideological commitment to the existence and survival of the State of Israel dates back to the beginning of his military career in the 1940s. To the Israelis he is a war hero and until his collapse the most dependable defender of the State to whom they turned when they felt let down by other leaders, while to the Palestinians he is a war criminal and ruthless adversary, the strongest supporter of the illegal settlements and responsible for the massacres at Sabra and Shatila amongst other atrocities.

During Arafat's last months it became clear how important to Sharon it was to break him. In the media the focus of the conflict became the siege of the compound itself and the day-to-day aspects of Arafat's survival and his contact with the outside world. In early 2003 he had given in to pressure to appoint Mahmoud Abbas as Prime Minister and to delegate a considerable amount of his authority to him. Now, although the PNA government was able to meet with him in Ramallah, he was unable to leave and became almost completely cut off from daily affairs. Keeping him under siege in such intolerable circumstances was an act of deliberate humiliation. The fear was that if he left the compound he might be killed or arrested, or if he was allowed to leave he might have been prevented from ever returning to the West Bank, which would have been a great blow to Palestinian morale.

Arafat died in November 2004 and, after funeral services in Paris and Cairo, was buried in Ramallah. A grand memorial now marks his grave. He was succeeded by Rawhi Fattouh as interim President until the election of Mahmoud Abbas by a comfortable majority in January 2005. Sharon collapsed with a stroke little more than a year later, in January 2006, and was succeeded as Prime Minister by Ehud Olmert.

The demise of these old soldiers left a void in terms of personality that could not be filled. Both were charismatic figures who held fast to twentieth-century ideologies and neither was fitted to be a peacetime leader. The best hope for both sides would be that they would be succeeded by a new generation of twenty-first-century practical politicians who might be able to seek realistic solutions. In reality, however, the obstacles look as insurmountable as ever. Divisions amongst the Palestinians themselves have made any kind of united front impossible and undermined their credibility. In Gaza in particular there had long been deeply rooted dissatisfaction with Fatah, which was active in 'the cause' but doing little for the people who lived in ever worsening conditions in the camps, deprived of most basic facilities. Meanwhile, Hamas was active on the ground, using its organizational expertise to help to provide welfare and services including schools and medical clinics. In elections in 2006 Hamas candidates, standing as the 'List for Change and Reform' (rather than Hamas as such, as this would not have been tolerated by Israel), won 72 out of 132 seats. This horrified Israel and its allies, for while America insisted that it was supporting democracy in the region, it was not prepared for the results of the exercise of this ideal. In the following months, attempts to bring about some form of coalition between Hamas and Fatah failed and a state of hostility between them prevailed. Hamas gained overall control of Gaza and the response by Israel has been effectively to close the Gaza Strip, and Western aid to Gaza has been cut off. As a consequence, Gaza has descended into a state of near third-world poverty and deprivation, with humanitarian agencies reporting malnutrition and an impending humanitarian disaster. Fatah retained control of the West Bank but this control is severely curtailed by the 'separation fence' that has continued to snake its way across the country. Much longer than the border it claims to secure (it is now over 700km long), it winds its way around towns and villages, strangling the economy and devastating communities and local agriculture. The West Bank is now so fragmented and debilitated that it is almost inconceivable that it could function as an independent state, even if an agreement on this could ever be achieved.

Since 2003 there have been events of enormous significance on the Middle-Eastern and the world stage that have occupied the US and its allies and overshadowed the situation of Israel and Palestine in the world media. These include the invasion of Iraq, the toppling of Saddam Hussein, and the inability of the Allies to extricate themselves from the country; the action in Afghanistan; and the so-called 'War on Terror'.

It is only since early 2007 that there have been any major new externally sponsored peace initiatives. In February 2007 talks were convened between US Secretary of State Condoleezza Rice, Ehud Olmert and Mahmoud Abbas, but little was achieved. The promise offered by the peace negotiations of the nineties has faded. Despite the fact that new generations of very able politicians have emerged, there does not appear to be any real drive for peace. These two communities have lived with a state of hostility for so long that it seems that they do not know any other way to live. Perhaps the most hopeful initiative is the Japanese-backed proposal announced in March 2007 to create joint economic development projects aimed at bringing prosperity to both communities. A shared interest in success and economic development may be the key to building a secure future.

At the beginning of 2008 George W. Bush visited Jerusalem as part of a tour of several countries in the Middle East. He expressed the US commitment to Israel and also pledged support for the Palestinians in their aspirations for a state of their own and in helping them build the institutions of democracy and prosperity. He urged Palestinians to oppose extremism and terrorism as the greatest threats to their aspirations. Meanwhile in Gaza, still blockaded and sliding into humanitarian crisis, the situation was approaching flashpoint. In late January Hamas led a breakout through the border into Egypt using explosives and bulldozers and tens of thousands of Gazans poured through the breach, desperate to buy food, medical supplies and all kinds of other products. These 'shopping expeditions' continued for several days while the Egyptians struggled to close the border and bring the situation under control. It is understandable then that to the people of Gaza it seems that it is not Hamas that threatens their aspirations but the powers that keep them in a stranglehold that prevents any possibility of economic or political development.

The truce agreed at the Annapolis Conference at the end of November 2007 did not survive long into the new year: rocket attacks were launched on Ashkelon from Gaza in late February 2008 and the IDF and Israeli Air Force responded swiftly and forcefully with Operation Hot Winter. This operation was supposed to target terrorist infrastructure in the form of ammunition stores, rocket factories and firing sites, but also included the office of the Hamas prime minister, Ismai'il Haniya. Air strikes failed to stop the rocket attacks and Israel went on to launch a ground attack in northern Gaza with a force of around two thousand soldiers focusing on the towns of Jabalya and Saja'iya. The operation lasted only four days but resulted in the deaths of at least 110 Palestinians, of whom more than half were civilians, according to Palestinian sources, and three Israelis, of whom one was a civilian killed in a rocket attack and the other two were soldiers killed during the incursions into Gaza. The European Union called for a halt in the rocket attacks from Gaza, but both it and the United Nations criticized what they called the disproportionate use of force by Israeli forces.

In June 2008 a six-month pause in hostilities was agreed involving Israel, Hamas and Egypt. Israel insisted that even a single rocket fired on southern Israel from Gaza would breach the ceasefire. Hamas agreed that all militant groups in Gaza would abide by the truce; Egypt committed itself to preventing smuggling, particularly arms smuggling through the tunnels from Sinai into Gaza and Israel agreed to ease the restrictions on goods imported into Gaza through legitimate channels. For some months there was a degree of calm and only relatively minor incidents were reported. The situation deteriorated later in the year, however, as each side accused the other of lack of good faith, and the truce started to break down in November as the IDF launched an attack on the residential area of Deir al-Balah in Gaza. The Israelis claimed that they were trying to destroy a tunnel under the border into Israel, although some sources said that the intention was to send a clear message to Hamas. Hamas responded with rocket attacks on southern Israel.

In mid-December both sides indicated their desire to extend the cease-fire, each putting the onus on the other to accept their terms. Hamas stated that it was ready to put a stop to all rocket and mortar attacks on Israel from Gaza, provided that Israel opened up the border crossings to Gaza and refrained from any incursions into the territory. After a Palestinian man was shot dead in northern Gaza on 17 December, Hamas declared an end to the truce the following day, just before the expiry of the six-month term, and refused to enter into negotiations to renew it. Palestinian sources indicated that there was a desire to continue the cease-fire but only if Israel agreed to open the border crossings with Israel and Egypt, refrain from all attacks on Gaza, and extend the truce to the West Bank. Over the following days, the situation broke down and on 27 December the IDF launched Operation Cast Lead, taking Hamas by surprise. In only a few minutes, fighter planes and attack helicopters fired upon 100 pre-determined targets and half an hour later they struck another 60, including the Police Headquarters, where forty people were killed including a large number of cadets at their graduation ceremony. On this first day of the operation at least 225 Palestinians were killed and some 700 injured, one of the highest Palestinian death tolls in a single day since the beginning of the conflict. On the following day a full-scale ground attack was launched into Gaza in accordance with pre-planned military strategies. As has consistently been the case, Palestinian casualties were of a different order of magnitude to Israeli losses. Estimates by different organizations vary but according to Amnesty International, Palestinian deaths numbered 1383, of whom 333 were children. Thirteen Israelis were killed, four of whom were soldiers killed by IDF friendly fire. The conflict continued until 17/18 January, when each side declared a cease-fire dependent on the cessation of hostilities by the other. The Israelis refused to allow access to media or observers throughout the operation. Following the cease-fire, Israel was severely criticized for its failure to distinguish between military and civilian targets.

The rest of 2009 continued relatively calmly. In November Israel declared a freeze on construction in its settlements in the occupied West Bank, apparently in response to pressure from the Obama government, although the Palestinians claimed that this was not a significant concession. There was a partial and token freeze on construction in East Jerusalem, but in March 2010 the construction of 1600 apartments in an East Jerusalem neighbourhood was approved. This caused diplomatic tension with the US, particularly as it was announced on the day Vice President Joe Biden arrived for talks.

In January 2010 there had been two Israeli air strikes on tunnels that were allegedly used to smuggle rockets and other weapons into Gaza. In May an aid convoy of ships from Turkey attempted to defy the blockade of Gaza that had been in place since the election of Hamas in 2007. Several previous unsuccessful attempts to break the blockade had been made and a few shipments had been allowed through before the Gaza war, but after the war the blockade was absolute. The flotilla carried more than six hundred activists and cargo including building materials, medical supplies and equipment, books, paper and clothing with an estimated value of $20 million. On 31 May Israeli forces boarded the ships from helicopters and speedboats with the intention of forcing the flotilla to divert to the port of Ashdod. Israel faced criticism for the assault on the flotilla in international waters in contravention of maritime law. Although it was not initiated as an attack with deadly force, they faced violent resistance from a minority of the activists, of whom nine were killed in clashes on board one of the ships. The ships were towed to Ashdod and the humanitarian aid was unloaded and subsequently delivered to Gaza, although a large part of the medical supplies were rejected as out of date and unfit for use. Construction materials were not allowed in. The ships and passengers were released within a few days, and the injured were treated and repatriated. Subsequent reports suggest that the majority of participants in the flotilla were genuine humanitarian activists, but a hardcore minority were bent on breaking the blockade by force and appeared to have been prepared for armed resistance.

In September 2010 after the construction freeze had been in place for nine months or so, the US succeeded in initiating two rounds of talks between Israel and the Palestinian Authority, the first in Washington and the second in Sharm El-Sheikh in Sinai. During the talks it was indicated that there could be an agreement, in principle, to a land swap. In response, Hamas led an alliance of militant groups in an attempt to use a campaign of violence to disrupt the talks. This was condemned by the Palestinian Authority and there were accusations that the real motive of the attacks was to undermine the Palestinian Authority itself. In late September the construction freeze came to an end and there were calls from the Israeli right wing for settlers to go forward with building as soon as possible. The end of the freeze brought international criticism and Mahmoud Abbas stated that negotiations could not continue until it was reinstated. Persuaded by the US, Israel offered a sixty-day freeze at the beginning of October and Palestinian negotiators indicated that this short extension would be acceptable as a basis for negotiation, provided that the two sides could agree borders within this period. On 11 October Benjamin Netanyahu stated in a speech to the Knesset that Israel was ready to offer a settlement freeze in return for the Palestinian Authority recognising Israel as the Jewish Homeland. The Palestinian Authority rejected this, saying that the Jewishness or otherwise of the state was nothing to do with the situation. The Palestinian Authority would never agree to this as it would damage the rights of Israeli Arabs and would effectively eliminate the right of Palestinian return to Israel. US incentives to Israel to extend the freeze in the form of military aid failed and the talks broke down.

In January 2011 Israel offered an interim peace deal with a Palestinian state initially on fifty per cent of the West Bank, with final borders to be agreed later; but the Palestinians rejected this, asserting that this was proof that Israel had no real intention of achieving peace. Soon afterwards Israel approved the building of 1400 apartments in another neighbourhood of East Jerusalem. No progress was made over the following weeks and the Palestinian Authority indicated that unless agreement was reached by September it would declare statehood unilaterally and request recognition by the United Nations. The new state would be ready to discuss all of the key issues in the conflict, focusing on a solution for the refugees. It was not ready to come back to the table unless there was a construction freeze, and the new state would not accept any Israeli military or civilian presence on its territory.

The year 2011 was marked by sporadic but relatively low-level acts of violence on both sides. News in the Middle East was dominated by the Arab Spring, which had started in late 2010 in Tunisia and was spreading across the region. In April Fatah and Hamas agreed to form a coalition government. Israel warned the Palestinian Authority that it could not have peace with Hamas and with Israel at the same time. In September 2011 the Palestinian Authority attempted to persuade the United Nations to pass a resolution recognizing Palestine as a state and admitting it as a member.

In October 2011 Gilad Shalit, an IDF soldier kidnapped from Israel in a raid through a tunnel under the border, was freed after being held hostage for five years by Hamas. There had been a tireless campaign in Israel and international pressure throughout his captivity, and ultimately Egyptian and German negotiators succeeded in securing his release in return for the release of 1027

Palestinian prisoners. This was the largest prisoner exchange to date, and Gilad Shalit was the first Israeli soldier to be released alive in 26 years.

In November Palestine was accepted as a member of UNESCO, leading the US to cut off funding to the organization, but the vote on statehood was deferred due to lack of support. The US in particular resisted Palestinian membership of the UN, which would have given Palestine access to the International Criminal Court and the ability to look into Israeli war crimes supported by the US. It would also have given Palestine the right to apply for membership of other UN agencies, which could lead to the US cutting off funding as it did with UNESCO. A year later, however, on 29 November 2012, the sixty-fifth anniversary of the UN General Assembly vote on partition, Palestine was admitted by a large majority vote to Non-Member Observer status.

This came in the wake of the latest Israeli military assault on Gaza, Operation Pillar of Defense, which started with the Israeli assassination on 14 November 2012 of the Hamas military leader, Ahmed al-Jabari. Israel stated that the operation, which lasted a week, was in response to rocket attacks on Israel from Gaza. The operation targeted some 1500 sites in Gaza and resulted in the deaths of 133 Palestinians, of whom more than fifty were civilians. More than 800 Palestinians were injured and many families were made homeless. Hamas and other factions responded with further rocket attacks, in which six Israelis were killed and more than 200 injured. Many Western countries, including the US, Canada and the UK, supported Israel's right to defend itself, while Russia and a number of Arab and Muslim countries condemned the operation.

In February 2013 John Kerry replaced Hillary Clinton as US Secretary of State and immediately became involved in diplomacy in the Middle East. As a result, by the end of July he succeeded in bringing Israeli and Palestinian negotiators together in

Washington for direct talks without US mediation. He had also been active in cultivating a rapprochement with Iran, however, and Israel reacted badly to this, doubting the good faith of Iran, which it sees as a long-standing supporter of Hamas and Hezbollah. Although initial talks were encouraging, over the following months they broke down as they failed to get beyond a number of the core issues that have been an obstacle to the resolution of the conflict over several decades including borders, settlement building, the status of Jerusalem, refugees and the right of Palestinian return.

As part of the agreement to the talks, however, Israel committed itself to releasing 104 Palestinian prisoners convicted of murder or attempted murder and sentenced prior to the Oslo Accords in 1993. By the end of 2013, three of the four proposed tranches of prisoners had been released, with the final group expected to be released in April 2014.

Following talks with Israeli and Palestinian leaders in the first days of January 2014, John Kerry said:

> The path is becoming clearer. The puzzle is becoming more defined. And it is becoming much more apparent to everybody what the remaining tough choices are, but I cannot tell you when, particularly, the last pieces may decide to fall into place or may fall on the floor and leave the puzzle unfinished.

In April there was a reconciliation between Hamas and Fatah, which led to the formation of a Unity Government in June. Israel condemned the agreement and made it clear that it would not be prepared to negotiate with what it considered to be a terrorist government.

Tensions were already rising, but the period of relative calm of early 2014 really began to break down in July after three Israeli teenagers were kidnapped on their way home from a religious seminary. They were later found murdered. Although this was perceived as the main trigger of the subsequent conflict, much less has been reported about the shooting dead of two Palestinian teenagers at the Nakba commemoration in May. The Israeli teenagers were abducted on 12 June, just two days after the release of an autopsy report indicating that the Palestinian boys were killed by live rounds and not rubber bullets. In the hunt for the kidnapped teenagers and their abductors, Israel launched Operation Brother's Keeper, in which hundreds of Palestinians were detained, including most of the Hamas leadership in the West Bank. It is believed that the Israeli authorities knew that the boys had been murdered some time before their bodies were discovered on 30 June. In the following days a Palestinian teenage boy was abducted, beaten and burnt to death by unknown assailants in what appeared to be a reprisal; his cousin, a Palestinian–American boy visiting from Florida, was beaten up by Israeli security, and several other attacks on Palestinians, mostly by settlers, were reported.

On 8 July, in response to Hamas rocket fire from Gaza and the fear of incursions via the Gazan network of tunnels, the IDF launched Operation Protective Edge. This turned into seven weeks of air strikes and ground operations in which more than 2000 Palestinians were killed, mostly civilians and many of them women and children. Many thousands more were injured and the bombing destroyed more than 17,000 homes and damaged more than 30,000 others. The air strikes included the bombardment of a number of UNRWA schools where civilians were sheltering. Israel lost some sixty-six IDF personnel and five civilians. Israel has been heavily criticized for the scale and brutality of its operation, which was completely disproportionate to the threat.

Following several abortive truces, a month-long cease-fire was agreed on 26 August. It had been hoped that the peace negotiations would lead to agreement to a port and airport in Gaza and an easing of the blockade, but Israel has indicated that it is not prepared to consider this. Hamas has lost much of its leadership, its tunnel infrastructure has been almost destroyed, perhaps 100,000 Gazans have been internally displaced and the rebuilding after the destruction may take a decade. It is estimated that the war has cost Israel something between three and four billion dollars. Meanwhile these events have been almost overshadowed by the atrocities of the so-called Islamic State in Iraq and Syria and it remains to be seen how this will affect the situation in Palestine and Israel.

Debate

Dan Cohn-Sherbok

In your discussion of the Balfour Declaration you make a number of serious claims about the moral legitimacy of Jewish settlement in Palestine. In chapter 8 you maintain that the Balfour Declaration was a great shock to the Arabs. You ask what grounds the British could have had to allow Zionists to settle in the Holy Land. This, you emphasize, is the basis of the Palestinian position. It was unjust, you assert, particularly at a time when native populations were beginning to throw off the oppression of foreign colonial influence. However, this is not simply a moral objection. You further assert that the Balfour Declaration had no legal substance. Even though the Declaration was incorporated into the body of the Mandate and given substance in the White Paper, you say this is of no legal significance.

Let me turn, first, to the moral issue. You must be aware that Jews through the centuries have been subject to persecution. Since the emergence of Christianity as the dominant religion in Europe, the Jewish community has been repeatedly attacked. Let me refer back to my discussion of early secular Zionism in chapter 1. In the nineteenth century, secular Zionists were unified in their contention that the Jewish people would never be able to overcome anti-Semitism unless they had a state of their own.

Hence, in *Rome and Jerusalem*, Moses Hess argued that Jews will inevitably be regarded as strangers among the nations. In his view, the restoration of Jewish nationalism is the only bulwark against Jew hatred. Similarly in *Autoemancipation*, Leon Pinsker stressed that the Jewish problem is as unresolved in modern society as it was in ancient times. In essence, he wrote, this dilemma concerns the unassimilable character of Jewish identity in countries where Jews are in the minority. In a similar vein, the father of modern Israel, Theodor Herzl, wrote in *The Jewish State* that the plan for a Jewish state is a realistic proposal arising out of the terrible conditions facing Jews living under oppression and persecution.

Arguably, the events of the Second World War demonstrate the validity of these early Zionist reflections on the future of the Jewish nation. Although German Jews were assimilated into German life and made a major contribution to the country, Hitler and his executioners embarked on a campaign to rid Germany and Europe of the Jewish population. The onslaught against European Jewry is one of the most horrific chapters of modern history.

Is this not sufficient moral grounds for the Jewish quest to obtain a foothold in their ancient homeland? In attempting to persuade the British of the justice of their cause, Zionists recounted the terrible legacy of anti-Semitism as it evolved through the ages. The Jews had been oppressed simply because of their faith. They constituted a small, vulnerable minority in alien cultures. In the face of rising anti-Jewish agitation particularly in Eastern Europe, these Zionist pioneers championed a Jewish homeland to safeguard the lives of their co-religionists. Was this truly an immoral act?

Inevitably Jews turned to those in power to attain this objective. There was no resort to arms. Rather, Herzl and the leaders of the Zionist movement sought to secure a homeland for the Jewish nation through appropriate legal and political channels. Repeatedly Herzl appealed to those in control of Palestine. Zionist leaders around 1900 continued this policy. What was required was the legitimate, legally recognized acquisition of territory in the Middle East. This was the Zionist quest from the inception of the movement until its realization through the authority of the United Nations. In no way did Jews seek to undermine the legal or political framework of the nation states with whom they dealt.

Let me turn to your discussion of the period following the First World War. You quote at length the Churchill White Paper, and then denounce British policy. You state that this White Paper appeared to offer something, but actually offered nothing at all. Facts, you maintain, were created on the ground. Repeatedly you allege that the White Paper contained meaningless statements. Yet, arguably, this document offers a reasonable solution to the conflict between Jews and Arabs. Recognizing the Jewish case for a homeland in Palestine, the British government was determined to uphold the Balfour Declaration. In the view of the British government, the Jewish people had the right to live in the Holy Land – they were not there on sufferance.

Nonetheless the British were determined not to oppress the Palestinian population. The Churchill White Paper asserts that the British government did not aim to transform Palestine into a Jewish state. Nor did the British seek the disappearance or subordination of the Arab population, language or culture. Further, the British wished to ensure that immigration into Palestine would not exceed the capacity of the country.

These were not empty aspirations. On the contrary, the British sought to provide a framework for peaceful co-existence between Arabs and Jews. Facts were not created; rather the Churchill White Paper sought to achieve a solution to the problem of Jewish settlement and immigration while at the same time recognize the legitimate concerns of the Arab community. At this stage there was every reason for both Jews and Arabs to accept the conditions of this statement, and work together in the quest for peace and harmony.

Seeking to fulfil the terms of this White Paper, Samuel promoted the issue of the legislative council. But, on returning from

London, the Palestinian delegates at their conference rejected the legislative council. To my mind, such determination to subvert the aims of the British was a tragedy. If a legislative body consisting of both Arabs and Jews had been created in 1922, there might have been a possibility for harmonious co-existence between Jews and Arabs, and the violent outbreaks of the early part of the twentieth century could have been avoided.

As we both noted, the British were undeterred by the Arab reaction and staged elections. But these were boycotted, thereby undermining the legislative council. Determined to implement British policy, Samuel sought to reconstitute an advisory council and create an Arab Agency. Again both of these bodies were rejected by the Arabs, who had embarked on a policy of non-co-operation as long as the British government supported the Balfour Declaration. Again, these were fatal errors on the road to peace. It was not the Jews who were intransigent, but the Arabs.

You refer further in chapter 9 to the Palestinian reaction to the founding of the Hebrew University. As you note, the Palestinian Arab Congress issued a call to all Palestinians to refuse to participate in this event and to boycott the celebrations. I cannot see that this was a reasonable response. Why should Jews living in Israel, for whom learning has always been of central importance, not have a university in the Holy Land. Since its inception, the Hebrew University in Jerusalem has been a pioneering institution and has engaged in important research. Moreover, it provided a haven for Jewish refugees from Nazi persecution, who were able to continue their teaching and scholarship.

Finally, I want to raise the problem of Arab violence against the Jewish community. Repeatedly the Grand Mufti encouraged the Arab population to rise up against Jewish settlers. Later, he sided with the Nazis against the Jews. In the light of the Holocaust, such anti-Jewish sentiment and agitation is incomprehensible. Where were refugees from European oppression to flee? Were Jews wrong to leave Germany after the Nazis rose to power? Surely there were compelling reasons for Jewish immigration to the Holy Land.

At the end of chapter 9 you summarize the policy of the Jewish Agency in 1937. There were three main conclusions: the interests of Jews and Arabs were inherently irreconcilable; the Churchill White Paper which supported the Balfour Declaration should be accepted and the language, culture and religion of the Arab population should not be prejudiced; Jews and Arabs should live in concord and mutual respect. As you note, Arab spokesmen repudiated this position and denounced the Jewish National Home. Yet, surely the stance adopted by the Jewish Agency was sensible and would have provided a framework for future development.

As you explain, a partition plan was proposed by the British. This was, however, rejected by the Arabs. At the Arab Summit in Bludanan in Syria, five resolutions were formulated which rejected the notion of a Jewish National Home, repudiated the Balfour Declaration, agitated for restriction of Jewish immigration and called for recognition of Palestinian sovereignty over the land. Such determination later served as the basis for rejecting the 1939 White Paper in which the British made various concessions to the Palestinian population. Throughout this period the Arab community was unwilling to negotiate over any of the issues facing those living in the Holy Land. Jews, on the other hand, continually sought to find a solution to the problems confronting the native population while retaining their conviction that a Jewish National Home must be established in the land of their ancestors.

In chapter 10 you outline the events surrounding the creation of the State of Israel. Thousands of Jewish and Arab lives were lost during the War of Independence. But why should this conflict have taken place? Let me review the events. In May 1947 the United Nations Special Committee on Palestine

(UNSCOP) was created and given responsibility to report by the autumn about the future of Palestine. During the summer, members of UNSCOP went to the Holy Land. On 31 August UNSCOP recommended the end of the British Mandate. A majority report stated that Palestine be partitioned into an Arab and a Jewish state with an international zone for the Holy Places. On 29 November the General Assembly formally considered the report, and thirty-three delegates voted in favour. Thirteen delegates were opposed and ten abstained.

The British resolved to continue their rule in Palestine until 15 May 1948. The Mandate would then come to an end. On 14 May 1948 Ben-Gurion and other leaders signed Israel's Declaration of Independence. This document described the Land of Israel as the birthplace of the Jewish nation and went on to explain that the Jewish people had long prayed for their return to the land of their ancestors. The Declaration further emphasized the destruction of European Jewry by the Nazis and the need for a Jewish state. The Declaration stated that the United Nations had accepted the right of the Jewish people to establish their own country which would be open for immigration. It was hoped that the Arabs of Israel would be active participants in this newly founded nation on the basis of equal citizenship rights.

The consequence, however, was an attack on Israel by the surrounding Arab nations. How could this response be justified? The Arab countries simply disregarded the authority of the United Nations, and instead of seeking peace with the Jews in their midst, subjected them to a ferocious onslaught. Is this not a violation of international agreements, of international law? Surely the Arabs were aware of the massacre of European Jewry during the Second World War, and conscious of the need for Jews to protect themselves from further attack. The Zionist cause was based on the recognition that Jews had been and no doubt would continue to be regarded as aliens in countries where they constituted a minority. By creating a Jewish commonwealth in the Holy Land, the Jewish people sought to defend themselves from future hostility.

The Palestinians who fled from their homes during this conflict could have been spared this tragedy if their fellow Arabs had accepted the authority of the United Nations. And so they should have. What point is there to being part of a democratic body – the United Nations – if its decisions are accepted only if they agree with one's own views? By rejecting the majority decision to partition Palestine, the Arab nations had placed themselves above the fundamental democratic process on which the United Nations is based. Since the creation of Israel over fifty years ago, Arab nations have repeatedly denied Israel's right to exist. Hatred and bloodshed have been the result of such intransigence. While Jews have sought peace with their neighbours, the Arabs have waged war.

In chapter 11 you discuss the acquisition of land by Jews. As you note, land was purchased from Palestinian and non-Palestinian landowners under Ottoman rule. Surely, this was a legitimate transaction. The vast tracts of land obtained before the State of Israel was created were purchased legally. Even though the mass of the Palestinian population was not involved in this transaction, this was a proper business venture, quite different from the seizure of land following the War of Independence.

As I explained in chapter 4, more than half a million Arab refugees fled from Israeli territory after the war. Most of these refugees went to Jordan, and others escaped to the Gaza Strip. Given the antagonism of the Arabs to the Jewish state, it is understandable that the Israeli government was opposed to their return. In June 1938 Ben-Gurion stated to his Cabinet that those who took up arms against the Jewish nation would have to bear the consequences.

One of the results of the war was Israel's determination to protect itself from further aggression. Is it surprising, therefore, that the Israelis took steps to restrict the activities of Palestinian refugees living in their midst? Although Israel's Declaration of Independence guarantees social and political equality to all its citizens, Israelis were ambivalent about the Arab population in the country. Could they be trusted? As events proved, the Arabs in Israel were a real threat to the stability of the country. Ben-Gurion was right that they were a dangerous presence.

For this reason the Jewish state took steps to control Arab agitators. Article 125 of the Emergency Regulations of 1949 granted military governors the power to declare any place or area forbidden. Under this provision, many Arab villages were designated as closed areas – no one was permitted to move without a permit. Further, Bedouin in the Negev were subjected to similar provisions. Other powers granted to the Israeli government included the right to banish, restrict the residence of or detain Arabs without trial. The justification for such regulations was state security. No doubt you object to such restrictions; you will say they undermine personal freedom. Yet, for Jews living in Israel they were of vital concern; the Israeli government was intent on safeguarding the life and property of its citizens.

Given the events of the Second World War, it is understandable why the Israeli government was determined to protect the Jewish state at all costs. As I noted, the main objective of this policy was to ensure that any form of Arab insurrection would be thwarted and that the Arab population was controlled. Many Arabs were prepared to accommodate themselves to such conditions, but Arab youth protested. Of particular concern was the confiscation of Arab land under the Absentee's Property Law of 1950 as well as the loss of Arab influence in the area.

But what was Israel to do? Throughout its history it has been besieged by Arab nations intent on driving Jews from the land. More recently the *Intifada* has sought to thwart Israeli control of its Arab inhabitants. No doubt you will object to all actions undertaken by Israel to defend itself from its enemies, including the attack on a nuclear reactor in Iraq and the attempt to drive the PLO out of Lebanon. Yet what alternatives did Israel have? Surrounded by its foes, isolated from external support, the Jewish nation has continually sought to safeguard itself from aggression. But it has not been the aggressor in these conflicts. Rather, as a young and relatively tiny country, it has continually sought to defend itself from attack; nonetheless, in doing so, Israel has constantly struggled to live in harmony with its neighbours.

In chapter 12 you outline the recent history of the quest for peace. As you note, the Oslo agreement provided a framework for negotiation between the Israelis and the Palestinians even though Israel remained in charge of East Jerusalem, the settlements, sovereignty and the economy of the country. Although Palestinians were to be allowed limited autonomy in the Gaza Strip and Jericho with regard to health, internal security, education, the postal services and tourism, Israel retained control over foreign affairs and overall security. In the West Bank, Israel would be the dominant partner. But, with the election of Benjamin Netanyahu, the Oslo plan was derailed.

However, with the victory of the Labour Party in the 1999 elections, there was renewed hope for a Middle East solution. As you explain, the Sharm al-Shaykh agreement signed on 5 September 1999 provides for Israeli withdrawal from the Palestinian areas, the release of prisoners, security passages, the construction of the Port of Gaza, and a final settlement. It appears that Barak was anxious to grant even further autonomy to the Palestinians. In recounting these recent events, you emphasize the Palestinian pain and displacement that continues after fifty years of exile. Yet, it must be accepted that there has been considerable Israeli suffering as well. It is not just the Palestinians who have endured great hardship through this conflict; Jews, too, have sacrificed their loved ones in this terrible struggle over what they believe to be their sacred homeland.

But what of the future? There are, I believe, a number of necessary ingredients to a lasting peace:

1. There should be a conscious recognition on all sides that Israel has a right to exist. This was the underlying assumption of the Balfour Declaration of 1917, which was resisted by the Arabs through the last century. Nonetheless, today after fifty years of existence, the Arab nations must accept the reality of the Jewish state as a precondition to any kind of mutual agreement. Since 9 September 1993, when Arafat sent a letter to Prime Minster Rabin confirming that the PLO recognized the State of Israel, this precondition has been given official approval. But there must be universal acceptance of this principle among all Arab peoples.

2. Similarly, the Jewish people in Israel and the diaspora should recognize the aspirations of the Palestinian people for a homeland of their own. As an empowered people, Israelis are obliged to consider the plight of those Palestinians who are homeless and seek to return to the land of their ancestors. Just as Jews sought to settle the Holy Land, Palestinians should be accorded the same right.

3. There are currently millions of Palestinians in the occupied territories and scattered throughout neighbouring countries who are anxious to form a Palestinian state. Yet, Israel is a tiny country. Where are these refugees to live? Obviously, no massive resettlement of Palestinians can take place in the Holy Land. What is required is more territory. The only practical solution is for neighbouring Arab countries to carve out from their lands a Greater Palestine which could be connected with a Palestinian homeland in the occupied territories. No doubt, you will resist such a proposal. You will say that such a plan is unwarranted and a violation of the sovereignty of other nation states. Yet, what other solution can there be? If there is to be a sizeable Palestinian state, land must come from somewhere.

4. The concept of bi-nationalism must be rejected. As we have surveyed in our respective parts of the book, Jews and

Palestinians have found it impossible to live together. The history of the Middle East is scarred by constant conflict. As suggested in the first few decades of the twentieth century, partition is the only way forward. Hence, instead of a unified Jewish–Arab state, two separate states should be formed in the Middle East, each with full autonomy and independence.

5. For an independent Palestinian state to flourish, Arab nations must be prepared to offer economic, political and cultural support. Not only will Arab countries need to provide additional land, they will also need to offer considerable assistance at every level. Only in this way will the Palestinian people be able to attain the level of economic stability required for political stability.

Dawoud El-Alami

The civilization of the Western world is founded to a great extent on the Judaeo-Christian tradition. Although religion may not play such an important role in public life as in previous generations, Western culture is permeated and patterned by it in ways of which we are aware and ways of which we are unaware. Until about the middle of the twentieth century throughout Europe and the New World, and to some extent until the present day, the folk history of a few Semitic tribes, passed down by narration and recorded at various times in various forms, much translated and with little of a true timescale, has been taught and learnt as if it were the documented history of Western culture. At the same time, general knowledge of the intervening history of the Holy Land is sketchy, encompassing little more than vague romantic notions of the Crusades of the early Middle Ages derived from school history books and novels of the *Ivanhoe* genre.

What is not commonly grasped, however, is that the history of Jewish Palestine ended effectively in 137 CE. Until the middle of the twentieth century, there had not been a Jewish majority in Palestine since that time over eighteen hundred years ago. In a kind of international aberration one of the most significant events of the twentieth century, involving the destruction and dispersal of a settled, indigenous population, has been based on a folk memory that, however vital to the cultural identity of the Jewish people, cannot possibly have entitled them to colonize an inhabited land at the very time when the rest of the world was turning against colonialism. Traditions and beliefs may have lingered on, the yearning to 'return' to a spiritual homeland may have remained through the centuries, but the hard reality of more than eighteen hundred years remains. It is inconceivable that in any other sphere of human existence an attempt might be made to turn back the clock almost two millennia.

In historical terms, the Jewish tribes are not the only people to have been conquered, defeated, dispersed. The history of the world is one of endless conquests and migrations over the centuries which are far too complex to unravel or reverse. My point is not to do with the moral issue of settlement as such. Palestine could easily have accommodated plenty of settlers had they come in moderate numbers simply to live and work alongside the indigenous population and developed organically as a community with no more ambitious agenda. A great deal of land was acquired by Jews by perfectly legitimate means, and this is not disputed, but the purchase of land in another country does not entitle one to establish one's own state therein. The Ottoman Empire, of which Palestine was a part at the time of the Balfour Declaration, had, over the centuries, provided refuge for Jews fleeing from persecution, including the Sephardim who fled the *reconquista* and the inquisition in Spain in the fifteenth century. There is, however, a vast difference between the scale of immigration represented by those seeking refuge from persecution, and the calculated usurpation and ethnic cleansing of an inhabited land.

My assertion about the legal status of the Balfour Declaration refers to the time it was issued, which was before the establishment of the Mandate. Palestine did not belong to Britain, nor did Britain have any legal authority in Palestine. At this point, British forces had not so much as set foot on Palestinian soil. Moreover, 'the Jewish people' had no juristic personality in international law; that is, it was not (and is not) a legal entity, and therefore could not be party to an agreement in international law. As Musa Mazzawi points out in his *Palestine and the Law*,[1] international law has spent centuries ridding itself of provisions based on religion and ethnicity and as late as the 1960s the US State Department explicitly did not recognize 'the Jewish people' as having juristic personality. So what possible legal significance could it have had at the time of the Balfour Declaration? By what right then did the British feel that they could in 1917 offer the territory of another country to an ill-defined religious/ethnic group represented with or without their agreement by self-appointed (not democratically elected) wealthy businessmen with the financial means to influence domestic and international politics and to promote their own agendas and ideals.

The Balfour Declaration gained its *de facto* legal effect when the Mandate, incorporating the policies of the Declaration, was imposed on Palestine. All of this opens a wider debate about the legitimacy of British government of Palestine. The Palestinian people did not choose to be governed by the British, rather they had British rule imposed on them. Jews were represented in the British government, whereas Palestinians were merely a subject population in a Middle East carved up between the interests of Britain and France. When you say that it was not the Jews who were intransigent but the Arabs, what you mean is that this indigenous population, this lesser race, should have done as it was told by its white masters.

I cannot accept that the dreadful events of the Second World War demonstrate the validity of the Zionist ambition. The creation of the apartheid state that is Israel represents the ultimate victory of the extreme separatist notions propounded by Nazism. Is not the very concept of a Jewish state the ultimate in discrimination? By definition the creation of a state based on religion and ethnicity in an inhabited land can only be achieved by a degree of ethnic cleansing. The state built by a people who have long been victims institutionalizes a form of ethnic and religious discrimination that would not be acceptable in any other modern state. The response to the Holocaust should have been, and in fact has been in the Western world, 'Never again will we allow this to happen.' Jews are no longer victims of institutionalized discrimination. They are a religious/social/ethnic group, or rather a number of such groups under one umbrella term, alongside innumerable other religious, ethnic and social groups. It does not undermine the horror of the Jewish experience to point out that the Jews are not the only group ever to have been the victims of discrimination, persecution or even genocide. The scale of the Holocaust is almost beyond comprehension, but there were other victims, including gypsies, homosexuals and those deemed physically inadequate or abnormal. In living memory there have been many other instances of genocide, such as in Cambodia and Rwanda. The black population of the United States, which historically has experienced slavery and utter disregard for the value of human life, and which is arguably still subject to greater discrimination and inequality of opportunity than Jews are, has not sought repatriation to a black homeland, but has fought and won civil liberties and equality of status before the law and in moral terms as absolutely equal members of a multicultural society.

Even if we accept the concept of a Jewish state, has it been the safe haven, the ideal society envisaged for all Jews? Look at the treatment of the Oriental Jews by their European co-religionists, who, fearing for their own interests in much the same way as any European anti-Semites, greeted Middle Eastern Jewish immigrants in the 1950s and 1960s by spraying them with DDT on arrival, forcing them to abandon their traditional dress, suppressing their culture, brainwashing their children, accommodating them in ghettos, using them for menial work and trying to make them conform to a national, in fact a European, ideal. How far removed is this from what Jews went to the Holy Land to escape?

No one would wish to deny the Jewish people peace and security, but true security in the modern world will never be attained simply by creating a fortress, maintaining military superiority and arming civilians with automatic weapons; rather it will be attained by establishing justice and recognizing that other peoples also have rights. To encourage continued immigration and tacitly to condone the relentless building of illegal settlements on Palestinian land makes a mockery of the 'peace process'. It suggests to Palestinians that Israel's declared desire for peace is nothing more than empty words intended to satisfy the international community.

As the situation stands, the law of this state supposedly created as a moral reaction to religious and ethnic discrimination incorporates a 'Right of Return' that gives any Jew from any part of the globe the right to settle in Israel. Immigrants do not have to be victims of discrimination or persecution who are seeking a place of safety. At the same time the indigenous population has been uprooted and scattered. Hundreds of thousands still live as refugees or stateless persons. The total number of Palestinians in the diaspora is in the region of four million. They have no right of return. How can this ever be the basis of a just society? From a Palestinian perspective it seems that Israelis, non-Israeli Jews and indeed the world are oblivious to or simply do not care about what has been done to the Palestinians. How can the Jewish people, whether in the Holy Land or elsewhere, a people themselves so badly wronged within living memory, in conscience accept that the creation of the Jewish state has been achieved by the displacement and the continued agony of another people?

You blame the Palestinians for putting up resistance to an incoming population with colonial ambitions, but who is the aggressor here and who is the victim? In any other context the Palestinians would be 'freedom fighters', defending their homeland. One day they are Palestinians living on their ancestral lands, going about their business, and the next their land is taken by Europeans and, if not expelled, they become 'the Arabs of Israel'. Where are their human rights? Where in all of this is their right to self-determination, which was not even given to them before it was taken away? The Palestinians did not have proper representation at the United Nations for them to. be governed by its authority. Does the United Nations have the authority then simply to hand over a populated territory to a colonizing people? This is an extremely worrying prospect. The Arabs would have been aware of the massacre of European Jewry during the Second World War, and no one would wish to see the experience of the Jewish people in the twentieth century repeated, but why should the price of the salvation of one people be the devastation of another? It was not Arabs who inflicted the Holocaust on European Jewry, but their fellow Europeans, yet it is the Arabs who have paid the price. The abused becomes the abuser. Terror tactics including massacres such as that at Deir Yassin were used to drive the Palestinians from their lands.

The core of the intractability of the situation is the absence of a level playing field. You talk of discrimination against Jews, but you should look more closely at the image of the uncivilized Arab in Western culture. This image is promoted and perpetuated in a way that would be totally unacceptable with regard to Jews or any other ethnic group. Israel is portrayed as a civilized

Western country surrounded by hostile barbarians. Israelis on the street may carry arms, but Palestinians may not. Would the world accept a Palestinian state with a nuclear capability and where civilians were allowed to carry M16 rifles? Why does a colonial state declared by a conquering people have full rights before the United Nations, while the original population of the land that it has usurped is deprived of any right of statehood and, in the struggle for equal treatment and gradually worn down over the years, is ultimately forced to beg for the minimum of what is expected by any other people. If the Palestinians 'behave themselves' over the next twenty years or so, the people who have dispossessed them may see fit to 'allow' them limited statehood in their own country.

This brings us to the future. The greater part of the Arab world does accept the existence of the State of Israel as a fact and is prepared to do business with it. This does not mean, however, that the injustices perpetrated against the Palestinian population can simply be written off. The Israelis must also recognize that the Palestinians have rights identical to their own in the present, and past grievances that deserve redress. Survivors of the Holocaust and their descendants and supporters have pursued claims for the restoration of property and payment of compensation over a period of more than fifty years. Moreover they have tracked down and brought to trial war criminals and those guilty of crimes against humanity without limit as to time and place. In this way they are setting legal precedents that may some day help to bring about, if not complete redress of the Palestinians' grievances, at least some token of recognition of wrongs done to them.

A right of return should exist for Palestinians in the same way as it exists for Jews. You cannot insist that any Jew anywhere in the world is entitled to settle in Israel, and then say, 'Obviously, no massive resettlement of Palestinians can take place in the Holy Land'.

Territory cannot be 'carved out' of other sovereign states. Would any European state agree to such a proposition? Would Germany or Italy, for instance, 'carve out' parts of their territory for the resettlement of Bosnian or Kosovan refugees on the basis that they are all Europeans? The Arab countries have carried the burden of Palestinian refugees for long enough and this suggestion simply adds insult to injury. The Palestinians do not want to seize parts of the territory of other countries; they want only what is theirs.

Israelis and Palestinians will not be able to live together in peace while they are not equal and while the Israelis hold the upper hand. Whether as a single state or as two states, Palestinians and Israelis must have absolutely identical legal, civil and democratic rights, and equality of opportunity. These are the intrinsic rights of the people and not favours to be bestowed by the patronage of Israel.

Dan Cohn-Sherbok

The prospects for peace in the Middle East, however, have been made increasingly difficult by the emergence of rabid anti-Semitism in Arab lands. Throughout the Arab world, Jews are continually vilified – as a consequence, the Zionist aspiration to solve the problem of anti-Semitism by creating a Jewish state in the Middle East has proved an illusion. In modern times the Arab community has regrettably become the greatest proponent of anti-Jewish attitudes, and has transformed the demonic image of the Jew to suit its own purposes.

During the last fifty years a vast quantity of anti-Semitic literature has been published in Muslim countries utilizing religious as well as racial motifs. Some of this literature, such as Hitler's *Mein Kampf*, Henry Ford's *The International Jew* and *The Protocols of the Elders of Zion*, has been translated into Arabic and is widely available. Other writings have exploited stereotypical images of the Jew inherited from the past. In all cases, these negative depictions of Jewry have been reinterpreted to express Arab antipathy towards Jews; repeatedly the Jew is portrayed as an evil force determined to corrupt and exploit the society in which he lives. In addition, Jews are presented as forming a global conspiracy intent on dominating world affairs.

Typical of such diatribes against the Jewish community is the tract *Holy War and Victory* written by Abd al-Halim Mahmoud, the former Rector of Cairo's al-Azhar University. In his view, the struggle for Islam is depicted as a struggle against Satan:

> Among Satan's friends – indeed his best friends in our age – are the Jews. They have laid down a plan for undermining humanity, religiously and ethically. They have begun their work to implement this plan with their money and their propaganda. They have falsified knowledge, exploited the pens of writers and bought minds in their quest for the ruination of humanity.[2]

Such denunciation of Jewry parallels medieval Christian polemics, as does the repeated allegation that Jews carry out acts of ritual murder. Thus in December 1984 the President of the World Muslim Congress, Dr Ma'ruf al-Dawalibi, claimed to quote the Talmud at the UN Centre for Human Rights Seminar alleging that it is necessary for Jews to drink the blood of non-Jews. 'If a Jew does not drink every year the blood of a non-Jewish man', he stated, 'then he will be damned for all eternity.' In his view the Talmud asserts that the whole world is the property of Israel including the wealth, blood and souls of gentiles. Another Muslim authority, Damil Safan, in his *Jews: History and Doctrine*[3] argued that there have been numerous cases of blood libel that have gone un-noted in history.

More recently, in an interview given to Al-Jazeera Arab television in 1998, the Arab terrorist Osama Bin Laden chillingly castigated the Jewish people as well as America, and encouraged Muslims to wage a holy war against these enemies of Islam. 'Our duty', he declared,

> is to incite the jihad against America, Israel and their allies . . . With the grace of God we have established [common cause] with a large number of our brothers in the International Islamic Front to confront Jews and the Crusaders. We believe that the affairs of many of those are moving in the right direction to have the ability to move widely. We pray to God to grant them victory and revenge on the Jews and Americans.[4]

Responding to the attack on the World Trade Center on 11 September 2001, the leader of the Nation of Islam and rabid Jew-hater Louis Farrakhan, condemned Israel for its treatment of the Palestinian people:

> The Palestinians believe they have sustained injustice since 1948. Whether you agree or disagree, from their point of view, they have not had justice. They have cried out in every forum for the redress of their grievances and justice has not come. They live in refugee camps, are scattered throughout the world and every day live with the horror of what they suffer. So more and more minds become imbalanced to the degree that life has no more meaning, for there is no joy in being free if there is no justice. Joy is the result of justice. Out of despair and hopelessness and waking up every day without the joy of justice, this is what causes children to strap themselves to bombs. They care nothing for the lives of others.[5]

As a result of such perceptions, many fundamentalist Muslims are intent on carrying out a jihad against the Jewish community.

Such intransigence highlights the ongoing presence of Jew-hatred in contemporary society. As humanity's most persistent hatred, anti-Semitism continues to flourish in the modern world. Nearly 4000 years of antipathy towards Jews has not diminished, despite the determination of the Jewish people to free them-selves from the scourge of prejudice and misunderstanding. Even though the Jewish people are now empowered in their own country, Jewish security is as imperilled as it was in previous centuries. In a world now faced with the very real threat of mass destruction, the flames of hostility continue to burn bright, with the threat of Jewish extermination as intense as ever.

Dawoud El-Alami

'So long as there is a military occupation of Palestine by Israel, there can never be peace. Occupation with tanks, soldiers, checkpoints and settlements is violence, and it is much greater than anything Palestinians have done by way of resistance.'[6] In July 2001 Edward Said recommended that all Palestinian spokespersons should begin their answer to any media question about the conflict with an opening statement along these lines, in the hope that repetition might imprint this concept on the minds of readers of newspapers and TV and radio audiences. He continues:

> These estimable people have to remember that 99 per cent of the people reading newspapers or watching TV news all over the world (including Arabs) have simply forgotten – if they ever knew – that Israel is an illegal occupying power and has been for 34 years [now 36]. So we must remind the world of that over and over. Repeat and repeat and repeat. This is not a difficult task, although it is, I believe, absolutely crucial. To remind everyone repeatedly about the Israeli occupation is a

necessary repetition, much more so than stupidly inconsequential and sentimental Israeli and American-style remarks about peace and violence.

This was in response to the media bias that does not allow Palestinians a voice but presents Palestinians/Arabs/Muslims (aren't they all the same?) as violent and intent on wanton killing and destruction while Israel with its military might is depicted as 'showing restraint'.

You present the blinkered view of those who see only what they want to see whilst remaining oblivious to what is really happening. In the Arab world, Jews are not vilified out of unprovoked spite and prejudice. The expression 'Arab anti-Semitism' is a contradiction in terms since Arabs are a Semitic people, and one should not forget that not all Arabs are Muslims, not all Palestinians are either Arab or Muslim, and only a fraction of the world's Muslims are either Palestinian or Arab. The Arabs simply resent the actions of the colonial Israeli state and its Apartheid regime and policy of ethnic cleansing. A Palestinian living in a refugee camp in Gaza or exiled from his homeland does not hate a Jewish settler because he is a Jew, but because he is an immigrant living in a settlement built on the destroyed remains of his village, supported morally and financially by the West, which has forgotten the plight of the Palestinian refugees and has abandoned them to statelessness and squalor for more than fifty years.

You have picked the most scurrilous examples of anti-Jewish rhetoric to quote to support your argument but these are not representative of the mainstream of Palestinian, Arab or Muslim opinion. You have not even considered the distorted picture of the Arab in the Western media. Vilification of Arabs and Muslims goes back centuries. In a more modern context, in his *Reel Bad Arabs*, Jack Shaheen has examined the permeation of film, perhaps the most powerful global medium, with anti-Arab

propaganda and stereotyping and has analysed its effects worldwide on attitudes towards Arabs, comparing it to the malicious
stereotyping of Jews that is no longer acceptable. The image of
the Arab is of a swarthy, devious, lascivious, perfidious, evil,
sadistic and brutal character who is likely to be a religious fanatic
and probably a misogynist to boot. In his introduction Shaheen
quotes one film producer as saying, 'You can hit an Arab free;
they're free enemies, free villains, where you couldn't do it to a
Jew and you can't do it to a black anymore'.[7]

The majority amongst the populations of the Arab countries
do not bear any ill will to Jews in general, although inevitably
some may hold prejudices and be influenced by propaganda.
They are not unique in this. It is not difficult to find examples
of hate literature. A brief internet search will quickly turn up
volumes of rabid anti-Arab, anti-Jewish, Zionist, Islamic fundamentalist, Christian fundamentalist, homophobic, racial and all
kinds of vile and brutal rhetoric.

Much has been made of reported incidents of Palestinians
celebrating on hearing the news of the attacks on the World
Trade Center towers and the Pentagon. No one would try to
deny that isolated incidents did occur but in any community
mobs can be incited without being genuinely informed of
the reality of the situation. The vast majority of Palestinians are
ordinary people with families who were as horrified as anyone
else by the events of September 11, 2001. A great number
have lost family members in the conflict and so are able to empa-
thize with those bereaved in the attacks.

The Palestinians are in an impossible position. Their legitimate cause has been hijacked by Bin Laden and his fanatics who
in no way represent the Palestinians and who have done nothing to promote and a great deal to harm them. The activities of
al-Qaeda have in turn been used to justify even more ruthless
repression of the Palestinians.

Phrases such as 'plucking out the terrorist network', 'destroying the terrorist infrastructure' and 'attacking terrorist nests' (note the total dehumanization involved) are repeated so often and so unthinkingly that they have given Israel the right to destroy Palestinian civil life, with a shocking degree of sheer wanton destruction, killing, humiliation and vandalism.[8]

From the perspective of a Palestinian survivor of the massacre of Jenin, or of a resident of the West Bank – the largest open prison in the world – it is difficult to comprehend how, as you suggest, 'the threat of Jewish extermination [is] as intense as ever'. The threat of Palestinian extermination, however, seems very real indeed.

Glossary

Aliyah
Term used specifically to refer to the immigration of Jews to Israel.

Al-Aqsa/Masjid al-Aqsa
'The Furthest Mosque', see footnote 10, chapter 9.

Dome of the Rock
See footnote 10, chapter 9.

Fatah
Reverse mnemonic for *Hizb al-Tahrir al-Filistini* – Palestinian Liberation Party – founded by Palestinian students, including Yasser Arafat, in Kuwait in 1958.

Haganah
Underground military organization of the yishuv in Palestine. It succeeded Ha-Shomer in 1920, and operated until 1948 when members joined the Israeli army.

Hamas
Harakat al-Muqawama al-Islamiyya. The word 'Hamas' itself means 'zeal'. Hamas bases its ideology on that of the Muslim Brotherhood which originated in Egypt in the 1920s. It was founded as an organization in the late 1970s and draws its main support from Gaza.

Harakat Al-Jihad al-Islami

A group formed by a split from the Palestinian Muslim Brother-hood by Palestinian students in Egypt in 1979–80.

Al-Haram al-Sharif

'The Noble Sanctuary'. Known to Jews and Christians as the Temple Mount, this is a large raised paved platform in the middle of the Old City of Jerusalem on which Al-Aqsa and the Dome of the Rock mosques stand.

Histadrut

Israeli federation of trade unions.

Hovevei Zion (lovers of Zion)

International Zionist movement. It grew up in the 1880s and served as the focus of early Zionist aspirations.

Intifada

'Shaking-off' or 'Uprising'. This refers both to the first *intifada*, 1987–93, and to *Al-Aqsa Intifada* which began in September 2000 and continues.

Jihad

Literally 'striving' or exerting oneself in the way of God, Jihad is often translated into English as 'Holy War'. Jihad may encompass armed struggle in defence of Islam but its true meaning can be any kind of 'striving' to do the will of God, including internal, spiritual striving.[1]

Kibbutz

Collective village in Israel which originated from 1918–21. Inspired by social ideals, the kibbutz movement played a pioneering role in the life of the country.

Knesset

The parliament of Israel. Created in 1949, it met in Tel Aviv, but later moved to Jerusalem.

Likud

Right-wing political party in Israel made up of a group of smaller parties. It was established in 1973, and in 1977 became the largest party in the Knesset.

Mahmoud Abbas/Abu Mazen

First Palestinian Prime Minister – appointed March 2003 – secretary-general of the executive committee of the Palestine Liberation Organization and a member of the Palestinian Central Council.

Moshav

Agricultural village of the type established in Palestine from about 1880.

Al-Nakba

'The Catastrophe'; the 1948 dispossession of the Palestinians caused by the creation of the State of Israel.

Nili

Underground intelligence organization which was active in Syria and Palestine under Turkish rule during the First World War.

Occupied Territories

The Palestinian territories outside the original borders of Israel declared in 1948, which Israel occupied during the 1967 war, and which it continues to occupy in contravention of international law and UN Resolution 242. These comprise East Jerusalem, the West Bank and the Gaza Strip.

PLO
Palestine Liberation Organization. Founded in Jerusalem in May 1964 under the auspices of the Arab League. The PLO later became a federation of organizations, of which Fatah was the largest. Arafat, as leader of Fatah, became chairman of the PLO.

PNA
Palestinian National Authority. The Palestinian Government in waiting, formed in 1994 it has limited autonomy in parts of the Occupied Territories and jurisdiction over internal affairs.

Shahid
Martyr. One who has died in the way of God. This has come to be used to refer to suicide bombers, fallen combatants and victims of Israeli forces whether civilian or paramilitary.

The Green Line
The border of Israel prior to the 1967 War and the Occupation of Gaza, the West Bank and East Jerusalem.

Yeshiva
Academy. Jewish school devoted to the study of the Talmud and rabbinic literature. The institution of the yeshiva is the continuation of the Babylonian and Palestine academies.

Yishuv
The Jewish community in Palestine before the creation of a Jewish state.

Zionism
International political and ideological movement devoted to securing the return of the Jewish people to the land of Israel. Modern Zionism was conceived by Theodor Herzl.

Notes

Acknowledgements

The authors would like to acknowledge their indebtedness to a number of important books from which they have obtained information and source material: Connor Cruse O'Brien, *The Siege*; Martin Gilbert, *Israel: A History*; *Israel: The Historical Atlas*; Arthur Hertzberg (ed.), *The Zionist Idea: A Historical Analysis and Reader*.

Chapter 1

1. Yehuda hai Alkalai, 'The Third Redemption', p. 105.
2. Ibid., p. 106.
3. Ibid.
4. Ibid. pp. 109–10.
5. Zwi Hirsch Kalischer, 'Derishat Zion', p. 53.
6. Abraham Isaac Kook, 'The Land of Israel', pp. 420–1.
7. Ibid., p. 430.
8. Ahad Ha-Am, *Nationalism and the Jewish Ethic*, pp. 74–5.
9. Moses Hess, *Rome and Jerusalem*, p. 133–4.
10. Leon Pinsker, *Autoemancipation*, p. 188.
11. Theodor Herzl, *The Jewish State*, p. 209.
12. David Vital, *Origins of Zionism*, p. 363.
13. David Vital, *Zionism: The Formative Years*, p. 143.

Chapter 2

1. Conor Cruise O'Brien, *The Siege*, p. 133.
2. Christopher Sykes, *Crossroads to Israel*, pp. 64–7.
3. Bernard Wasserstein, *The British in Palestine*, p. 109.
4. O'Brien, *The Siege*, p. 167.

5. *Ibid.*, p. 176.
6. Wasserstein, *The British in Palestine*, p. 156.
7. Yehoshua Porath, *The Emergence of the Palestinian-Arab National Movement 1918–1929*, p. 256.
8. O Brien, *The Siege*, p. 186.
9. Hansard, Vol. 248, Cols 751–7, 13 February 1931.
10. O'Brien, *The Siege*, p. 198.
11. Peel Commission Minutes, in ibid., pp. 224–5.
12. Jacob Coleman Hurewitz, *Struggle for Palestine*, p. 92.

Chapter 3

1. *Survey of International Affairs*, 1, 1938, pp. 469–70.
2. O'Brien, *The Siege* , p. 243.
3. J.B. Schechtman, *Mufti and the Fuehrer*, pp. 110–22.
4. Ibid., pp. 306–8.
5. Arthur D. Morse, *While Six Million Died*, pp.16–17.
6. Francis Williams (ed.) *Prime Minister Remembers*, p. 189.
7. Hurewitz, *Struggle for Palestine*, p. 253.
8. Ibid., p. 255.
9. Ibid., p. 288.
10. Nicholas Bethel, *The Palestine Triangle*, p. 313.
11. Martin Gilbert, *Israel*, pp. 186–8.
12. Michael Brecher, *Decisions in Israel's Foreign Policy*, p. 282.
13. Ibid., p. 287.
14. O'Brien, *The Siege*, pp. 398–9.

Chapter 4

1. *Israel: The Historical Atlas*, p. 71.
2. Ibid., p. 72.
3. Ibid., pp. 74–5.
4. O'Brien, *The Siege*, p. 422.
5. Ibid., p. 423.
6. Eitan Gabatello, 'The Population of the Administered Territories', p. 9.

7. George Kossaifi 'Demographic Communities of a Palestinian People' p. 422.
8. Yitzhak Rabin, *The Rabin Memoirs*, pp. 118–19.
9. *Israel: The Historical Atlas*, p. 99.
10. Ibid., p. 101.
11. Ibid., p. 107.
12. Gilbert, *Israel*, pp. 525–6.

Chapter 5

1. Gilbert, *Israel*, p. 533.
2. Ibid., p. 538.
3. Ibid., p. 547.
4. Ibid., p. 551.
5. Ibid., p. 569.
6. Ibid., pp. 576–8.

Chapter 6

1. www.us-israel.org/jsource/Peace/Taba.html
2. www.al-bab.com/arab/docs/pal/mitchell1.htm
3. www.globalpolicy.org/security/issues/israel-palestine/2001/1017bushpal.htm
4. ww.palestinefacts.org/pf_1991to_now_defensive_shield_2002.php
5. www.palestinefacts.org/sharon_speech_8apr02.php
6. www.mideastweb.org/basiclaw.htm
7. www.mideastweb.org/bushspeech1.htm

Chapter 8

1. Mary Eliza Rogers, *Domestic Life in Palestine*, p.13.
2. Hut Bayan Nawayhad, *Al-Qiyadat wa'l Mu'assasat al-Siyasiyya fi Filastin 1917–1945*.
3. Edoardo Vitta, *The Conflict of Laws in Matters of Personal Status in Palestine*, pp. 1–6.

4. ESCO Foundation, *Palestine, A Study of Jewish, Arab and British Policies*, Vol. 1, p. 2.

5. Governor of Egypt, 1805–48.

6. Ali Muhafaza, *Al-Fikr al-Siyasi fi Filastin min Nihayat al-Hukm al-Uthmani hata Nihayat al-Intidab al-Britani 1918–1948*, pp. 50–80.

7. Ibid., pp. 19–20.

8. Henry Lammens, *al-Mashriq*, 2, 1899, pp. 1088–94.

9. ESCO Foundation, *Palestine*, Vol. 1, pp. 43–5.

10. Hut, *Al-Qiyadat*,p.14.

11. William Pitt (Pitt the Younger) was the youngest ever British Prime Minister, 1783–1801, 1804–6 (Tory), son of William Pitt, First Earl of Chatham (Pitt the Elder), British Prime Minister, 1757–61, 1766–8 (Whig).

12. Beverley Milton Edwards, *Contemporary Politics in the Middle East*, pp. 21–3.

13. Musa Mazzawi, *Palestine and the Law. Guidelines for the Resolution of the Arab Israeli Conflict*, pp. 19–24.

14. Walter Laqueur and Barry Rubin (eds), *The Israel–Arab Reader. A Documentary History of the Middle East Conflict*, pp. 30–1.

Chapter 9

1. It was decided at the San Remo Conference on 24 April 1920 that the Mandate for Palestine under the League of Nations should be assigned to Britain. This was confirmed by the Council of the League of Nations on 24 July 1922 and came into force in September 1923.

2. Laqueur and Rubin, *The Israel–Arab Reader*, pp. 30–1.

3. ESCO Foundation, *Palestine*, Vol. 1, pp. 213–22. For details of King-Crane findings see Laqueur and Rubin, *The Israel–Arab Reader*, pp. 21–7.

4. Haifa, 13 December 1920. The Second Congress was never actually held. The Palestinian delegates had decided to hold the Second Congress in Jerusalem in May 1920 to protest against the confirmation of the British Mandate over Palestine and the incorporation of the Balfour Declaration in the instrument of the Mandate at the San Remo Conference. The Palestine government forbade its convening,

however, out of concern that it might lead to disturbances. Muhammad Y. Muslih, *The Origins of Palestinian Nationalism*, p. 204.

5. Mazzawi, *Palestine and the Law*, pp. 29–49.
6. Laqueur and Rubin, *The Israel–Arab Reader*, pp. 39–42.
7. ESCO Foundation, *Palestine*, Vol. 1, p. 291.
8. As'ad Muhammad Darwasa, *Al-Qadiyya al-Filastiniyya fi Mukhtalaf Marahiliha*, Vol. 1, pp. 43–60.
9. ESCO Foundation, *Palestine*, Vol. 1, Vol. 2, p. 695.
10. The two mosques that stand on the Haram al-Sharif, the 'Noble Sanctuary', are often confused. The Aqsa Mosque was originally built by the Caliph Umar in the seventh century CE. The first structure was of timber but was rebuilt in stone in the early eighth century. Twice in its early history it was destroyed by earthquakes and the present structure dates from the eleventh century. The Dome of the Rock with its unmistakable golden dome is built around the rock from which the Prophet Muhammad is said to have ascended on the 'Night Journey' to the seven heavens. It was built by the Caliph Abd al-Malik ibn Marwan between 687 and 691 CE.
11. ESCO Foundation, *Palestine*, Vol. 1, pp. 294–6, for a detailed account of the Shaw Commission findings.

Chapter 10

1. Nicholas Bethell, *The Palestine Triangle*, p. 194ff. Christopher Sykes, *Crossroads to Israel*, pp. 245–78.
2. Approximately half a million acres.
3. For more information on Musa Alami, see Bethell, *The Palestine Triangle*,
4. p. 194, and Geoffrey Furlonge, *Palestine Is My Country – The Story of Musa Alami*.
5. The number of people killed has long been believed to be in the region of 250 and the reader will find such figures in many references, but recent (Palestinian) research indicates that the number was exaggerated by the Israelis to cause panic and drive local people out of the area, the actual figure being not more than 107. Sherif Kana'neh, *Demolished Arab Villages*, No. 4.

Chapter 11

1. Mohamed Heikal, *Secret Channels – The Inside Story of the Arab–Israeli Peace Negotiations*, pp. 3–139.
2. Helena Cobban, *The Palestinian Liberation Movement – People, Power and Politics*, pp. 21–34.
3. Ahmad al-Shukairy was a Palestinian lawyer and Chairman of the Palestine Liberation Organization, 1964–7.
4. Andrew Gowers and Tony Walker, *Arafat – The Biography*, pp. 3–65.
5. Robert Stephens, *Nasser*, pp. 493–510.
6. Heikal, *Secret Channels*, pp. 150–9.
7. Ahron Bregman and Jihan Tahri, *The Fifty Years War – Israel and the Arabs*, Vol. 2, pp. 60–99.

Chapter 12

1. Gowers and Walker, *Arafat*, p. 147.
2. Heikal, *Secret Channels*, pp. 180–213.
3. Ibid., pp. 259–60.
4. Dilip Hiro, *Sharing the Promised Land – An Interwoven Tale of Israelis and Palestinians*, p. 192.
5. Bashir Gemayel was a Lebanese Maronite Christian militia leader. He was elected President of Lebanon in September 1982 (under patronage of Ariel Sharon) but assassinated by bomb attack before he could take office.
6. Abu Iyad (1933–91). One of the founders of the PLO and of the Fatah movement; assassinated, probably by a PLO splinter group.
7. See, for detail, Edward W. Said, *Peace and Its Discontents – Gaza – Jericho 1993–1995*.
8. A US citizen of Palestinian Christian origin, Edward Said is Professor of English and Comparative Literature at Columbia University but is perhaps more widely known outside his field of specialization as one of the most prominent and eloquent spokespeople on Palestinian issues. For some of his most important writing on Palestine see the bibliography.

9. www.ariga.com/treaties/wye.htm
10. www.ariga.com/treaties/sharmelsheikh.htm

Chapter 13

1. *The Middle East*, January 2003, pp. 6–9.
2. Abu Jihad – Khalil al-Wazir. Senior aide to Arafat and No. 2 in Fatah chain of command.

Debate

1. Mazzawi, M. E., *Palestine and the Law*. Reading, Ithaca Press, 1997, pp. 19–24.
2. Abd al-Halim Mahmoud, *Al-Jihad wa al-Nasr* (*Holy War and Victory*). Cairo, 1974
3. Quoted in Cohn-Sherbok, D., *Antisemitism*. Stroud, Sutton, 2002.
4. http://www.guardian.co.uk/waronterror/story/0,1361,565446,00.html
5. World Press Conference from Mosque Maryam, 16 September 2001; http://www.noi.org/statements/transcript_us.attacked09-16-2001.htm
6. Said, E., 'Israel Sharpens its Axe'. *Counterpunch*, 13 July 2001.
7. Shaheen, J., *Reel Bad Arabs*. Northampton, MA, Interlink Publishing, 2001, p. 6.
8. Said, E., 'What Israel has Done'. *The Nation*, 18 April 2002.

Glossary

1. Seyyed Hossein Nasr. *Traditional Islam in the Modern World*. London, Kegan Paul International, 1994 (reprint).

Bibliography

A Jewish perspective

Alkalai, Y. hai, 'The Third Redemption', in A. Hertzberg (ed.), *The Zionist Idea: A Historical Analysis and Reader*. New York, Atheneum, 1959.

Avineri, S., *The Making of Modern Zionism*. New York, 1981.

Bauer, Y., *From Diplomacy to Resistance: A History of Jewish Palestine, 1939–1945*. New York, Atheneum, 1973.

Bethel, N., *The Palestine Triangle*. London, Deutsch, 1979.

Brecher, M., *Decisions in Israel's Foreign Policy*. London, Oxford University Press, 1974.

Chomsky, N., *The Fateful Triangle: The United States, Israel, and the Palestinians*, Boston, South End Press, 1983.

Cohn-Sherbok, D., *Israel: The History of an Idea*. London, SPCK, 1992.

Eban, A., *Heritage, Civilization and the Jews*. London, Weidenfeld & Nicolson, 1984.

Frankel, W., *Israel Observed, An Anatomy of the State*. London, Thames & Hudson, 1980.

Gabatello, E., *The Population of the Administered Territories*. Jerusalem, West Bank Data Project, 1983.

Gilbert, M., *Israel: A History*. London, Black Swan, 1999.

Goldberg, D., *To the Promised Land, A History of Zionist Thought from Its Origin to the Modern State of Israel*. London, Penguin, 1996.

Ha-Am, A., *Nationalism and the Jewish Ethic*. New York, Basic Books, 1962.

Hertzberg, A. (ed.), *The Zionist Idea: A Historical Analysis and Reader*. New York, Atheneum, 1959.

Herzl, T., *The Jewish State*, in A. Hertzberg (ed.), *The Zionist Idea: A Historical Analysis and Reader*. New York, Atheneum, 1959.

Hess, M., *Rome and Jerusalem*, in A. Hertzberg (ed.), *The Zionist Idea: A Historical Analysis and Reader*. New York, Atheneum, 1959.

Hiro, D., *Sharing the Promised Land, An Interwoven Tale of Israelis and Palestinians*. Hodder & Stoughton, 1996.

Hurewitz, J.C., *Struggle for Palestine*. New York, Norton, 1950.

Israel: The Historical Atlas. New York, Macmillan, 1997.

Kalisher, Z.H., 'Derishat Zion', in S. Avineri, *The Making of Modern Zionism*, New York, Basic Books, 1981.

Kook, A.I., 'The Land of Israel', in A. Hertzberg (ed.), *The Zionist Idea: A Historical Analysis and Reader*, New York, Atheneum, 1959.

Kossaifi, G., 'Demographic Characteristics of a Palestinian People', in K. Nakhlek and E. Zureik (eds), *Sociology of Palestine*. London, Croom Helm, 1971.

Laqueur, W., *A History of Zionism*. Weidenfeld & Nicolson, 1972.

Lewis, B., *The Middle-East and the West*. London, Weidenfeld & Nicolson, 1968.

Lucas, N., *The Modern History of Israel*. London, Weidenfeld & Nicolson, 1974.

Morse, A.D., *While Six Million Died*. New York, Random House, 1968.

O'Brien, C.C., *The Siege*. London, Weidenfeld & Nicolson, 1986.

Pinsker, L., *Autoemancipation* in A. Hertzberg (ed.), *The Zionist Idea: A Historical Analysis and Reader*. New York, Atheneum, 1959.

Porath, Y., *The Emergence of the Palestinian–Arab National Movement 1918–1929*. London, Routledge & Kegan Paul, 1974.

Rabin, Y., *The Rabin Memoirs*. London, Weidenfeld & Nicolson, 1979.

Rodinson, M., *Israel and the Arabs*. London, Penguin, 1982.

Sachar, H., *A History of Israel from the Rise of Zionism to Our Time*. New York, Knopf, 1976.

Schechtman, J.B., *Mufti and the Fuehrer*. New York, Thomas Yoseloff, 1969.

Shindler, C., *Ploughshares into Swords? Israelis and Jews in the Shadow of the Intifada*. London, I. B. Taurus, 1991.

Sykes, C., *Crossroads to Israel*. Bloomington, Indiana University Press, 1973.

Vital, D., *Origins of Zionism*. Oxford, Clarendon Press, 1975.

Vital, D., *Zionism: The Formative Years*. New York, Oxford University Press, 1982.

Wasserstein, B., *The British in Palestine*. London, Royal Historical Society, 1979.

Williams, F. (ed.), *Prime Minister Remembers*. London, Heinemann, 1961.

A Palestinian perspective

Asali, K.J. (ed.), *Jerusalem in History*. London, Scorpion Publishing, 1989.

Brand, L.A., *Palestinians in the Arab World*. New York, Columbia University Press, 1988.

Carey, R. (ed.), Chomsky, N., Svirsky, G., Weir, A., *The New Intifada: Resisting Israel's Apartheid*. London, Verso Books, 2001.

Christison, K., *Perceptions of Palestine: Their Influence on U.S. Middle East Policy*. Berkeley, University of California Press, 2001 (updated edition).

Cohen, N.W., *The Year After the Riots*. Detroit, Wayne State University Press, 1988.

Finkelstein, N.G., *The Rise and Fall of Palestine: A Personal Account of the Intifada Years*. Minneapolis, University of Minnesota Press, 1996.

Green, S., *Taking Sides – America's Secret Relations with a Militant Israel*. Vermont, Amana Books, 1988.

Hadawi, S., *Palestinian Rights and Losses in 1948*. London, Saqi, 1988.

Heikal, M., *Secret Channels*. London, Harper Collins, 1996.

Hiro, D., *Sharing the Promised Land*. London, Hodder & Stoughton, 1996.

Kerr, M.H. (ed.), *The Elusive Peace in the Middle East*. New York, SUNY Press, 1975.

Khalidi, R., *Palestinian Identity*. New York, Columbia University Press, 1998.

Laqueur, W. and Rubin, B. (eds), *The Israel–Arab Reader*. London, Penguin, 1995.

Lockman, Z., *Comrades and Enemies – Arab and Jewish Workers in Palestine 1906–1948*, Berkeley: CA, University of California Press, 1996.

Masalha, N., *Imperial Israel and the Palestinians: The Politics of Expansion*. London, Pluto Press, 2000.

Palumbo, M., *The Palestinian Catastrophe*. London, Faber, 1987.

Pappe, I., *The Israel/Palestine Question*. London, Routledge, 1999.

Quandt, W.B., *Peace Process: American Diplomacy and the Arab Israeli Conflict Since 1967*. Washington D.C., Brookings Institution, 1993.

Said, E., *After the Last Sky: Palestinian Lives*. London, Faber, 1986.

Said, E., *The Question of Palestine*. New York, Vintage Books, 1992.

Said, E., *Peace and its Discontents: Gaza-Jericho 1993–1995*.London, Vintage, 1995.

Said, E., *The Politics of Dispossession: The Struggle for Palestinian Self-Determination: 1969–1994*. London, Vintage Books, 1995.

Said, E., *The End of the Peace Process – Oslo and After*. New York, Vintage, 2001.

Said, E. and Hitchens, C., *Blaming the Victims: Spurious Scholarship and the Palestinian Question*. London, Verso, 1988.

Segev, T. and Kay, S. (eds), Watzman, H. (trans.), *One Palestine, Complete: Jews and Arabs Under the British Mandate*. New York, Owl Books, 2001.

Segev, T. and Weinstein, A.N. (trans.),*1949, The First Israelis*. New York, Henry Holt, 1998 (reprint).

Shahak, I. and Mezvinsky, N., *Jewish Fundamentalism in Israel*. Sterling, VA, Pluto Press, 1999.

Sherman, A.J., *Mandate Days: British Lives in Palestine*. London, Thames and Hudson, 1997.

Index